LEGAL RIGHTS

LEGAL RIGHTS

The Guide for Deaf and Hard of Hearing People

Sixth Edition

NATIONAL ASSOCIATION OF THE DEAF

Gallaudet University Press
Washington, DC

Gallaudet University Press
Washington, DC 20002
http://gupress.gallaudet.edu

Library of Congress Cataloging-in-Publication Data

Legal rights : the guide for deaf and hard of hearing people / National
Association of the Deaf.—Sixth Edition.
        pages   cm
    Includes index.
    ISBN 978-1-56368-644-3 (pbk. : alk. paper)—ISBN 978-1-56368-645-0
    (e-book)
    1. Deaf—Legal status, laws, etc.—United States.   2. Hearing impaired—
Legal status, laws, etc.—United States.   I. National Association of the Deaf.
    KF480.5.D4L43 2015
    346.7301'3—dc23   2015005783

♾ This paper meets the requirements of ANSI/NISO Z39.48-1992
(Permanence of Paper).

Authors

National Association of the Deaf Law and Advocacy Center

Howard A. Rosenblum, NAD Chief Executive Officer and
Director of the Law and Advocacy Center
JD, Illinois Institute of Technology/Chicago–Kent

Marc Charmatz, Senior Attorney
JD, Northwestern University

Debra Patkin, Staff Attorney
JD, University of California Los Angeles

Andrew Phillips, Policy Counsel
JD, University of California Hastings

Caroline Jackson, Staff Attorney and Skadden Fellow
JD, Stanford University

*To the Executive Directors of the National
Association of the Deaf for their longstanding
support of the goals of the NAD Law Center
and
in memory of Fred Schreiber, the happy warrior for
Deaf people's rights*

Contents

Preface   xi

Acknowledgments   xiii

CHAPTER 1   Communicating with People Who Are
                        Deaf or Hard of Hearing   1

CHAPTER 2   The Americans with Disabilities Act   25

CHAPTER 3   The Rehabilitation Act of 1973   53

CHAPTER 4   Public School Education   71

CHAPTER 5   Postsecondary and Continuing Education   101

CHAPTER 6   Health Care and Social Services   119

CHAPTER 7   Employment   149

CHAPTER 8   Housing   177

CHAPTER 9   The Legal System   191

CHAPTER 10   Video Media   217

CHAPTER 11   Telecommunication Services   243

Index   263

Preface

Established in 1880, the National Association of the Deaf (NAD) is the oldest civil rights organization in the United States. Throughout these many years, the mission of the NAD has been to preserve, protect, and promote the civil, human, and linguistic rights of deaf and hard of hearing people in this country. The NAD has advocated for equality on behalf of deaf and hard of hearing individuals by seeking to implement and enforce various statutes, regulations, policies, and practices that are designed to eradicate discrimination. There have been many victories in the creation of rights for deaf and hard of hearing individuals, but equality remains an elusive goal on many fronts. Litigation has become necessary to secure rights that are often already accorded in legislation but not recognized or given in many areas of life. For this reason, the NAD founded the National Center for Law and Deafness (NCLD) in 1976.

The NAD hired its first attorney, Marc Charmatz, in 1977, and in the nearly four decades since then, the NCLD (now the Law and Advocacy Center) has grown to succeed in many areas of law: special education; higher education; employment; housing; access to state and local government services; access to professional services, including health, mental health services, financial, and legal services; captioning on many levels (television, movie theaters, schools, public accommodations, sports stadiums, the Internet, and more); transportation; and telecommunications. The legal staff of the NCLD wrote the first editions of *Legal Rights* to doc-ument the areas where deaf and hard of hearing people had suc-cessfully secured rights under the law.

This sixth edition of *Legal Rights* is being published a decade and half after the last edition, and many of the chapters required a major overhaul. This edition includes new rights provided by the Twenty-First Century Communications and Video Accessibility Act of 2010, as well as the ADA Amendments Act (ADAAA) and several rulings and orders from the Federal Communications Commission. New technologies have transformed how communi-cation access is provided, and laws and regulations have adapted to recognize new means of communication such as videophones, Internet streaming services, and numerous new forms of social media such as Twitter, Facebook, Instagram, and many more.

This book is a testament to all those lawyers and advocates who came before us to ensure that deaf and hard of hearing people achieve true equality in all aspects of life. All of us at the National Association of the Deaf share this new book with the hope that it will be useful and helpful to everyone—deaf and hard of hearing individuals, parents and family members, teach-ers, interpreters, allies and friends, advocates, attorneys, legisla-tors, and policy makers.

HOWARD A. ROSENBLUM
Chief Executive Officer and Director,
Law and Advocacy Center

Acknowledgments

We would like to thank the coauthors of the first four editions of this book from the National Center for Law and Deafness (NCLD): Sy DuBow, legal director of the NCLD from 1976 to 1996; Larry Goldberg, associate director of the NCLD from 1976 to 1983; Elaine Gardner, associate legal director of the NCLD from 1983 to 1996; Andrew Penn, NCLD staff attorney from 1978 to 1981; and Sheila Conlon Mentkowski, NCLD staff attorney from 1981 to 1988. In addition, we recognize and thank the coauthors from the NAD who produced the fifth edition of this book: Marc Charmatz, director of the NAD Law Center; Sarah Geer, senior attorney of the NAD Law Center; Mary Vargas, staff attorney and Skadden Fellow of the NAD Law Center; Kelby Brick, staff attorney of the NAD Department of Government Affairs; and Karen Peltz Strauss, staff attorney of the NAD Department of Government Affairs.

We also thank several former law students who interned at the NAD Law and Advocacy Center, provided valuable research, and contributed to many chapters in this book: Elise Ko, Franklin Kanin, Kathryn Robertson, and Michelle Sliwinski.

LEGAL RIGHTS

Chapter 1

Communicating with People Who are Deaf or Hard of Hearing

More than forty-eight million Americans are deaf or hard of hearing.[1] It is difficult to generalize about them because of their wide range of hearing levels, the variety of communication methods, and the differences in the age of onset. Being deaf or hard of hearing can entail more than having a barrier to sound perception; it usually requires a different form of communication and understanding.

Deaf and hard of hearing people frequently rely on information they can see because they process information through their eyes to a greater extent than other people do. Sign language, speech, amplification, and writing are some of their preferred methods of communication. In order to communicate as effectively as possible, many of these individuals use more than one method, and with the use of an auxiliary aid or reasonable accommodation, along with the sensitivity to establish clear lines of communication, they can communicate and participate fully and easily in most settings.

Too often, because of the failure to provide appropriate auxiliary aids or reasonable accommodations, deaf and hard of hearing people have not received fair treatment from professional, social, and government service providers, including those working in law enforcement and the courts. Such aids or accommodations can make a critical difference in whether this group of people receives necessary services and can participate equally in society. The material cost of such accommodations is modest in comparison with the benefits.

As we review the various methods that these individuals use to communicate, one general rule to bear in mind is that each person has a preferred method that is effective for that specific person because he or she has spent a lifetime knowing what works most successfully. What works for that particular person may not work for a different person who is deaf or hard of hearing. Whatever method is natural for that person is the approach that should always be used, preferably from the first moment of contact.

COMMON COMMUNICATION STYLES

Due to variation in the degree of hearing and the age of onset, as well as competing theories on how to ensure success for deaf and hard of hearing children, these individuals use a variety of means to communicate as a matter of daily living. Many, although not all, of them use American Sign Language (ASL) as their primary mode of communication. ASL is a visible language that is linguistically independent of English. It consists of handshapes and movements that represent words, grammar, and concepts, and it is a complete language with rich cultural associations.

In recent decades, educators have developed variants of signing to relay the specific words and grammar of the English language through visual means. Communication systems such as Signing Exact English (SEE) and Conceptually Accurate Signed English (CASE) are commonly used in school settings, although most individuals who learned SEE or CASE in school are able to learn and use ASL as adults.

Other deaf and hard of hearing individuals, including some who have been profoundly deaf since birth, use spoken English as their primary mode of communication. These individuals understand English words based on the movement of the speaker's lips, a technique called *speechreading* or *lipreading,* and will respond to the speaker in English. Other individuals use a system of handshapes designed to represent the sounds of English, called *cued speech,* and may respond using spoken English.

COMMUNICATION BARRIERS

The Limitations of Speechreading

A common misconception about deaf and hard of hearing people is that they all speechread and do so with good comprehension. In fact, very few people can read lips well enough to understand speech, even under optimum conditions. One survey concluded that "even the best speechreaders in a one-to-one situation were found to understand only twenty-six percent of what was said and many bright deaf and hard of hearing individuals grasp less than five percent."[2]

This low level of comprehension occurs because many English speech sounds either are not visible or look the same on the mouth or lips. Certain spoken words or sounds create similar lip movements. The ambiguity of speechreading is demonstrated by the fact that the sounds of *t, d, z, s,* and *n* all look almost identical on the lips. The words *right, ride,* and *rise* would be indistinguishable to a deaf or hard of hearing person, as would the sentences "Do you have the time?" and "Do you have a dime?" The meaning of entire conversations can be lost because a key word is missed or misunderstood.

Speechreading and speaking are separate skills. Skilled speechreaders typically have dedicated decades to learning this craft or can hear well enough for sound to help them distinguish between words while speechreading. Although developing the ability to speak English helps with speechreading, a deaf or hard of hearing individual's ability to speak clearly gives no indication of that person's ability to speechread effectively. Even among skilled speechreaders, many factors can hinder the ability to understand what someone is saying, such as when:

+ there is more than one speaker (e.g., group settings or conversations)
+ the speaker is not directly in front of the speechreader
+ the speaker is in motion or not directly facing the speechreader
+ the lips are obscured by hands, beards, or mustaches
+ the speaker does not articulate carefully or has distorted speech
+ the speaker has a regional or foreign accent
+ the speaker is using technical or unfamiliar words
+ the speechreader is not familiar with the grammar or vocabulary of spoken English
+ the speaker is not well lighted
+ the speechreader must look into a glare or light
+ the speechreader has poor vision

Speechreading often supplements other modes of communication, but it is seldom sufficient by itself to ensure effective communication. Deaf and hard of hearing persons should not rely extensively on speechreading for communication unless they indicate such a preference. In those situations, the following guidelines will help them understand more easily:

+ Speak directly to the person without moving around, turning away, or looking down at papers or books.
+ Use gestures freely, for example, pointing to a wristwatch to indicate time.
+ Speak naturally at a normal rate of speed without shouting or distorting normal mouth movements.
+ If you have not been understood, repeat the utterance more slowly. If this is not successful, try using different words.

For a person who is born deaf or hard of hearing or becomes so early in life, appropriate measures must be taken to ensure age-appropriate language and speech acquisition. Some of these people have intelligible speech. Others do not use their voices at all. Many of those who speak do so with unusual tones, inflections, or modulations. Whether or not a deaf or hard of hearing person uses speech is a matter of individual preference. Difficulty in understanding the person's voice can often be relieved by listening without interruption for a while until the person's particular voice patterns become familiar.

Regardless of a deaf or hard of hearing person's use or nonuse of speech, the use of "mute" (whether deaf-mute or deaf and mute) and "deaf and dumb" is considered insulting by deaf and hard of hearing people and should never be used to describe them.

The Limitations of Note Writing

When interacting with hearing people who do not sign or whose speech is difficult to lipread, many deaf and hard of hearing people rely on written notes for communication. However, this may pose problems and may not always be effective or appropriate. A written version of an ongoing communication is usually tedious, cumbersome, and time consuming. The writer omits much of the information that would otherwise be exchanged, so the deaf or hard of hearing person receives an abbreviated version, which lacks the amount of detail that a hearing person would receive.

A common misconception is that deaf and hard of hearing people compensate for their inability to hear by reading and writing with greater proficiency than hearing people. This is false. Deaf and hard of hearing people are just like the general population. Some are highly literate whereas others are not. Therefore, one should not assume that these individuals are able to communicate easily or effectively in writing.

Most people in the United States learn English by hearing it spoken from birth. But a person who is born deaf or hard of hearing or who loses the ability to hear when very young typically does not learn English in this way. Therefore, these children must be deliberately taught English in school. Some techniques for doing so succeed, whereas others fail, yielding wide variation in English literacy levels among deaf adults.

The extensive use of figurative language in English also poses significant reading problems for people who are deaf or hard of hearing. For example, the expression "under arrest" in the *Miranda* warnings (discussed in chapter 9) might be puzzling in written form to some deaf or hard of hearing people. This confusion may stem from the fact that the word *under* might be perceived to mean *beneath* to someone who is not fluent in English. By contrast, American Sign Language is a completely separate language with its own terminology, grammar, and context.

Because a person often cannot fully convey all the necessary information by writing notes and because everybody has different levels of literacy, the limitations of note writing as a communication method should be observed carefully to avoid miscommunication, especially in legal settings.

Environmental Factors

Environmental factors can also affect the ease of communication with a deaf or hard of hearing person. Any room used should have adequate lighting but minimal glare. One should try to talk in a quiet place, away from the noises of machinery, other conversations, and distractions. Although profoundly deaf people are typically not affected by background noises, they often will be distracted by a great deal of background movement or changes in lighting. A person who uses a hearing aid or who has residual hearing may be significantly distracted by background noises.

COMMUNICATION SOLUTIONS

Because written communications and speechreading are not always appropriate for complex communication, auxiliary aids and services must be provided to ensure comprehension. Such auxiliary aids and services include "qualified interpreters, notetakers, computer-aided transcription services, written materials, telephone handset amplifiers, assistive listening devices, assistive listening systems, telephones compatible with hearing aids, closed caption decoders, open and closed captioning, telecommunications devices for deaf persons (TDD's), videotext displays, or other effective methods of making aurally delivered materials available."[3] Which auxiliary aid or service is required depends on the nature and complexity of the interaction, as well as the communication style and background of the deaf or hard of hearing participant. This section briefly explains the various types of aids and services currently available.

Interpreters

As with spoken language interpreters, interpreters who facilitate communication between deaf and hearing individuals are skilled professionals who have spent years developing their craft. Although individuals with less skill or experience may be easier to find or cheaper to hire than professional interpreters, they are not able to convey information as effectively, completely, accurately, or efficiently as the situation requires. For this reason, professional, trained interpreters should be used whenever possible.

Sign Language Interpreters

A sign language interpreter is a skilled professional who can translate the meaning of spoken English words into a signed language, usually ASL, and can translate the signed language into English. It takes as much time and effort to learn sign language as any other language. Moreover, interpreting between any two languages is a unique skill that goes beyond simply knowing two or more languages and requires years to develop. Interpreting written or spoken English into ASL entails extensive training in addition to the time and effort spent acquiring ASL initially. Legally, sign language interpreters are considered "qualified" only if they can "interpret effectively, accurately and impartially both receptively and expressively, using any necessary specialized vocabulary."[4]

This definition of a "qualified interpreter" requires a subjective assessment of whether the interpreter and the deaf or hard of hearing persons involved are able to understand each other and whether the interpreter is able to interpret effectively, accurately, and impartially for them. Each deaf individual may have different fluency in ASL, Signed English, written English, or other means of communication. As a result, an interpreter's ability to interpret effectively for any specific deaf individual will vary according to the circumstances. Consequently, ensuring successful communication is not as simple as just calling up any interpreter to communicate with a deaf or hard of hearing client. Individual language and communication skills affect an interpreter's capacity to provide truly effective communication for each client.

However, the optimal way to ensure that an interpreter is most likely qualified to interpret for any deaf or hard of hearing person is to retain the services of a nationally certified and, where appropriate, licensed interpreter. The Registry of Interpreters for the Deaf (RID) and the National Association of the Deaf (NAD) are two separate organizations that have issued professional national certifications for sign language interpreters since the mid-1970s. The testing and the labeling for specific sign language certification have changed over time, but the various interpreter certifications are considered equivalent to one another. Most recently, the RID and the NAD created a joint certification called the National Interpreter Certification (NIC).

In addition to national certification, some states issue their own assessment, permits, or certification for sign language interpreters. In most of these, the state process for assessment, permits, or certification is more lenient than the national certification process, requiring fewer hours of training and/or a written exam. Many states now license sign language interpreters to regulate the profession, but the majority recognize the national certification system as a qualification for licensure as most states appear reluctant to create their own license examination.[5]

National or state certification does not automatically make an interpreter "qualified" for every assignment. Interpreters are ethically obligated to decline assignments when they lack the skill or familiarity with the subject matter to interpret effectively and accurately or when they cannot be impartial. Given that every deaf person's background and sign language skills vary, not all such clients may understand a particular sign language interpreter. As a result, the deaf client is usually the best judge of an interpreter's ability to understand and be understood by the client. If a deaf individual indicates an inability to understand the interpreter or feels that the interpreter does not understand him or her, such expressed statements should be regarded as a strong indication that the interpreter is not qualified to interpret for that deaf person in the assignment. In addition, if a deaf person indicates a preference for working with another interpreter, that request should be respected in an effort to ensure successful interpretation.

Certified Deaf Interpreters

Not every deaf or hard of hearing person who signs uses conventional ASL. Some individuals may have circumstances in their past or individual limitations that have prevented them from learning ASL well enough to understand a conventional ASL interpreter. Typically, regular sign language interpreters do not have the capacity to provide effective communication under such circumstances, and it is necessary to bring in a specialized interpreter who has training in this particular type of communication. This specialized interpreter is deaf and is used to facilitate communication between a deaf person with limited language skills and a regular hearing interpreter who is able to translate from spoken English to ASL. The role of the deaf interpreter is to interpret the hearing interpreter's signed ASL into a mode of visual communication that is understandable to a deaf person who is not fluent in ASL or possibly any formal language. Thus, a deaf person who does not use conventional ASL often requires two interpreters: a deaf interpreter to translate between the individual's communication style and ASL, and a hearing interpreter to translate between ASL and English.

The RID has issued a professional certification for deaf interpreters, known as a Certified Deaf Interpreter (CDI). The CDI is equivalent to the National Interpreter Certification, reflecting extensive training and expertise in dealing with the needs of this unique population.

Oral Interpreters

Individuals who do not sign and prefer to communicate through speechreading may require an "oral" interpreter who silently mouths the speaker's words to them. Although such interpreters may not be needed for one-on-one interactions, they play an important role where other factors make speechreading difficult. For this reason, they are most often used for lectures, where the speaker will be far away or moving around, or in group settings, where conversation would otherwise be impossible to follow. An oral interpreter may be necessary for a deaf person who does not know sign language but needs to lipread during a court proceeding involving many people in various parts of the courtroom.

As with sign language interpreters, oral interpreters have extensive training. Their training focuses on mouthing words in a manner that is easy to speechread, on substituting synonyms for words that are difficult to speechread, and on adding gestures in a manner that facilitates speechreading. They have also developed the ability to understand and repeat the message and intent of the speech and the mouth movements of the person who is deaf or hard of hearing. The RID issues a professional interpreter certification for oral interpreters, called the Oral Transliteration Certificate (OTC).

Video Remote Interpreters

When a live interpreter cannot be secured either because of distance or time constraints, an off-site interpreter may be used through a process called video remote interpreting (VRI). With VRI, both the deaf and the hearing people occupy the same room. The off-site interpreter accesses the setting through a camera, a screen, and an Internet connection that allows the interpreter to both see and be seen by the deaf person and to hear and be heard by the hearing person. Although this system serves well when an interpreter is needed quickly or when a sufficiently skilled interpreter is not available, VRI is not appropriate in every setting; in certain situations it is important to have the interpreter physically present so that he or she can interact with all parties easily and clearly. For example, when a deaf person is involved in a trial, it is essential for the interpreter to be able to hear everyone in the courtroom and move about the room to hear and see what is going on to effectively relay communications between the deaf person and the rest of the people participating in the trial. In addition, it may be important for an interpreter to be physically present during a difficult discussion about a medical diagnosis and/or prognosis.

Specifically, the National Association of the Deaf recommends the following guidelines to determine when it is inappropriate to use VRI:

+ VRI requires a strong Internet connection. It will not be effective when the Internet connection is weak or when other demands interrupt the process of streaming video.
+ VRI requires the deaf individual to see the screen clearly. It is not appropriate for deaf individuals with vision problems or who cannot be positioned to see the screen due to injury or some other factor.
+ Relying on VRI for intermittent communication with the deaf person, such as during an extended hospital stay, can cause serious translation problems. ASL is a highly context-dependent language; for example, the question "Did you take your medicine?" is interpreted differently depending on whether the medicine is a pill, a liquid, or an injection. Using VRI for ongoing communication increases the risk that each new interpreter will be unfamiliar with the history of the interaction and will not be able to provide an accurate translation. For this reason, live interpreters should be used whenever possible for ongoing interpreting needs.
+ Intensive multiparty communications involving a deaf person, such as those that occur during a court trial, may be inappropriate for VRI.

Locating a Sign Language Interpreter

Qualified sign language interpreters can be found through the Registry of Interpreters for the Deaf (RID) or state registries of interpreters. Deaf and hard of hearing people may themselves suggest local interpreters. Other sources of interpreters include the following:

+ local interpreting agencies specifically serving deaf and hard of hearing people
+ organizations of deaf and hard of hearing people
+ your state association of deaf and hard of hearing people

+ state commissions or agencies for deaf and hard of hearing
  people
+ schools and programs for deaf and hard of hearing
  children

Professional offices and service agencies should be prepared
to provide sign language interpreters at any time by developing and
maintaining their own lists of reliable and competent interpreters.

Best Practices in Using Sign Language Interpreters

Simply adding a sign language interpreter to a situation does not
automatically create successful communication, especially when
the parties are not familiar with the use of sign language interpreters. The following tips can help ensure dialogue that is as
effective as possible.

What to Expect of an Interpreter.   Professional interpreters have
extensive training in how to conduct themselves in professional
situations. Further, they are bound by a code of professional conduct that requires certain behaviors and proscribes others. For
this reason, interpreters should do the following:

+ Prepare for assignments ahead of time by asking the contact person or the agency who places them for the details of
  the assignment.
+ Decline assignments if they notice that they lack the skill or
  background knowledge to interpret effectively or accurately or if they cannot be impartial.
+ Keep all assignment-related information confidential,
  including the identity of all parties involved and the information exchanged before, during, and after the assignment.
+ Relay all information faithfully and accurately between the
  parties regardless of the complexity or sensitivity of the
  information.
+ Refrain from interjecting themselves into the interaction
  unless necessary to clarify information or otherwise adequately perform their role as an interpreter.
+ Dress appropriately for the setting, including matching the
  formality of the attendees and refraining from wearing
  distracting clothing, accessories, or fragrances.
+ Treat all participants in a professional, respectful manner.

If an interpreter does not meet these expectations, it is important that you inform the agency or other entity who supplied the interpreter or referred that interpreter to you. Because interpreters work almost exclusively independently or in pairs, misconduct may not be identified unless the individuals working directly with the interpreter bring the matter to the attention of the agency or other hiring body.

Hiring an Interpreter.   Not every interpreter, even if professionally certified, is appropriate for every assignment. Following these tips will give you the best chance of obtaining an interpreter who is both qualified and prepared to interpret effectively.

- Give the interpreting agency (or other entity charged with hiring the interpreter) as much information as possible about the situation requiring the interpreter, including:
  - the purpose of the interaction
  - the information to be discussed, including background information that may be helpful to completely understand a complex assignment
  - the likely length and complexity of the interaction
  - the importance of the interaction
  - the identity of the deaf and hearing attendees, if known
  - any visual materials that will be used during the interaction (these can be supplied ahead of time or when the interpreter arrives)
- Ask any potential interpreters about their professional certification (including licensure if required in your state) and their work experience.
- Avoid hiring individuals who lack certification, training, and/or experience as a professional interpreter. Definitely do not hire individuals who do not have any requisite licensure mandated by the state.
- For ongoing assignments, try to use the same interpreter each time. The interpreter's familiarity with the content of the interaction and sequence of events will allow the person to perform even more effectively.

Using a Sign Language Interpreter

When communicating with a deaf person through a sign language interpreter, keep in mind the following guidelines:

+ When addressing the deaf person, look directly at him or her, not at the interpreter. Speak to the person as if the interpreter were not present. For example, say "The meeting will be on Tuesday" rather than "Tell her that the meeting will be on Tuesday." The interpreter will sign exactly what is said.

+ Some deaf people use their own voice while signing. Others do not, so the interpreter will say in English what the person signs. In both cases, respond by talking to the deaf person, not to the interpreter.

+ The interpreter should stand or sit directly beside the speaker so that he or she is easily visible to the deaf person.

+ The interpreter should not be standing or placed in shadows or in front of any source of bright light, such as a window.

+ Do not expect or allow the interpreter to participate in the conversation. The interpreter's only role is to facilitate communication between you and the deaf person.

+ No private conversation should occur with the interpreter or with anyone else in the deaf person's presence. The interpreter is to interpret everything that is said in front of the deaf person even if the person intended to have a private conversation. Ask the deaf person, not the interpreter, if he or she understands what is being said.

+ Speak naturally and not too fast. Remember that names and some other words must be fingerspelled and that this takes more time than signing. The interpreter will indicate whether it is necessary to slow down. Avoid jargon or other technical words with which the interpreter (a layperson) may be unfamiliar. If possible, meet with the interpreter before the interview to discuss the best way to interpret certain technical concepts into ASL without losing any of the meaning.

Although professional certification may be useful in evaluating the skills of an interpreter, the ultimate authority on whether the interpreter is understandable and able to understand is the deaf or hard of hearing person. An interpreter who is unable to provide effective communication for a particular person is unqualified regardless of any level of professional certification.

The Hazards of Using Unqualified Interpreters

A lack of fluency in ASL or another sign language will prevent amateur or beginning signers from interpreting effectively. First, they will have a limited vocabulary and often will not know the ASL equivalent of a given word or phrase. They may attempt to work around this limitation by fingerspelling English words, creating the same comprehension problems that exist when attempting to communicate in written English. Second, they may have a poor command of ASL grammar, so even if they know the appropriate vocabulary terms, they will not produce them in a way that conveys a complete or an accurate thought. For example, for the English phrase "have to," they may spell out the letters or produce the signs "have" and "to." With either translation the signer will be producing an utterance about possession instead of the English concept of obligation or requirement. Similarly, the word "fine" in the context of a parking ticket might be translated as "well-being" instead of conveying the idea of a financial penalty. Thus, the phrase "You have to pay this fine" could be mistranslated as "You have payment. Good."

Moreover, a beginning or an intermediate signer will not be able to understand deaf or hard of hearing signers well enough to translate their signing statements into English. Even where the amateur signer believes he or she has understood the deaf signer, a mistranslation may nonetheless result, causing a serious miscommunication and a lack of access.

Even fluent signers who have not been formally trained as interpreters are often unable to interpret successfully. English and ASL have very different ways of communicating ideas. Without training, even a fully bilingual individual will struggle to produce a truly equivalent translation in the time allowed (usually only a couple of seconds), resulting in misunderstandings. Untrained persons fluent in sign language also may not understand their role. They may not grasp the need to convey information completely to both sides and as a result leave out important concepts. They may not recognize the need to refrain from participating in the interaction and to keep the communication confidential.

Interpreting for Clients with Special Requirements

Under circumstances such as the following, a different kind of interpreter or one with a particular skill set may be necessary to ensure effective communication:

+ When a deaf or hard of hearing person also has a visual impairment
+ When a disability (e.g., intellectual impairment, mental illness) or other condition (e.g., insufficient exposure to language as a child) affects a deaf or hard of hearing person's ability to understand mainstream American culture
+ When a deaf or hard of hearing person grew up in a foreign country and has not yet learned ASL
+ When participating in situations that necessitate accurate interpretation, such as a discussion or treatment of a serious medical condition, a police interrogation, or a trial court proceeding

Deaf-Blind Individuals.   Deaf and hard of hearing people rely entirely on vision for most communications; however, those who are also blind or have some other visual impairment have a unique set of communication needs that vary based on how these conditions have manifested themselves over time.

Individuals who became deaf or hard of hearing early in life and then developed a visual impairment as a teenager or an adult typically use sign language to communicate. Many prefer to rely on their residual vision to communicate and simply require that interpreters wear certain colors that contrast with their skin tone or adapt their signing style to fit within a smaller visual field. Others may not have enough residual vision to rely on for extensive communication or simply prefer not to do so. They will require an interpreter with expertise in tactile forms of signed communication. Tactile signed communications occur when a person understands sign language by placing one of his or her hands on the hands of the person who is signing (either another deaf person or an interpreter) and using the sense of touch to determine what is being signed.

Other deaf-blind individuals, especially those who became blind or developed a visual impairment early in life and became deaf or hard of hearing as a teenager or an adult, typically do not use sign language to communicate. They may rely on a range of other communication methods, including amplification or reading real-time captions with Braille or enlarged text.

At the present time, there is no specialized certification for these communication styles. Where possible, the person hiring the interpreter should inquire in advance about the deaf-blind person's communication preferences and inform the agency or potential interpreter. Every effort should be made to accommodate the specific needs and preferences of a deaf-blind individual.

Individuals with Language Deprivation or an Intellectual or Mental Impairment.   Due to circumstances of the past or a co-occurring disability, not every deaf or hard of hearing person has the capacity to understand a standard sign language interpreter. The overwhelming majority of ASL interpreters learned ASL as a teenager or an adult and do not sign with native proficiency. For this reason, their translations into ASL tend to assume strong familiarity with English and with dominant American culture. Although most deaf and hard of hearing people have enough familiarity with English and with American culture to understand such interpreters, some do not, and communication will not be effective without a CDI to fully match the client's communication style and level of world knowledge.

These circumstances arise most frequently for deaf or hard of hearing individuals with cognitive impairments or mental illness or whose advanced age has affected their ability to perceive communication, much as advanced age may affect a hearing individual. These circumstances can also arise when a deaf or hard of hearing person was not exposed to conventional ASL until adulthood and acquired either an extremely localized dialect of ASL not commonly understood by outsiders or has created a system of gestures that does not resemble ASL.

Immigrants.   Deaf or hard of hearing individuals who have immigrated to the United States may know only their native country's sign language and may not yet have learned ASL fluently enough to understand an ASL interpreter. Where possible, an interpreter should be found who is sufficiently fluent in that country's sign language to interpret. Such an interpreter would translate between the foreign sign language and ASL, and an additional interpreter would translate between ASL and English. When such an interpreter who is familiar with the deaf person's native sign language cannot be found, a CDI can be effectively used to form a language bond with the deaf person who uses a different sign language and thereby utilize a common set of signs to translate into ASL.

Suspects, Witnesses, and Defendants.   When an accurate translation is crucial, such as in a police interrogation or a court hearing, a CDI should be used with a standard ASL interpreter to ensure the highest degree of accuracy. These measures are often necessary even if the deaf or hard of hearing person being questioned is fluent in ASL and/or English, as minor misinterpretations can have very serious consequences.

CAPTIONING

For deaf and hard of hearing people who have excellent reading skills, captioning can be at least as effective as interpreters in providing access to a given setting, and at times even more so. For example, presentations involving highly technical information can be relayed more easily through captioning, as it does not require the captioner (who is usually a layperson) to understand the content of the presentation. Videos also can be more easily understood with captioning than with interpreters due to the interaction between the visual and the auditory information in the video, the proximity of the captioning and the visual information, and the speed at which speakers change.

Real-Time Captioning

For live events, captioning can be made available through a variety of methods, such as communication access real-time translation (CART) or C-Print captioning. With both services, an individual with extensive training in stenography or other captioning systems types the speaker's words into a program that displays them on a projection screen or monitor. The deaf or hard of hearing person can then read a simultaneous transcript during the live proceeding.

Captioning is ideal for individuals who have excellent reading skills and for those who do not know sign language and therefore cannot use a sign language interpreter. Because of the speed of the transcription, however, it is not appropriate for slow readers or for those who may not be familiar with any technical vocabulary used. It also may not be suitable as the only auxiliary aid or service in a setting where a deaf or hard of hearing person is expected to participate in a discussion but does not speak. In such a setting, captioning may help the individual to understand what is being said, but another form of service such as a sign language interpreter may be needed in order to enable the person to express his or her thoughts or opinions.

CART systems are frequently used in courts since they were first developed using the skills of court stenographers. The system is also widely used in classrooms, lecture halls, and other settings. The success of the transcription depends on the skill of the stenographer and the sophistication of the translation program. One advantage of a CART system is that the stenographer can also produce a printed transcript of the spoken information for use by all participants. Despite advancements in the technology, significant misleading errors can still appear in a real-time transcription.

Despite the widespread use of computers and the resultant availability of skilled typists, laypeople are not qualified to provide real-time captioning. Only the most exceptional typists can keep up with the rate of human speech while typing on a standard keyboard. Both CART and C-Print use special software designed to utilize phonemes, shorthand, or abbreviations that allow the captioner to keep up with the flow of speech. Anyone untrained in the use of such software or who does not have access to it will not be able to keep up with the rate of speech and should not be used as a captioner.

Closed Captioning

For videos and other prerecorded media, closed captioning (which the viewer can turn on or off) can make the information visible to only a specific subset of viewers, such as the deaf and hard of hearing members of an audience. The most effective way of developing closed captioning at present is to feed the script into software that uses voice recognition to synchronize the display of captions with the speakers' words. Voice recognition software is not yet reliable enough to provide genuine access to video content. The accuracy of any captioning produced by voice recognition software should be vetted and corrected by a human before it is made available for widespread use.

Open Captioning

In certain settings, captioning can take the form of open captions, which are captions displayed on a movie screen, jumbotrons, or LED boards in movie theaters, regular theaters, and stadiums. The captions can be turned on and off with the press of a button and can be seen by the entire audience when displayed.

Due to the unreliability of closed captioning and assistive listening devices, movie theaters and stadiums are encouraged to turn on captions when requested by deaf or hard of hearing patrons. Live theater productions can also be made accessible through open captioning, which is encouraged as a way to provide access to the theater for deaf and hard of hearing individuals who do not sign.

Assistive Listening Systems

Background noise and reverberation make it difficult for individuals who are deaf or hard of hearing—whether or not they wear hearing aids or use cochlear implants—to distinguish the words and sounds around them. Thus, they have difficulty participating on equal terms with hearing people in rooms that are not equipped with an assistive listening system. Even the best in sound systems technology, combined with the best in hearing aid technology, cannot solve these problems. Therefore, the 1990 Americans with Disabilities Act included requirements for installing assistive listening devices in places of public accommodation.

The purpose of an assistive listening system is to transmit sound as directly as possible to the ear. Such systems should not be confused with audio systems (such as public address systems), which are generally designed to enhance sound quality or simply amplify sound. Rather than enhancing all the sounds in a room, an assistive listening device can bring specific sounds directly to the user's ears. Three basic wireless technologies are available for this purpose: induction loop, FM broadcast, and infrared light. No single technology is best for all applications. All three types of assistive listening systems can be installed in new and old facilities alike, as long as their individual limitations are kept in mind.

Induction Loop Technology

Induction loop technology is based on electromagnetic transmission. It has a unique advantage in that the signal is received directly by the user's hearing aid or cochlear implant if that device is equipped with a telecoil circuit, or "T" switch. Since the hearing aid or cochlear implant itself acts as a receiver, there is no need for an additional receiver as is required by all other technologies. For example, by turning on the telecoil, users can receive the signal in their own hearing aid or cochlear implant rather than using headphones. However, if the listeners do not have a hearing aid or cochlear implant equipped with a telecoil or have no hearing device at all, then induction receivers must be used. An induction receiver takes the place of a hearing aid or cochlear implant with the telecoil function by bringing the sound directly to the ear, like headphones. There are three types of receivers: a wandlike device, a pocket-sized device with headphones, and a telecoil installed inside a plastic shell that looks like a hearing aid. The first two are the most common.

FM Broadcast Technology

The Federal Communications Commission (FCC) has designated certain frequencies for the operation of FM systems. Since each system may use its own broadcast frequency, several systems may operate simultaneously at one location without interfering with one another. However, unlike the loop system, the FM system requires a special receiver for each person, regardless of whether the person has a hearing aid or cochlear implant. Several options for coupling a hearing aid to an FM system are available. The most convenient methods for public places employ either a neck-loop or a silhouette inductor used with the telecoil circuit of the hearing aid or cochlear implant.

Infrared Light Technology

From a practical point of view, the infrared receiver system is in many ways similar in operation to the FM system. However, receivers must be in the line of sight of the emitter (transmitter); the signal can be received only inside the covered room. As with FM technology, each person—hearing aid or cochlear implant user or not—must use a receiver. The options for coupling the infrared receiver to the hearing aid or cochlear implant are the same as for FM systems.

The communication techniques and the assistive listening systems described here are methods of crossing and thus eliminating many of the communications barriers that separate deaf, hard of hearing, and hearing people from one another.

TELECOMMUNICATIONS

Although amplification devices can be used to make telephones accessible to some deaf or hard of hearing people, others find communication through a conventional telephone unsuccessful. For exclusively written communication, the proliferation of email, text messaging, and online chat software allows instant communication to occur between hearing and deaf people without any specialized equipment. For this reason, teletypewriters (known as TTYs, or telecommunications devices for deaf people [TDDs]), which rely on a much slower form of technology for data transmission, have become virtually obsolete.

When written communication alone is not possible, either because the communication is too complex or because the entity requires telephone communication only (as is often the case with banks and doctors' offices), a variety of devices can be used, depending on the deaf person's preference. Deaf and hard of hearing individuals who use sign language most commonly place phone calls with a videophone (VP). A VP is a freestanding device that allows one individual to make a video-based phone call to another using a regular ten-digit phone number, much as a webcam can be used for video-based communication over the Internet. In addition, VP software can be downloaded to a computer or smartphone to allow that device to operate as a VP. The major advantage of a VP is that the callers can use ASL or any other sign language to communicate.

Relay Services

When a deaf or hard of hearing caller places a call through a device that is not compatible with a standard telephone, a relay service serves as an intermediary. Because the FCC funds these relay services, neither the deaf nor the hearing caller is charged for them. All businesses and government entities have an obligation to accept calls placed through relay services just as they accept calls from hearing callers. The use of the intermediary does not interfere with the legally recognized confidentiality of any phone call.

Calls between VPs and standard telephones are placed through a video relay service (VRS). In a VRS, the intermediary is an ASL interpreter who uses a VP to communicate directly with the ASL-using caller and a standard telephone to communicate directly with the hearing caller. Calls can also be placed from online chat or text messaging systems through Internet protocol (IP) relay. In IP relay, the intermediary reads the typing caller's text out loud through a standard telephone and types the words of the hearing caller.

A deaf or hard of hearing caller with intelligible speech may use a standard telephone in conjunction with a captioning system or a VRS. When doing so, the caller speaks directly to the hearing caller through a standard telephone, but an intermediary relays the hearing caller's words back to the deaf or hard of hearing caller. The intermediary may either interpret the response into ASL, use a VRS, or type out the response through IP relay, a captioned telephone, or a TTY.

Alerting Devices

Devices that traditionally use auditory cues to alert users have adaptations for deaf and hard of hearing consumers. For instance, VPs alert users of incoming calls through flashing lights or a blinking screen. Conventional telephones and cell phones can also be set up to flash lights when they ring. Doorbells, smoke alarms, fire alarms, and other devices are also available with visual alert systems.

This chapter demonstrates the myriad ways that the channels of communication between hearing and deaf or hard of hearing people can be opened to ensure easy and effective dialogue. Although the variety of these methods may seem overwhelming, most deaf and hard of hearing people are intimately familiar with their preferred method and can be consulted about the provision of auxiliary aids and services. Similarly, providers of these services, such as interpreters and captioners, likewise have a wealth of knowledge on how to bridge this communication gap. With minimal effort, you can make a tremendous difference by ensuring that the deaf and hard of hearing people in your personal or professional life have full and equal access to our society.

NOTES

1. Johns Hopkins University, "One in Five Americans Has Hearing Loss," November 14, 2011, http://www.hopkinsmedicine.org/news/media/releases/one_in_five_americans_has_hearing_loss.
2. McCay Vernon and Eugene D. Mindel, *They Grow in Silence: The Deaf Child and His Family* (Silver Spring, MD: National Association of the Deaf, 1971), 96.
3. 28 C.F.R. Part 36.
4. 42 U.S.C. 12101–12213.
5. http://www.360translations.com/burnsat/stateregs.htm.

Chapter *2*

The Americans with Disabilities Act

The Americans with Disabilities Act (ADA) of 1990 was land-mark civil rights legislation for all citizens with disabilities.[1] It has been of tremendous benefit to deaf and hard of hearing people in their efforts to gain equal access to all aspects of society, especially in its provisions to remove communication barriers in many significant places.

Prior to passage of the ADA, federal and state laws prohibited discrimination against people with disabilities in limited areas. For example, the Rehabilitation Act of 1973 prohibited discrimination in federal employment, federally conducted programs and activities, and programs and activities receiving federal financial assistance (see chapter 3). The Architectural Barriers Act of 1968 mandated the removal of obstacles to physical access and to communication in federally funded buildings (see chapter 3). The Individuals with Disabilities Education Act of 1990 (IDEA, originally the Education for All Handicapped Children Act of 1975) provided important procedural and substantive protections for deaf or hard of hearing students who attend public schools (see chapter 4). All of these federal laws established critical principles of equal access, but their impact was limited to the specific areas addressed.

The ADA took the important principles in these laws and extended them to the broad mainstream of American public life. The ADA prohibits discrimination in almost every aspect of society. This legislation provides legal protections in employment (Title I), access to state and local government and public transportation (Title II), public accommodations (Title III), and telecommunications (Title IV). Under Title I of the ADA, virtually all employers with fifteen or more employees must eliminate discriminatory practices, not just those with federal contracts or receiving federal financial assistance, as was required under the Rehabilitation Act of 1973. Under Title II of the ADA, all state and local government activities must be accessible, even if the government entity does not receive federal funds. Under Title III of the ADA, private businesses and professionals and nonprofit organizations must make their facilities and services accessible to people with disabilities. Because the statute applies to a wide range of new construction of private buildings and workplaces, new construction standards will include accessibility features as a matter of standard practice.

Congress adopted the ADA with strong bipartisan support, and President George H. W. Bush signed it into law. It was received with wide acclaim, and even though it has not eliminated all disability-based discrimination, it does provide a powerful tool for alleviating such discrimination. Over the years, courts, including the Supreme Court, have made rulings that have narrowed the impact of the ADA. However, in 2008, Congress passed the ADA Amendments Act (ADAAA) with the intent to broaden interpretation of the ADA and reject Supreme Court decisions that worked to narrow it.

DEFINITION OF "DISABILITY"

Federal disability laws protect people with many different kinds of physical and mental disabilities. The definition of "disability" in the ADA includes any person who (1) has a physical or mental impairment that substantially limits at least one major life activity, (2) has a record of such an impairment, or (3) is regarded as having such an impairment.[2] Under Title III of the ADA, private businesses and professionals and nonprofit organizations must make their facilities and services accessible to people with disabilities.

Defining Disability in the Courts

According to the ADA, a disability is a condition that "substantially limits" a person's ability to perform a major life activity. A person need not be profoundly or severely deaf to be protected by the ADA. People who are hard of hearing may be significantly affected in their ability to hear, and so they may be entitled to the protections of the statute. The ADA regulation for employment reiterates that the term "substantially limits" generally means that a person is unable to perform a major life activity that the average person in the general population can perform.[3]

In June 1999 the US Supreme Court decided three cases dealing with the definition of an "individual with a disability." The major issue in these cases was whether corrective devices and medications should be considered in determining whether a person is an "individual with a disability." In these three cases, the Supreme Court ruled that the plaintiffs did not meet the definition of "disability" under the ADA.

In *Sutton v. United Airlines,* United Airlines would not hire two airline pilots as commercial pilots because they were nearsighted. With glasses, their vision could be corrected to 20/20. These pilots said that they were individuals with disabilities because, without eyeglasses, their vision was 20/100 or less. The Supreme Court found that the two pilots had no disability because, with glasses, their vision was corrected to 20/20.[4] In *Murphy v. United Parcel Service,* an individual was fired from his job as a mechanic because he had high blood pressure, even though it was controlled by medication. The Supreme Court held that the plaintiff had no disability when he was on medication that controlled his high blood pressure.[5] In *Kirkingburg v. Albertsons,* an individual with vision in only one eye was denied continued employment as a truck driver, and in this case the Supreme Court stated that he had no disability because he could still see out of one eye.[6]

These cases affected many individuals who believed they were entitled to the legal protections afforded by the ADA and the Rehabilitation Act. The Supreme Court decisions, however, established that a person does not have a disability if corrective measures (such as glasses or medication) render them not "substantially" impaired in a major life activity.

In the ADAAA of 2008 Congress broadened the definition of an "individual with a disability" under the ADA, explaining that the US Supreme Court had created "an inappropriately high level of limitation." Congress rejected the Court's decisions in *Sutton, Murphy,* and *Kirkingburg* by deciding that the substantial limitation caused by one's impairment should not consider ameliorative affects.[7] Since Congress revoked the decisions in those three cases, mitigating measures such as hearing aids or cochlear implants can no longer be considered in determining whether an individual is substantially limited in the major life activity of hearing.

Even before the ADAAA, these decisions were not as restrictive as they might have seemed at first for deaf or hard of hearing people. The US Supreme Court stressed that determining whether a person has a disability needs to be done on a case-by-case basis. As a result, these decisions should not have seriously affected deaf and hard of hearing individuals. Under the ADA and the Rehabilitation Act, a deaf or hard of hearing individual is considered an "individual with a disability" because of a substantial impairment to the major life activity of hearing.

A key concern relates to hearing aids and cochlear implants and to people with mild or moderate hearing loss. Some people have argued that a deaf or hard of hearing individual does not have a disability if the person wears a hearing aid or has a cochlear implant, but this is an overreaction.

For most individuals, eyeglasses correct vision to 20/20. This is simply not the case with hearing aids, cochlear implants, and assistive listening devices. Many hearing aid and cochlear implant users still have great difficulty understanding speech, especially in noisy work settings. Before the ADAAA, the primary legal issue was whether an individual who uses a hearing aid, assistive listening device, or cochlear implant had a substantial impairment to a major life activity. If that person had a "substantial impairment," then the individual is entitled to the legal protections of the ADA and the Rehabilitation Act. This would be true for most deaf or hard of hearing individuals. After the ADAAA, the primary legal issue is now whether an individual is substantially limited in the major life activity of hearing or speaking without the use of a hearing aid, assistive listening device, or cochlear implant. Thus, while some people have a degree of hearing loss that can be brought within "normal" limits with a hearing aid, cochlear implant, or other assistive listening devices, this does not mean that these individuals are not covered under the ADA or Rehabilitation Act because they would still be entitled to the legal protection of these federal statutes if they could show, absent the hearing aid, assistive listening device, and/or cochlear implant, that they have a substantial impairment to a major life activity.

Title I: Employment

Title I of the ADA and regulations adopted by the US Equal Employment Opportunity Commission (EEOC) prohibit an employer from discriminating against a "qualified individual with a disability" in the following areas: (1) job application procedures, (2) hiring, (3) discharge, (4) compensation, (5) advancement, and (6) any other terms, conditions, and privileges of employment.[8]

Employers Covered under the ADA

Employers with fifteen or more employees (including part-time and seasonal) are covered by Title I. Employment agencies, unions, and joint labor/management committees also are covered by Title l. Exempted from ADA's requirements are the US government, Indian tribes, and tax-exempt private membership clubs.[9]

Discrimination Prohibited

The ADA and the EEOC regulations make it unlawful for an employer to discriminate against a qualified individual on the basis of disability in the following areas:

+ recruitment, advertising, and job application procedures
+ hiring, upgrading, promotion, award of tenure, demotion, transfer, layoff, termination, right of return from layoff, and rehire
+ rates of pay
+ job assignments, job classifications, position descriptions, and seniority lists
+ leaves of absence, sick leave, or any other leave
+ fringe benefits
+ selection and financial support for training
+ activities sponsored by the employer, including social and recreational programs
+ any other term, condition, or privilege of employment[10]

Employers are required to provide reasonable accommodations to people with disabilities during the application process and on the job. A reasonable accommodation is any change or adjustment to an environment that permits a qualified applicant or employee to participate in the job application process, perform the essential functions of a job, or enjoy the benefits and privileges of employment.

Some examples of prohibited discrimination against a deaf or hard of hearing person are the following:

+ being denied a qualified interpreter for a job interview
+ not being hired or promoted because the employer says communication is required and does not consider an accommodation to be reasonable
+ receiving a lower rate of pay for doing the same job as hearing workers
+ not being provided special equipment
+ being denied an opportunity to participate in training because the employer refuses to pay for a qualified interpreter

Employer's Defense of "Undue Hardship"

An employer who is asked to make a reasonable accommodation may claim that the requested accommodation would be an "undue hardship," meaning a significant difficulty or expense. In deciding whether an accommodation would be an undue hardship for the business, the following conditions should be considered:

1. the nature and net cost of the accommodation needed, taking into consideration the availability of tax credits and deductions and/or outside funding
2. the overall financial resources of the business site providing the accommodation, the number of employees, and the effect on resources
3. the overall financial resources of the business, including its size in terms of number of employees and number and type of business sites
4. the type of operation of the business and the relationship of the facility to the overall business

The EEOC analysis of the regulations gives the following example involving a deaf applicant: An independently owned fast-food franchise receives no money from the parent company, which gives out the franchises. The franchise refuses to hire a deaf person because it says it would be an undue hardship to provide an interpreter for monthly staff meetings. Since the financial relationship between the local franchise and the parent company is only a franchise fee, only the financial resources of the local franchise would be considered in deciding whether providing the accommodation would be an undue hardship. However, if a financial or an administrative relationship exists between the parent company and the local franchise, then the parent company's resources should be considered in determining whether the hardship is undue.

Enforcement Provisions

Employment practices under the ADA are enforced by the EEOC, along with state and local civil rights agencies who work in conjunction with the EEOC. Individuals with disabilities have the same remedies available to all groups protected under Title VII of the Civil Rights Act of 1964, as amended by the Civil Rights Act of 1991. An employer found in violation of the employment section of the ADA may be ordered to discontinue discriminatory practices, to correct policies and practices, to hire a qualified individual with a disability, or to rehire the person with back pay and provide the person with a reasonable accommodation. Compensatory and punitive damages may be available for intentional discrimination, but damages may not be awarded where the employer demonstrates "good-faith efforts" to identify and make reasonable accommodations. Employers who lose a case will be required to pay attorney's fees and costs to the individual with a disability. (See chapter 7 for extended discussion of employment rights under the ADA and other laws.)

EEOC Amendments of Its ADA Regulation to Reflect the ADA Amendments Act of 2008

On September 25, 2008, the ADA Amendments Act was signed into law and became effective on January 1, 2009. Both the US Senate and the US House of Representatives unanimously passed the ADAAA. The EEOC amended its ADA regulation to reflect the ADAAA's changes to the term "disability." The following is a summary of the ADAAA's most significant changes to the EEOC's ADA regulation:

+ Emphasized that the definition of "disability" is be interpreted broadly, that is, to the maximum extent permitted by the terms of the ADA
+ Expanded the definition of "major life activities" by providing two nonexhaustive lists:
    ◇ The first list includes many activities that the EEOC has recognized (e.g., walking) as well as those that the EEOC has not specifically recognized (e.g., reading, bending, communicating).
    ◇ The second list includes major bodily functions (e.g., "functions of the immune system, normal cell

growth, digestive, bowel, bladder, respiratory, neurological, brain, circulatory, endocrine, and reproductive functions").

+ Stated that mitigating measures other than "ordinary eyeglasses or contact lenses" shall not be considered in determining whether an individual has a disability

+ Clarified that an impairment that is episodic or in remission is a disability if it would substantially limit a major life activity when active

+ Revised the definition of "substantially limits" by providing that a limitation need not "significantly" or "severely" restrict a major life activity in order to meet the standard

+ Changed the definition of "regarded as" so that it no longer requires showing that the employer perceived the individual to be substantially limited in a major life activity and instead provides that an applicant or employee is "regarded as" having a disability if he or she is subject to an action prohibited by the ADA (e.g., failure to hire) based on an impairment that is not transitory or minor. Individuals covered only under the "regarded as" prong are not entitled to reasonable accommodations

+ Listed impairments that will "consistently meet the definition of disability," which include, but are not limited to, autism, cancer, cerebral palsy, diabetes, epilepsy, HIV/AIDS, multiple sclerosis, muscular dystrophy, major depression, bipolar disorder, posttraumatic stress disorder, obsessive compulsive disorder, and schizophrenia

TITLE II: STATE AND LOCAL GOVERNMENTS

Title II of the ADA requires state and local government agencies to make all of their programs, activities, and services accessible to individuals with disabilities. It also requires public transportation agencies to be accessible. Title II became effective in 1992. The US Department of Justice (DOJ) adopted a regulation implementing and explaining the requirements of Title II.[11]

These requirements are important because they extend protection against discrimination to all state and local governmental agencies, even those programs, activities, and services that were not covered by Section 504 of the Rehabilitation Act of 1973 because they did not receive any federal financial assistance (see chapter 3). For example, some state and local courts and police departments may not receive federal financial assistance. Deaf people could not use Section 504 to complain about discrimination when these courts and law enforcement agencies did not provide interpreter services. Now, however, they can look to the ADA to require equal access.

The goal of Title II is to make sure that people with disabilities may use all services, programs, and activities of state and local governments. Any person with a disability who meets the essential eligibility requirements for obtaining services or participating in or benefiting from a government program is protected by the ADA.

Agencies That Must Be Accessible

Title II of the ADA applies to all state and local "public entities," as well as to Amtrak and commuter transportation agencies. The term is defined broadly to include "everything a state or local entity does." Public agencies include the following:

+ school systems
+ motor vehicle departments
+ police and fire departments
+ parks and recreation programs
+ jails and prisons
+ libraries
+ food stamp offices
+ welfare and social service agencies
+ public hospitals, clinics, and counseling centers

Although federal courts are not covered by Title II, state and local courts, as well as the legislatures of cities, counties, and states, must comply with the statute.[12] State and local government activities carried out by private contractors may also be covered by the ADA. For example, state park concession activities are often operated by private contractors, and shelters and halfway houses may be operated by private nonprofit agencies but receive state and local government contracts.

Federal government agencies, however, are not covered by Title II. Federal buildings and federal executive agencies are required to be accessible, but they are covered by the Rehabilitation Act and the Architectural Barriers Act, not by the ADA.

Defining Discrimination under the ADA and the Rehabilitation Act

If a person with a disability meets the "essential eligibility requirements" for a state or local government program, activity, or service, that entity cannot use the individual's disability as a reason to (1) exclude the person from participating, (2) deny the person the benefits of the program, activity, or service, or (3) subject the person to discrimination. In addition, state and local government agencies must comply with the following requirements:

1. A government agency cannot exclude or refuse to serve an individual because of a disability. For example, city recreation programs may not turn away or impose additional requirements on people who are deaf. A counseling or health service may not refuse to accept a deaf client because of difficulty in communication.
2. A government agency must modify policies and practices that are unfair to people with disabilities. For example, an agency that requires a driver's license as the only acceptable means of identification must change its policy because blind individuals or individuals with other disabilities may not be able to obtain drivers' licenses. If the agency imposes safety requirements that are necessary for the safe operation of the program (such as a requirement to have a valid driver's license), the requirement must be based on actual risk and not on mere speculation, stereotype, or generalizations about individuals with disabilities. If an agency has a "no pets" policy, it may be required to modify that policy for dogs or other animals that are trained to provide assistance to deaf or blind people.
3. A public park that leases boats or other equipment cannot ask a deaf individual to pay a higher deposit than that for hearing people or take out additional insurance to rent equipment.

4. A government agency must remove architectural, communication, or transportation barriers. The agency does not have to remove physical barriers in every part of every public building, as long as the programs it offers can be made available to people who cannot use the facility. For example, the agency could serve a person with a disability in an accessible location or provide an aide, an assistant, or a device that would enable the person to use the service.
5. Most important to deaf individuals, a government agency must also provide the "auxiliary aids and services" that are needed to ensure effective communication between a deaf individual and a hearing individual.

Auxiliary Aids and Services

Which Auxiliary Aids Should Be Provided?

Government agencies are required to provide auxiliary aids so that a deaf or hard of hearing individual may have an equal opportunity to participate in and enjoy government services, programs, and activities.[13] The appropriate auxiliary aid will depend on the type of service, program, or activity being accommodated and the needs of the person wanting to take part in it. For example, a deaf person who uses sign language may need an interpreter to understand a school board meeting or to talk to a county social worker or police officer. However, an interpreter would be useless for a deaf or hard of hearing person who does not use sign language. In that case, the appropriate auxiliary aid may be a transcription service or an amplification system.

The DOJ defines a qualified interpreter as "an interpreter who, via a video remote interpreting (VRI) service or an on-site appearance, is able to interpret effectively, accurately, and impartially, both receptively and expressively, using any necessary specialized vocabulary. Qualified interpreters include, for example, sign language interpreters, oral transliterators, and cued-language transliterators."[14] An interpreter who is qualified for one type of interpreting assignment may not have sufficient skills for interpreting in another situation.

What Are Auxiliary Aids and Services?

State and local governments must ensure effective communication with individuals with disabilities.[15] In order to make sure that communication for a person who is deaf or hard of hearing is as effective as communication for others, the public agency must provide appropriate auxiliary aids.

Auxiliary aids include any device or service that is needed to make spoken information accessible to a deaf person. The DOJ regulation specifically lists the following:

qualified interpreters (on-site or through video remote interpreting services)

notetakers

real-time computer-aided transcription services

written materials or exchange of written notes

telephone handset amplifiers or telephones compatible with hearing aids

assistive listening systems (loop, FM, and infrared systems)

television captioning and decoders; open and closed captioning

voice-, text-, and video-based telecommunications products and services, including TTYs, videophones, and captioned telephones

videotext displays

accessible electronic and information technology

readers

taped texts

However, this list is not inclusive, and additional types of auxiliary aids will be required under ADA standards as new technology becomes available. Also, just having the assistive equipment is not enough. A state or local government must adopt and publicize procedures on available equipment and how to request it.

In determining whether an interpreter or other auxiliary aid is necessary, a government agency should consider the context in which the communication is taking place, the number of people involved, the importance of the communication, and whether the information being communicated is complex or lengthy. A family member or friend should not be considered qualified to interpret because of factors such as emotional or personal involvement or considerations of confidentiality.[16]

Although a state or local government may have the final word on the type of auxiliary aid that will be provided, the deaf individual is in the best position to evaluate his or her own needs and the effectiveness of the service. The DOJ regulation states that in determining what type of auxiliary aid or service is necessary, the public agency must give "primary consideration" to the requests of the individual concerned.[17] The DOJ's analysis of its ADA regulation states the following:

> The public entity must provide an opportunity for individuals with disabilities to request the auxiliary aids and services of their choice. This expressed choice shall be given primary consideration by the public entity. The public entity shall honor the choice unless it can demonstrate that another effective means of communication exists or that use of the means chosen would not be required under the regulation.[18]

Deaf individuals should notify government agencies if interpreters are not sufficiently skilled or if an auxiliary aid does not give them equal access to a program.

Who Pays for the Interpreters and Other Auxiliary Aids?

A state or local governmental agency may not charge a deaf or hard of hearing person any extra fee for providing an interpreter or other auxiliary aid.[19] For example, courts may not include an interpreter fee as "court costs" when a deaf person is involved in a trial and is ordered to pay the "costs" of the trial.[20] The ADA does not require a governmental agency to provide an auxiliary aid if it would result in an undue burden or if it would fundamentally alter the nature of the services the agency provides. Interpreters would seldom be considered an undue burden on a state or local government since the cost is compared to its entire budget. Even if a particular auxiliary aid is considered to be too expensive or burdensome, the state or local government must then offer another auxiliary aid, if available, that does not cause a fundamental alteration to or an undue burden on the agency.

Filing a Complaint

A person who believes that he or she is a victim of discrimination by a state or local government may file a lawsuit or an administrative complaint under the ADA. The remedies, such as damages and injunctive relief, are the same as those provided under Section 504 of the Rehabilitation Act of 1973 (see chapter 3). Administrative complaints may be filed with any agency that provides financial assistance to the entity in question, with the DOJ, or with the federal agency with enforcement authority over that entity or subject area. Complaints should be made in writing and signed by the complainant or an authorized representative. The complaint must contain the complainant's name and address and a description of the alleged discrimination by the public entity. For more information or to file a complaint, contact:

U.S. Department of Justice
950 Pennsylvania Avenue NW
Civil Rights Division
Disability Rights Section—NYA
Washington, DC 20530

TITLE III: PUBLIC ACCOMMODATION

The most dramatic expansion of disability rights is the application of Title III of the ADA to give full and equal access to "places of public accommodation." Title III requires thousands of private businesses, professionals, and nonprofit organizations to remove communication and physical barriers for people with disabilities. For deaf and hard of hearing people, Title III and the DOJ regulation implementing it are of tremendous help in removing communication barriers.[21] The title states that "No individual shall be discriminated against on the basis of disability in the full and equal enjoyment of the goods, services, facilities, privileges, advantages, or accommodations of any place of public accommodation by any person who owns, leases (or leases to), or operates a place of public accommodation."[22]

Title III covers a wide range of commercial and nonprofit places such as hotels, theaters, restaurants, doctors' offices, lawyers' offices, retail stores, banks, museums, parks, libraries, daycare centers, and private schools. A "place of public accommodation" is a facility operated by a private entity whose operations affect commerce and that falls within at least one of the following categories:

1. an inn, hotel, motel, or other place of lodging (except for an establishment in a building that has not more than five rooms for rent and is the residence of the proprietor)
2. a restaurant, bar, or other establishment serving food or drink
3. a movie theater, theater, concert hall, stadium, or other place of exhibition or entertainment
4. an auditorium, convention center, lecture hall, or other place of public gathering
5. a bakery, grocery store, clothing store, hardware store, shopping center, or other sales or rental establishment
6. a Laundromat, dry cleaner, bank, barbershop, beauty shop, travel service, shoe repair service, funeral parlor, gas station, office of an accountant or a lawyer, pharmacy, insurance office, professional office of a healthcare provider, hospital, or other service establishment
7. a terminal, depot, or other station used for public transportation
8. a museum, library, gallery, or other place of public display or collection
9. a park, zoo, amusement park, or other place of recreation
10. a nursery, elementary, secondary, undergraduate, or postgraduate private school, or other place of education
11. a day-care center, senior citizen center, homeless shelter, food bank, adoption agency, or other social service establishment
12. a gymnasium, health spa, bowling alley, golf course, or other place of exercise or recreation[23]

The examples in each category help illustrate and define the category, but they are not the only entities that are covered. For example, even though the "sales or rental establishment" category does not list jewelry stores, all stores, including jewelry stores, are covered. Even though the "service establishment" category does not list photo-finishing shops or housecleaning services, all service and professional service agencies are included. Even though the "education" category does not list driving schools or computer training specialists, all such educational activities are covered.

Title III of the ADA applies no matter how many employees a public accommodation employs—even just one. If the public accommodation fits within the definition of one of the twelve categories, it is covered by Title III of the ADA. However, not all "public" activities are covered by Title III of the ADA. For example, television broadcasters offer services to the general public, but they do not fit within any of the twelve categories. Furthermore, Title III of the ADA does not cover private clubs, religious organizations, or places of worship.

Auxiliary Aids

A public accommodation must provide an "auxiliary aid or service" when necessary for effective communication. The DOJ regulation to implement Title III of the ADA provides a comprehensive list of auxiliary aids and services required by the ADA, including qualified interpreters.[24]

Other examples of auxiliary aids listed in the regulation are notetakers, transcription services, written materials, telephone handset amplifiers, assistive listening devices, assistive listening systems, telephones compatible with hearing aids, closed-caption decoders, open and closed captioning, telecommunication devices for deaf people, and videotext displays. The list is not intended to be exhaustive. The DOJ has noted that new devices will become available as technology advances, and they will be considered "auxiliary aids and services."

The costs of compliance with the auxiliary aids requirements may not be financed by charging a fee to a deaf person. Requiring a deaf person to pay for hiring an interpreter is considered an impermissible "surcharge."[25] However, if a public accommodation loans special equipment (such as a decoder or an assistive listening device) to a customer, it is permitted to charge a reasonable, refundable deposit to ensure that the equipment will be returned. Such deposits would be permissible only if the business also demands a deposit for the loan of equipment to people without disabilities.

Defense of the Requirements

The ADA does not require a public accommodation to provide any auxiliary aid that would result in an "undue burden" or in a fundamental alteration to the nature of the goods and services it provides. An undue burden is defined as a "significant" difficulty or expense to the public accommodation. However, this entity is not exempted from the duty to furnish an alternative auxiliary aid, if available, that would not result in an undue burden.

The DOJ strongly encourages public accommodations to consult with an individual before providing him or her with a particular auxiliary aid or service. The department's analysis of the regulation points out that an interpreter may be necessary to ensure effective communication. It mentions the existence of a wide range of communication situations, including areas such as health, legal matters, and finances that would be sufficiently lengthy or complex to require an interpreter for effective communication. However, unlike the DOJ regulation implementing Title II of the ADA, the DOJ regulation implementing Title III of the ADA does not contain language requiring a public accommodation to give "primary consideration" to the auxiliary aid requests of an individual with a disability.

Decoders and Captioning

Hospitals that provide televisions for patient use and places of lodging that provide televisions in five or more guest rooms must provide a means of decoding captions upon request. Other public accommodations that impart verbal information through soundtracks on films, videotapes, DVDs, or slide shows are required to make such information accessible through means such as captioning.

Movie Captioning

In 2013 the DOJ published a Notice of Proposed Rulemaking (NPRM) to increase the accessibility of movie theaters to people who are deaf or hard of hearing. This process started in 2008, when the DOJ considered revising the regulations implementing Title III of the ADA to make movie theaters more accessible and issued an NPRM to seek comment on the issue. The public comments persuaded the DOJ that captioning at movie theaters should be required. With unresolved questions on how to frame and implement the new requirements, the DOJ issued an additional NPRM in 2010 to elicit more public input on the issue.

Movie theaters are specifically listed in Title III of the ADA as places of public accommodation. DOJ regulations require public accommodations to provide reasonable accommodations, including auxiliary aids and services to individuals with disabilities. Many movie theaters, however, do not offer captioning for the movies they show. The DOJ noted that even though the legislative history of the ADA indicates that Congress did not require open captioning of movies in 1990, it did leave the door open for the DOJ to eventually require captioning as the technology developed. As various types of closed captioning now exist that are cheaper and easier for movie theaters to acquire than open captioning, the DOJ believes it is time for new regulations requiring captioning at movie theaters. Further, recognizing that movie theaters are updating its screens to digital ones, the DOJ published the NPRM in 2013 so the theaters could take the new regulations into account when updating their technology.

In its ANPRM in 2010, the DOJ sought guidance from the public on how to implement the regulations, specifically how many screens should be required to have captioning and the proper method of captioning. In its comments to the ANPRM in 2010, the NAD strongly opposed the suggestion that just 50 percent of movie screens need to comply with new captioning standards within five years and instead suggested that the regulations require all movie theaters to display captions at every movie in every theater, absent a showing of undue burden. The NAD noted that Title III of the ADA already requires movie theaters to provide auxiliary aids and services so that people with disabilities can have full and equal enjoyment of their services. It also suggested that the regulations require movie theaters to make the transition to captioned movies as soon as possible and opposed a five-year transition period. The NAD urged the DOJ to require closed captioning, which is available for display when the movie is first released, and encouraged the DOJ to adopt standards to ensure that the captioning text is readable.

Website Accessibility

The DOJ is considering revising the regulations implementing Title III of the ADA to establish requirements for making websites of public accommodations accessible to individuals with disabilities. In its advance notice of proposed rulemaking in 2010, the DOJ noted that, when the ADA was enacted in 1990, the Internet did not play the large role in the daily lives of Americans that it does today. However, when enacting the ADA, Congress expected that its application would evolve with the times, so the DOJ states that the ADA should be interpreted to keep pace with developing technologies and that businesses that operate virtual "places" solely on the Internet may be considered as "places of public accommodation" under the ADA, provided that they fall into one of the twelve categories listed in the statute. The DOJ put out a notice of proposed rulemaking in December of 2013 regarding website accessibility.

The DOJ has recognized that the inability to fully access websites puts individuals at a great disadvantage in obtaining goods and services, acquiring an education, socializing and seeking entertainment, and obtaining healthcare information. The DOJ noted that deaf individuals are often unable to access information in web videos or other multimedia presentations because these do not have captions. Although some courts have found liability in cases where a business operates an inaccessible website, there is thus far no clear requirement to provide the disability community consistent access to websites and covered entities with clear guidance on what the ADA mandates.

Among other issues, the DOJ sought guidance from the public in its ANPRM on what accessibility standards should apply to covered websites and whether certain types of online activity should be excluded. In its comments to the ANPRM on web accessibility, the National Association of the Deaf recommended that any standards used to determine web accessibility should include a requirement that captions be of high quality and that transcripts of captions also be readily available. Additionally, the NAD agreed with the DOJ that businesses that operate solely on the web should not be exempted in view of the fact that a virtual place can be a "place of public accommodation." It thus urged the DOJ to explicitly state this in the proposed regulations.

Stadiums

Great strides have recently been made in the courts in providing deaf and hard of hearing individuals with captioning at sporting events. In 2006 three deaf Washington Redskins fans sued Pro-Football, Inc., alleging a failure to provide equal access to aural content available to fans with no hearing loss. The plaintiffs requested that the defendant "provide and display captioning on . . . video monitors at FedEx Field for all announcements made over the public address system, including all of the plays that just occurred, all of the penalties called, safety and emergency information, and any other announcements made over the public address system."[26] On March 25, 2011, the US Court of Appeals for the Fourth Circuit Court affirmed the decision of a Maryland federal district court that required that "music with lyrics, play information, advertisements, referee calls, safety/emergency information, and other announcements"[27] be captioned. The appeals court reasoned that the plaintiffs must be able to enjoy the services provided by the Redskins "as equally as possible with hearing spectators." It continued by stating that the defendants must provide "full and equal enjoyment" of the goods and services in view of the fact that, without auxiliary aids to provide such access, the plaintiffs would be treated differently, which would put the defendants in violation of the ADA.

On October 12, 2010, the Ohio State University (OSU), the attorney general of Ohio, and Vincent Sabino entered into a consent decree to resolve the lawsuit that Sabino had filed against OSU regarding the use of captioning at athletic events. Sabino's lawsuit alleged that OSU's athletic department discriminated against him and other deaf and hard of hearing individuals by failing to provide adequate auxiliary aids and services at Ohio Stadium and Value City Arena at the Jerome Schottenstein Center. This consent decree requires that OSU provide scoreboard captions for all public address announcements, emergency information, music, and other auditory information broadcast into Ohio Stadium before, during, and after home football games. It also requires OSU to activate the captioning of television broadcasts in the concourse of Ohio Stadium on at least half of the television monitors there and continue to handle accessible seating requests under its existing policies. Additionally, OSU must update its websites for its athletic department and the Value City Arena to include a guide for guests with disabilities, information about requesting accommodations, contact information for OSU's ADA coordinator, and an outline of the complaint procedure for guests with disabilities.

Conferences and Performances

Educational and training organizations, trade associations, or performing artists that lease space for a conference or performance at a hotel, auditorium, convention center, or stadium must comply with the ADA.[28] The analysis to the DOJ regulation states that the renter is responsible for providing auxiliary aids and services for the participants in its conference or the audience at its performance. The determination of who actually provides auxiliary aids (the landlord or the renters) can be decided during the lease negotiations. For example, if a theater rents space to a performing artist, the question of who provides an interpreter will be decided by their contract. Both the landlord and the tenant are subject to the requirements of the ADA.

Use of Service Animals

The DOJ Title III regulation provides broad protections for the use of service animals.[29] Public accommodations must modify their policies and practices to allow the use of service animals, which are broadly defined to include any dog or other animal that is trained to provide assistance to a person with a disability. The ADA does not require service animals to be professionally trained or certified by state agencies.

Examinations and Courses

Title III of the ADA requires private organizations that offer examinations or courses for licensing, certification, or credentials to provide appropriate auxiliary aids such as interpreters.[30] This applies to high school or college education and to professional and trade training. The private organization would not be required to provide an auxiliary aid if it could show that such provision would fundamentally alter the skills or knowledge the examination intends to test. The examinations must be designed and administered in a way that best reflect an individual's aptitude or achievement level rather than the person's impaired sensory, manual, or speaking skills. The only exception is where the examination seeks to measure those skills.

Existing vs. New Facilities

The ADA requires the removal of structural communication barriers from existing facilities.[31] This can be accomplished by installing flashing alarm systems, permanent signage, assistive listening systems, and adequate sound buffers. For newly constructed buildings, the US Architectural and Transportation Barriers Compliance Board (Access Board) has developed ADA Accessibility Guidelines (ADAAG).[32] According to these guidelines, all new construction and building alterations must be accessible to people with disabilities. The requirements for telephones, assistive listening devices, and visual alarm systems are as follows:

1. One TTY must be provided inside any building that has four or more public pay telephones, including both interior and exterior phones. In addition, one TTY must be provided whenever there is an interior public pay phone in a stadium or an arena; a convention center; a hotel with a convention center; a covered shopping mall; or a hospital emergency, recovery, or waiting room.

2. One accessible public pay phone must be provided for each level of a public accommodation. If a level has two or more banks of phones, there must be one accessible phone for each bank.

3. Fixed-seating assembly areas that accommodate fifty or more people or that have audio-amplification systems must have a permanently installed assistive listening system.

4. Hotels must make 8 percent of the first one hundred rooms and approximately 4 percent of the remaining rooms accessible to deaf and hard of hearing people. These rooms must contain visual alarms, notification devices, volume-control telephones, and an accessible electrical outlet for a TTY. Half of these rooms must also be accessible to people with physical disabilities.

Enforcement

Individuals with disabilities can bring lawsuits for court orders to stop discrimination under Title III, but they cannot collect money damages. If the individuals win their court case, they can recover attorney's fees and costs. Individuals with disabilities can also file complaints with the US attorney general, who has the power to initiate lawsuits in cases of public importance or where a "pattern or practice" of discrimination is alleged. In such cases, the attorney general may seek money damages and civil penalties. In many cases, the Justice Department will refer a case for mediation rather than investigating.

The 2010 Amendments to the DOJ Regulations Implementing Title III of the ADA

In September 2010 the Department of Justice published amendments to its regulations that implement Title II of the Americans with Disabilities Act, which applies to public entities, and Title III of the ADA, which applies to public accommodations and commercial facilities. These final regulations became effective on March 15, 2011. The following summary describes the significant effects these new regulations have specifically on the deaf and hard of hearing community and the requirement that public entities and accommodations provide effective communications under Title III:

+ Clarify that a qualified interpreter means an interpreter who, via a video remote interpreting service or an on-site appearance, is able to interpret effectively. Moreover, the DOJ provides examples of qualified interpreters, including sign language interpreters, oral transliterators, and cued-language transliterators.
+ Expand the definition of what auxiliary aids and services a place of public accommodation should offer to ensure that individuals who are deaf or hard of hearing are not excluded. The following items have been added under the term "auxiliary aids and services": qualified interpreters on-site or available through video remote interpreting services; computer-aided real-time transcription services; exchange of written notes; open and closed captioning, including real-time captioning; voice, text, and video-based telecommunications products and systems, including text telephones, videophones, and captioned telephones, or equally effective telecommunications devices; videotext displays; accessible electronic and information technology.
+ Explain that effective communication must be provided not only to individuals with disabilities but also to "companions" (family, friends, or associates) if they have disabilities and are seeking access to or are participating in the goods, services, facilities, privileges, advantages, or accommodations of a public accommodation and are appropriate persons with whom the public accommodation should communicate.

- State that public entities shall not require an individual with a disability to bring another individual to interpret for him or her. Moreover, if an individual is accompanied by an adult, the public entity shall not rely on that adult to interpret or facilitate communications except (1) in an emergency where no interpreter is available (this exception extends to minors, who may act as interpreters) or (2) when the individual with a disability specifically requests that the accompanying adult interpret if he or she agrees to do so and such assistance is appropriate under the circumstances.
- State that public accommodations that use automated-attendant systems require those systems to provide effective real-time communication for individuals using auxiliary aids and services, including text telephones and all forms of FCC-approved telecommunications relay systems, including Internet-based relay systems. Moreover, a public accommodation may use relay services in place of direct telephone communication to receive or make telephone calls incident to its operations and shall respond to telephone calls from a telecommunications relay service established under title IV of the ADA in the same manner in which it responds to other telephone calls.
- Set forth standards that govern the use of video remote interpreting services to provide interpretation. VRI uses video conference technology over dedicated lines or wireless technology offering a high-speed, wide-bandwidth video connection that delivers high-quality video images. The DOJ has established performance standards for VRI and requires training for users of the technology and other involved individuals so that they may quickly and efficiently set up and operate the system.

TITLE IV: TELECOMMUNICATIONS

Title IV of the ADA requires telephone companies to provide both local and long-distance telecommunications relay services across the nation. (See chapter 11 for a complete discussion of telecommunications issues.) These relay services enable deaf and hard of hearing people to have telephone conversations with people who use conventional voice telephones any time, any place, and for any reason whatsoever. In addition, Title IV also requires all television public service announcements that are produced or funded by the federal government to include closed captioning. Occasionally, federal agencies develop television announcements about AIDS, aging, drug use, and other general health and consumer issues. In the future, the vital information in these and other federally assisted announcements will finally reach individuals who rely on closed captions to receive the verbal content of television.

Notes

1. Pub. L. No. 101–336; 42 U.S.C. 12101 et seq.
2. 42 U.S.C. 12102(2). See also *Rehabilitation Act*, 29 U.S.C. 706(8) (A); *Fair Housing Act Amendments Act*, 42 U.S.C. 3602(h) (1988); *Air Carrier Access Act*, 49 U.S.C. 1374(c)(2).
3. 29 C.F.R. §1630.2(j)(1).
4. *Sutton v. United Airlines*, 119 S.Ct. 2139 (1999).
5. *Murphy v. United Parcel Service*, 119 S.Ct. 2133 (1999).
6. *Kirkingburg v. Albertsons*, 119 S.Ct. 2162 (1999).
7. Pub. L. No. 110-325(b)(2).
8. 29 C.F.R. §1630.
9. 29 C.F.R. §1630.2.
10. 29 C.F.R. §1630.4.
11. 28 C.F.R. Part 35.
12. Federal courts are covered by 28 U.S.C. §1827.
13. 28 C.F.R. §35.160(b).
14. 28 C.F.R. §35.104.
15. 28 C.F.R. §35.160.
16. *56 Fed. Reg.* 35,701 (July 26, 1991).
17. 28 C.F.R. §35.160(b).
18. *56 Fed. Reg.* 35,711–35,712 (July 26, 1991).
19. 28 C.F.R. §35.130(f).
20. The analysis to the Justice Department ADA regulation states that "the costs of interpreter services may not be assessed as an element of court costs. The Justice Department has already recognized that imposition of the cost of courtroom interpreter services is impermissible under section 504 . . . Accordingly, recouping the costs of interpreter services by assessing them as part of court costs would also be prohibited" (*56 Fed. Reg.* 35,706 [July 26, 1991]).

21. 28 C.F.R. §35.161.
22. 28 C.F.R. §35.162.
23. 28 C.F.R. Part 36.
24. 42 U.S.C. §12182(a).
25. 28 C.F.R. §36.301(c).
26. *Feldman, Kelly, & Singleton v. Pro Football, Inc., & WFI Stadium, Inc.,* (4th Cir. 2011).
27. *Feldman, et al. v. Pro Football, Inc., et al.,* No. AW-06-2266 (Md. Dist. Ct. 2011).
28. 28 C.F.R. §36.201(b)(4).
29. 28 C.F.R. §36.104.
30. 28 C.F.R. §36.303.
31. 28 C.F.R. §36.302.
32. U.S. Access Board, "ADA Accessibility Guidelines (ADAAG)," September 2002, http://www.access-board.gov/guidelines-and-standards/buildings-and-sites/about-the-ada-standards/background/adaag.

Chapter 3

The Rehabilitation Act of 1973

In 1920 Congress passed the first federal laws to help people with disabilities get job training and find employment.[1] But these laws were clearly inadequate; even highly qualified people with disabilities could not find good jobs because of widespread discrimination by private employers and by federal, state, and local governments. Congress helped address the problem by enacting the Rehabilitation Act of 1973.

At the time of its passage, Title V of the Rehabilitation Act was hailed as a "bill of rights" for people with disabilities. The purpose of Title V is to make sure that programs receiving federal financial assistance can be used by individuals with disabilities, so that the federal government will no longer be implicated in discriminatory activities. This chapter focuses on the implementation, regulation, and application of Section 504, which prohibits discrimination in federal programs and federally supported programs and on recent changes to Section 508.

Synopsis of Title V

The five major sections of Title V prohibit discrimination and require accessibility in employment, education, health, welfare, and social services.

Section 501 applies to federal government employment practices.[2] It requires that the federal government not discriminate against applicants and employees of the federal government and that it make reasonable accommodations for applicants and employees. It also requires each executive department and agency to adopt an affirmative action plan for the hiring, placement, and advancement of qualified people with disabilities. (For more information see chapter 7.)

Section 502 created the Architectural and Transportation Barriers Compliance Board, or Access Board.[3] The Access Board's primary functions are to ensure compliance with the Architectural Barriers Act (a 1968 federal law prohibiting architectural barriers in federally funded buildings) and to eliminate barriers from public buildings. (For more information on the Access Board see chapter 2.)

Section 503 requires that federal contractors not discriminate against applicants and employees with disabilities.[4] It also requires affirmative action in the hiring, placement, and promotion of qualified people with disabilities by employers who have contracts or subcontracts with the federal government of more than $10,000 a year. Contractors with fifteen or more employees or contracts for more than $50,000 are also required to have written affirmative action plans. (See chapter 7.)

Section 504 prohibits discrimination against qualified people with disabilities by recipients of federal financial assistance with respect to the provision of any federally supported program or activity.[5] Recipients of federal financial assistance include many public and some private institutions.

Section 508 requires federal agencies to procure and use electronic and information technology that is accessible to individuals with disabilities. Examples of this technology are hardware and software for computers, telecommunications equipment, Internet-based information and applications, and multimedia applications. The Architectural and Transportation Compliance Board has the responsibility of establishing accessibility standards under Section 508. Each federal agency must use these standards to develop its own policies for procuring and using electronic and information technology.

Section 504

As amended in 1978, Section 504 of the Rehabilitation Act reads as follows:

No otherwise qualified individual with a disability in the United States . . . shall, solely by reason of his or her disability, be excluded from the participation in, be denied the benefits of, or be subjected to discrimination under any program or activity receiving Federal financial assistance or under any program or activity conducted by any Executive Agency or by the United States Postal Service.

Section 504 is implemented by detailed regulations that every federal agency giving financial assistance must promulgate, spelling out the Section 504 obligations of its recipients. In 1977 the US Department of Health, Education, and Welfare (HEW)[6] became the first agency to publish its regulation and detailed analysis.[7] The department also issued a set of standards for other agencies to use in developing their own Section 504 rules. A 1980 executive order gave the Department of Justice primary authority to monitor the agencies' regulations.[8]

Who Must Obey Section 504?

The federal government assists many programs and activities around the country. The Section 504 regulation defines "federal financial assistance" as any grant, loan, contract, or other arrangement by which the department provides assistance in the form of funds or services of federal personnel or property.[9] Procurement contracts are specifically excluded. As a result, private manufacturers of items purchased by the government do not have to obey Section 504. However, they may be subject to Section 503, which prohibits employment discrimination by federal contractors. Organizations that have procurement contracts and also receive federal financial assistance must obey both Section 503 and Section 504.

Section 504 applies to an organization regardless of whether it receives federal assistance directly or indirectly, for example, through a state or local government. A "recipient" is defined as any institution that receives federal assistance or indirectly benefits from such assistance.

Certain types of significant federal involvement are not considered to be assistance in the form of funds or services. For example, the federal government awards broadcast licenses to radio and television broadcasters, but these licenses are not considered either federal assistance or federally conducted programs.[10] Commercial airlines benefit from the federal air traffic control system furnished by the government, but the US Supreme Court has held that operation of the federal system is not federal financial assistance to the airlines themselves.[11]

Notwithstanding these narrow exceptions, the definition of federal financial assistance is so broad that many private and public institutions must obey Section 504. The types of institutions that usually receive some form of federal financial assistance include elementary and secondary schools, colleges and universities, hospitals, nursing homes, vocational rehabilitation agencies, public welfare offices, state and local governments, police and fire departments, correction and probation departments, libraries, museums, theater programs, parks, recreational facilities, mass transit systems, airports and harbors, subsidized housing programs, legal services programs, and most of the judicial system.

Sometimes it is difficult to determine whether and from what agency an institution gets federal financial assistance. If the institution is public, citizens can usually examine its financial records and reports to see whether it receives federal assistance. Many federal agencies keep public lists of the programs and activities they fund. If an agency does not have such a list or if the particular institution is not listed, a request can be filed under the Freedom of Information Act (FOIA) of 1966 with each federal agency thought to be the funding source.[12]

The FOIA request should identify the possible recipient, state that the information is being sought under the Freedom of Information Act, and ask whether the particular institution receives federal financial assistance and, if so, for what purpose. It is important to identify the institution fully and correctly and to give the name and address of any parent organization(s) to which it belongs. For example, a local branch library may not be listed as a direct recipient of federal assistance. Instead, the state, regional, or county association may be the formal recipient. The federal agency is supposed to respond to a FOIA request within ten days.

A complaint against an institution for violation of Section 504 can be filed with a federal agency even if it is not clear whether the institution gets financial assistance from that agency. If the agency does not financially support that institution, the agency will simply refuse to accept the complaint. If an institution receives any federal financial assistance for one part of its activities, then it must obey Section 504 in all of its activities that benefit from the financial assistance even if those other activities do not receive any direct aid. Section 504 was again amended in 1987 to clarify that the law applies to all of the operations of an agency, department, college, hospital, or other organization that receives any federal financial assistance.[13]

Section 504 applies to federal executive agencies and recipients of federal financial assistance. Because the original 1973 law did not apply to federal agencies, most of the Section 504 regulations apply only to recipients of assistance from the agency and not to the agency itself. Since the adoption of the 1978 amendments,

however, the agencies themselves must obey Section 504 regardless of whether they have adopted specific regulations that apply
to their own activities.[14]

Defining a "Qualified Person with a Disability"

Section 504 does not guarantee access to jobs or services merely
because a person has a disability. To be protected by Section 504,
a person with a disability must also be qualified for the job or
service in question. The 504 regulations define a "qualified person
with a disability" as follows:

+ With respect to employment, a person with a disability
  who, with reasonable accommodation, can perform the
  essential functions of the job in question.
+ With respect to public preschool, elementary, secondary, or
  adult education, a person with a disability (i) of an age
  during which other students are provided such services,
  (ii) of any age during which it is mandatory under state law
  to provide such services, or (iii) to whom a state is required
  to provide a free appropriate public education under the
  Individuals with Disabilities Education Act (IDEA).
+ With respect to postsecondary and vocational education
  services, a person with a disability who meets the academic
  and technical standards requisite to admission to or participation in the recipient's education program or activity.
+ With respect to other services, a person with a disability
  who meets the essential eligibility requirements for the
  receipt of such services.[15]

A person must fall under the applicable definition in order to
be protected by the nondiscrimination provisions of Section 504.

GENERAL NONDISCRIMINATION PROVISIONS

The Section 504 regulations list general categories of discriminatory behavior that are prohibited. They also establish broad policy
guidelines to determine whether a particular discriminatory act is
prohibited by Section 504.

Equal Opportunity

The most significant principle of Section 504 is that no recipient or federal agency may deny a qualified person an opportunity to participate in or benefit from its programs or services.[16] A federally funded program cannot refuse to serve a person with a disability merely because of that disability. For example, a deaf person cannot be denied admission to a federally funded mental health counseling program merely because he or she is deaf. If a counseling program is available only to people who live in a certain county, however, and the deaf person does not live in that county, he or she can be denied admission to the program for that nondiscriminatory reason.

A person with a disability must be given an opportunity to participate in or benefit from a program in a manner that is equal to and as effective as the opportunity provided to other people.[17] To be equally effective, a program does not have to produce the identical result or level of achievement for participants with a disability and those without; the requirement is only that people with disabilities must be provided an equal opportunity to obtain the same result, to gain the same benefit, or to reach the same level of achievement as other people.[18] For example, the administrator of an adult education program might tell a deaf person simply to read the written materials for a class rather than attending lectures and discussions. This would be unfair. Because the lectures and discussions help to explain and amplify the written material, the deaf person would not have an equal opportunity to benefit from the class. More important, others benefit from the availability of lectures and discussions, and Section 504 requires the same availability for deaf persons.

Different or Special Treatment

Sometimes people with disabilities need different treatment in order to give them genuine equal opportunity. In the area of race or sex discrimination, equal opportunity usually means treating people in exactly the same way. However, a person with a disability may need some special assistance or accommodation in order to obtain benefits or services equivalent to those that other people obtain. Failure to provide that accommodation or assistance would constitute discrimination. The analysis accompanying the original Section 504 regulation explains this as follows:

> Different or special treatment of handicapped persons because of their handicaps may be necessary in a number of contexts in order to assure [sic] equal opportunity. Thus, for example, it is meaningless to "admit" a handicapped person in a wheelchair to a program if the program is offered only on the third floor of a walk-up building. Nor is one providing equal educational opportunity to a deaf child by admitting him or her to a classroom but providing no means for the child to understand the teacher or receive instruction.[19]

At the same time, Section 504 also prohibits unnecessary special or different treatment if it would tend to stigmatize people with disabilities or set them apart from other people. Different or separate aids, benefits, or services are prohibited unless the separation is necessary to provide services that are as effective as those provided to others.[20] A legal services organization, for example, may designate a special office to serve clients who have disabilities if the office is physically accessible and has lawyers trained in disability law. But it would be unfair to require all clients with disabilities, regardless of their legal problems, to use only that special office.

Communication Barriers

The general nondiscrimination provisions in the Section 504 regulation apply to the communication barriers faced by deaf people as well as to physical barriers encountered by people in wheelchairs. A deaf woman may be able to walk up a flight of stairs to a job counseling center without difficulty. But if she cannot understand the intake worker's explanations about filling out the forms, she will not be able to complete them correctly. She will not know what services are available or how to get them. A deaf man may be able to walk into a hospital or mental health center, but if he cannot communicate with the doctor or counselor, then he does not have meaningful, equivalent access to the program and its facilities.

The HHS analysis of the regulation gives an example of a welfare office that uses telephones to communicate with clients. Clients can call the office for information or to reach caseworkers. Staff can call clients to schedule appointments. This office must provide an accessible means to communicate with its deaf clients, such as through the telecommunications relay system. Another example is a museum exhibit that includes monitors with videorecorded interviews or explanations. The exhibit video must be captioned to enable deaf or hard of hearing people to obtain the same information.

Communication problems are specifically addressed in the Justice Department's Section 504 regulations. These rules require recipients to ensure that communications are effectively conveyed to people with a visual or hearing impairment.[21] The regulation requires recipients to provide appropriate auxiliary aids in order to give this population equal access to programs and services.[22]

When the Justice Department implemented the ADA, it clarified Section 504's definition of auxiliary aids and services. The ADA regulation defines auxiliary aids and services to include "qualified interpreters on-site or through video remote interpreting (VRI) services; notetakers; real-time computer-aided transcription services; written materials; exchange of written notes; telephone handset amplifiers; assistive listening devices; assistive listening systems; telephones compatible with hearing aids; closed caption decoders; open and closed captioning, including real-time captioning; voice, text, and video-based telecommunications products and systems, including text telephones (TTYs), videophones, and captioned telephones, or equally effective telecommunications devices; videotext displays; accessible electronic and information technology; or other effective methods of making aurally delivered information available to individuals who are deaf or hard of hearing."[23] The Justice Department also defined a qualified interpreter as one "who, via a video remote interpreting (VRI) service or an on-site appearance, is able to interpret effectively, accurately, and impartially, both receptively and expressively, using any necessary specialized vocabulary. Qualified interpreters include, for example, sign language interpreters, oral transliterators, and cued-language transliterators."[24]

Interpreters should be available for any meeting, conference, class, or other group activity held by an agency that receives federal financial assistance. Section 504 requires interpreters for cultural events, city government meetings, adult education classes, park programs, or any other event that deaf people may wish to attend. Publicity for meetings should announce the availability of special services and interpreters and describe the procedures for requesting them.

The needs of deaf people are specifically addressed by one HHS regulation that requires funding recipients to ensure that people with a visual or a hearing impairment can obtain information about the various services that are accessible to them.[25] For example, televised public service announcements that are federally funded should be signed or captioned. If federally funded programs or services are announced by radio, a recipient might ensure that deaf people receive the same information by direct mail or by announcements inserted in local newsletters or newspapers distributed by associations of people who are deaf or hard of hearing.

Program Accessibility

The Section 504 regulation requires that programs be offered in a way that permits people with disabilities to use them easily and have equal opportunity to benefit from them.[26] For people in wheelchairs, "program accessibility" means removing architectural and physical barriers. For deaf people, it means removing communication barriers. Deaf people cannot fully utilize programs and facilities that they do not have equal access to or in which they are unable to communicate effectively. Programs and facilities must be usable by everyone. This requirement of the Rehabilitation Act suggests much more than physical accessibility to a site or building. In effect, it requires that people with disabilities have functionally equivalent services and programs.

As a policy concept, program accessibility should be invoked aggressively to prevent the exclusion of deaf people from many programs and services.

The Section 504 regulations list methods of making programs accessible.[27] Although the list provides little guidance for making specific programs accessible to deaf people, the phrase "redesign of equipment" encompasses modifications to telephones and auditory alarm systems; captions for films and videos; and stage, podium, and audiovisual system designs that include facilities and lighting for interpreters. The phrase "assignment of aides" can be interpreted to mean the provision of appropriate interpreters, notetakers, transcribers, or other aides needed by deaf people. Because this list is not inclusive, deaf people should feel free to request any other accommodation that would make a program or activity accessible.

ENFORCEMENT OF SECTION 504

A person who believes that a recipient of federal financial assistance has discriminated against him or her on the basis of disability has several alternative procedures for seeking redress.

Administrative Enforcement

There is no central enforcement mechanism for Section 504. Although the Justice Department has overall supervision, every agency that provides federal financial assistance is required to adopt its own regulations and enforcement procedures. Each agency must make its recipients sign assurances of compliance with Section 504 and use the same enforcement procedures as those established to enforce Title VI of the Civil Rights Act of 1964. Within this framework, the procedures used by the various agencies can differ substantially. However, most of the agencies have adopted procedures that are modeled on those originally developed by HEW and now used by the Department of HHS and the Department of Education.

Self-Evaluation

All recipients must conduct a self-evaluation of their Section 504 compliance, assisted by interested parties, including people with disabilities or organizations representing them.[28] Recipients must complete their self-evaluations, modify any policies or practices that were not in compliance with Section 504, and take appropriate remedial steps to eliminate the effects of any discrimination that resulted from past policies and practices. If a recipient has not yet conducted a self-evaluation or made appropriate modifications, a person bringing a complaint can use this fact to focus attention on discriminatory practices. If a recipient refuses to conduct a self-evaluation, any interested person can file a complaint asking the appropriate federal agency to compel compliance.

Internal Grievance Procedure

The Department of Education and the HHS require recipients with fifteen or more employees to adopt grievance procedures for complaints alleging discrimination under Section 504. Such recipients must also designate at least one person to coordinate Section 504 compliance. The grievance procedure must incorporate appropriate due process standards and provide for the "prompt and equitable" resolution of complaints.[29] Complaint procedures need not be established for applicants seeking employment or admission to postsecondary institutions.

A grievance procedure can be a useful, inexpensive mechanism to resolve simple complaints, especially those stemming from ignorance of or misunderstandings about disabilities and Section 504 obligations. Correspondence, memoranda, and other documents generated in grievance proceedings can be used later as evidence of the recipient's discriminatory attitudes or policies. Because the grievance procedure is set up and operated by the recipient itself, however, it will usually be ineffective to resolve major or contested complaints.

Complaint to the Federal Agency

A person who believes that a recipient of federal financial assistance has violated Section 504 can file a complaint with the federal agency that provided the financial assistance. Complaints against recipients of funding from either the Department of Education or HHS should be filed with that agency's regional Office for Civil Rights.

Filing Complaints

Complaints must be filed within 180 days of the alleged discriminatory act. For example, if a deaf person went to a hospital on March 1 and was not provided with an interpreter, the person must send a complaint to HHS within 180 days of the date of the discrimination, which would be August 28. If the complainant waits longer than that, the department will not be required to do anything about the grievance. However, the time for filing can be extended at the discretion of the department. Many discriminatory acts are continuous; they represent a general policy or course of conduct. When this is the case, the 180-day limit may not be a problem. The complainant can try to use the program or service again (e.g., reapply for benefits or employment; renew the request for auxiliary aids) so there will be no question that the discriminatory act took place within the time limits.

The complaint can be a simple letter that merely notifies the federal agency of an alleged discriminatory act. However, it will have more impact if it sets out all of the important facts of the discrimination and fully identifies the parts of the Section 504 regulation that have been violated. The complaint should include the following information:

+ the name, address, and telephone number of the person lodging the complaint ("complainant") and any special instructions for contacting a deaf complainant
+ the name, address, and telephone number of the complainant's attorney or other representative, if any; a statement that the complainant is a "qualified person with a disability" under Section 504

- the name, address, and telephone number of the program or facility that discriminated and a statement that this program receives financial assistance from the federal agency
- a complete description of the discriminatory acts in chronological order. The complaint should be as specific as possible about the dates, places, names, and titles of the people involved and should explain why the conduct was discriminatory and how the complainant was qualified for the job, benefit, service, or program
- a description of any attempts to complain about the discrimination and the organization's response
- any other information or documents that help explain the discrimination and describe what happened
- a list of witnesses, including names, addresses, titles, and telephone numbers
- if possible, an analysis of the parts of the Section 504 regulation that have been violated

Any relevant documents should be photocopied and attached to the complaint. Do not send original documents. Any attached documents should be numbered and clearly identified by number in the text of the complaint.

Agency Investigation

The federal agency will then investigate the matter and determine whether a violation of Section 504 has occurred. Agency investigators should interview the complainant, representatives of the program, and other relevant witnesses. Although the complainant is not a formal "party" to the investigation and has no role in it or in the resolution reached by the agency, the complainant should attempt to be actively involved. Make sure that the federal investigator has contacted important witnesses and is familiar with the issues. This is particularly important in complaints involving deafness; few investigators are knowledgeable about deafness and the types of auxiliary aids or reasonable accommodations that may be necessary to overcome communication barriers. The investigator may need to meet with experts or other people who can provide relevant information.

If the federal agency finds that a recipient has violated Section 504, it will notify the complainant and the recipient in writing. It will then try to negotiate with the recipient to provide the appropriate relief. The agency can require the recipient to take necessary remedial action to overcome effects of the discrimination. The agency can also require a remedial action plan that shows what steps the recipient will take within a specific time period to come into compliance. Such a plan requires the recipient to document its efforts. If the recipient fails to take the required corrective steps or if negotiations do not result in a satisfactory resolution, the federal agency will then institute enforcement proceedings to terminate the recipient's federal financial assistance.

Judicial Enforcement

A person has the right to bypass Section 504 agency complaint procedures by bringing a lawsuit in federal court. Investigations by federal agencies can take a long time; by the time they are completed, it may be too late to help the person with a disability. A lawsuit in federal court might provide a quicker, more effective remedy, as well as monetary damages; attorney's fees and other court costs can be awarded. For example, a deaf woman who was about to have a baby learned that her hospital would not allow an interpreter in the delivery room. She could not wait for a federal agency to investigate her complaint, so she filed a lawsuit in federal court and received immediate help. Federal injunctions have also been upheld in cases involving college students needing classroom interpreters.

Each of these methods to enforce Section 504 should be reviewed carefully to determine which will be most effective in a particular case.

Section 508

The US Congress originally enacted Section 508 in 1986. At that time, all federal agencies were directed to make their electronic equipment accessible in compliance with guidelines developed by the General Services Administration. Although a few federal agencies did comply with these mandates, most of them ignored the directives of Section 508 during the decade that followed. As the need for access to electronic and information technology grew in the 1990s, consumers with disabilities became frustrated with the federal government's failure to comply with Section 508. In the mid-1990s, consumers went back to the US Congress to ask for a new version of Section 508 that contained stronger enforcement mechanisms. In 1998 consumers were successful, and an amended version of Section 508 was enacted in the Workforce Investment Act of that year.[30] The regulations implementing Section 508 were updated in 2013.

The amended version of Section 508 contains strict requirements for federal agencies to obtain and use electronic and information technology that is accessible to federal employees with disabilities and to individuals with disabilities outside the federal government who need government information. Under this law, access to and use of information and data must be comparable to access and use available to federal employees and members of the public who do not have a disability unless doing so would impose an undue burden on the agency. If providing access would result in an undue burden, a federal agency must (1) provide documentation on why access would result in such a burden and (2) provide the information that was requested through an alternative means of access. Consumers will be able to bring a complaint against agencies that do not comply with these requirements.

Section 508 has had a significant impact on the ability of deaf and hard of hearing individuals. In addition to requiring access to technologies themselves, the new law requires mainstream technologies to work with adaptive technologies. It requires all materials presented in an audio format to have either open or closed captions. Any piece of technology that transmits information must do so in a manner that does not eliminate access. For example, if a particular software program contains captions, the technology used to transmit that program may not eliminate those captions.

NOTES

1. The earliest laws regarding people who are deaf include Pub. L. No. 236-66 and the *Smith-Fess Act of 1920*.
2. 29 U.S.C. §791.
3. 29 U.S.C. §792.
4. 29 U.S.C. §793.
5. 29 U.S.C. §794.
6. The HEW was divided into two cabinet-level departments, the Department of Education and the Department of Health and Human Services (HHS), effective May 4, 1980. Hereafter, references to HEW will be restricted to actions taken before that date. Unless noted otherwise, HEW policies remain in effect at HHS and the Department of Education.
7. Pub. L. No. 105-220, Title IV, §408(b), codified at 29 U.S.C. §794(d).
8. Exec. Order No. 11,914 (1976), 41 *Fed. Reg.* 17,871 (April 28, 1976).
9. 45 C.F.R. Part 84.
10. Exec. Order No. 12,250 (1980), 45 *Fed. Reg.* 72,995 (1980); 28 C.F.R. Part 41.
11. 45 C.F.R. §84.3(h).
12. Pub. L. No. 105-220, Title IV, §508(b), codified at 29 U.S.C. §794(d).
13. 47 C.F.R. §1.1830(b)(6).
14. *United States Department of Transportation v. Paralyzed Veterans of America*, 477 U.S. 597 (1986).
15. 5 U.S.C. §552.
16. *Civil Rights Restoration Act*, Pub. L. No. 100-259, 29 U.S.C. §794(b) (1987).
17. See regulations of the U.S. Department of Justice, which apply to its own "federally conducted" programs, 28 C.F.R. §39.
18. 45 C.F.R. §84.3(k); 34 C.F.R. §104.4(k).
19. 45 C.F.R. §84.4(b)(1)(i).
20. 45 C.F.R. §84.4(b)(1)(ii and iii).
21. 45 C.F.R. §84.4(b)(2).
22. 42 *Fed. Reg.* 22,676 (1977).
23. 45 C.F.R. §84.4(b)(3).
24. 28 C.F.R. §42.503(e).
25. 28 C.F.R. §35.104.
26. Ibid.
27. 45 C.F.R. §84.22(f).
28. 45 C.F.R. §84.22.
29. Ibid.
30. 28 C.F.R. §41.5(b)(2).

Chapter 4

Public School Education

In these days, it is doubtful that any child may reasonably be expected to succeed in life if he is denied the opportunity of an education. Such an opportunity, where the state has undertaken to provide it, is a right which must be made available to all on equal terms.

BROWN V. BOARD OF EDUCATION

Education is one of the essential civil rights issues for deaf and hard of hearing children and their families. Although the importance of education has been broadly recognized since the *Brown v. Board of Education* case was decided in 1954, many children with disabilities are still denied their right to equal educational opportunity. In 1975 Congress found that more than half of this nation's eight million children with disabilities were not receiving appropriate educational services, and one million were excluded from the public school system entirely.[1] Since then, Congress has taken action to guarantee children the right to qualified teachers, accessible classrooms, and appropriate materials and programs. Nevertheless, given the individual nature of each child's needs, parents still have a responsibility to advocate for their children to receive the services they need.

The Individuals with Disabilities Education Act (IDEA) imposes on states the procedural and substantive requirements on how education should be provided to students with disabilities.[2] It covers students from birth to age twenty-one (or until high school graduation, if that occurs earlier) who need special education and related services as a result of their disability.

The law originally passed as Public Law 94-142 in 1975 and was known as the Education for All Handicapped Children Act; it was implemented in 1977. This statute has been amended several times in the ensuing decades. As part of the 1990 reauthorization, the law was renamed the Individuals with Disabilities Education Act (IDEA). Updates to IDEA in 1997 improved educational opportunities for children with disabilities and gave families and other community-based entities a greater role in the decision-making process.[3] In 2004 the IDEA was again amended, this time to bring it in line with the No Child Left Behind Act of 2002 and to give students with disabilities the same right to high-quality instructors and the same expectations for making adequate yearly progress as students without disabilities.[4] At the time of this book's publishing, the IDEA is awaiting reauthorization and possible amendment.

The IDEA and its regulations are intended to fulfill four major purposes:

+ to ensure that all children with disabilities have access to a free, appropriate public education that emphasizes special education and related services designed to meet their unique needs and prepare them for employment and independent living
+ to ensure that the rights of children with disabilities and their parents are protected
+ to assist states, localities, educational service agencies, and federal agencies to pay for the education of all children with disabilities
+ to assess and ensure the effectiveness of efforts to educate children with disabilities[5]

As is true for all federal legislation, the IDEA establishes minimum substantive and procedural requirements that all states must follow. Most states have adopted their own laws or regulations to complement the IDEA. In a few states, such as Michigan, students are entitled to a higher standard of services under state law than under IDEA.[6] Several states have also passed a deaf child's bill of rights (DCBR), which may create additional rights for deaf and hard of hearing students.[7] These bills of rights will be discussed in more depth later in this chapter.

The IDEA is divided into different parts to serve the needs of various segments of children with disabilities. Part C addresses the needs of infants and toddlers—children from birth to the age of two years. Part B addresses the needs of children from age three to twenty-one (or graduation from high school). The following sections cover those parts of the IDEA and the requirements thereunder.

PART C: INFANTS AND TODDLERS

Education begins at birth, and for parents of deaf and hard of hearing children, this period is of special importance because it is the optimal time for learning language. Although the responsibilities of school systems under IDEA do not begin until a child reaches age three, under Part C of the IDEA, the federal government provides money to states to make programs and services available to children with special needs from birth through age two.[8] Each state participating in this program must offer a comprehensive statewide interagency system for providing early intervention services for toddlers and infants with disabilities and their families.[9] To be eligible, a child must be experiencing developmental delays in cognitive, physical, communicative, social, or emotional development or have a physical or mental condition that has a high probability of causing developmental delays.[10]

The office providing early intervention services varies by state: Some manage these services through the state department of education, and others through the state health or social service agency. The tool for identifying services for a child younger than age three is an individualized family service plan (IFSP).[11] An IFSP for each child must be developed annually and reviewed every six months.[12] It must include specific descriptions of the child's present levels of development and expected outcomes, as well as the resources available to support the child and where and how these supports will be implemented.[13] Parents, caregivers, and service providers must all be involved in the development of the IFSP, and interpreters or other auxiliary aids must be provided for deaf or hard of hearing parents. Ideally, the IFSP puts the child in the best possible position to start school and in some situations eliminates the need for an individualized curriculum once the child reaches school age.

The IFSP should cover the following:

+ any necessary family training, counseling, special instruction, speech-language and audiology services
+ occupational therapy, physical therapy, psychological services
+ diagnostic medical services, health services, social work, vision services, and assistive technology devices and services
+ transportation, day care, and related costs that are necessary for the child's family to take advantage of these services

Each IFSP must include the following:

+ a statement of the child's present levels of development
+ a statement of the family's resources, priorities, and concerns as they relate to the child's development
+ a statement of major outcomes expected for the child and the family, as well as how and when they should be achieved
+ a statement of which early intervention services are to be provided
+ a statement of the setting in which the services will be provided and a justification for any services that will not be provided in a "natural environment"
+ a statement of when services will begin and how long they will continue
+ the name of the case manager responsible for carrying out the provisions of the IFSP and the steps to be taken to help the child transition to a preschool program

The team that develops the IFSP must include the following:

+ the child's parents
+ other family members or an advocate whose participation is requested by the parent

+ the service coordinator
+ a person directly involved in conducting the evaluation of the child
+ any appropriate service providers

PART B: STUDENTS AGES 3–21

The bulk of the substantive and procedural requirements of the IDEA come under Part B, which applies to students from age three until high school graduation or their twenty-first birthday, whichever comes first.[14] To receive IDEA services, a student must first be deemed eligible. Once a student is found eligible, the student becomes entitled to an individualized education program (IEP), which delivers a free, appropriate public education in the least-restrictive environment. These elements are explained in the following sections.

Eligibility

To receive IDEA services, a student must have a disability that falls into one of ten categories, including the label "hearing impairment."[15] In addition, to qualify for services, the disability must affect the child's educational performance, so that the child needs at least some specialized instruction as a result of the disability. Students whose disability does not require specialized instruction still have the right to an accessible education under the ADA and/or Section 504 but do not have the right to the individually tailored curriculum that the IDEA requires.

The "hearing impairment" category under the IDEA comprises three categories:

+ "Deafness" means a hearing disability that is so severe that the child is impaired in processing linguistic information through hearing, with or without amplification, and that adversely affects a child's educational performance.
+ "Deaf-blindness" means concomitant hearing and visual impairments, the combination of which causes such severe communication and other developmental and educational

needs that they cannot be accommodated in special education programs designed solely for deafness or children with
blindness.

✦ "Hearing impairment" means a permanent or fluctuating
impairment that adversely affects a child's educational
performance but is not included under the definition of
deafness in this section.[8]

General IDEA Entitlements

The heart of the IDEA is the guaranteed right of every child to a
free, appropriate public education administered in the least
restrictive environment. The IDEA includes certain procedural
mechanisms designed to ensure that these rights are enforced.
These provisions are explained briefly here and in greater depth
later in this chapter.

A Free, Appropriate Public Education

Under IDEA and Section 504, every child with a disability has a
right to (1) specially designed instruction meeting the child's
unique needs and (2) related services that are necessary to help
the child benefit from the special program.[16] The IDEA does not
oblige schools to maximize the potential of every eligible student,
however, but to provide personalized instruction with sufficient
support services to permit the child to benefit educationally from
that instruction.[17]

The question of what satisfies this standard depends entirely
on the student's needs, as evidenced by expert evaluations and
the progress that the student makes each year. For this reason,
the specific services that a school must provide will vary from
child to child, even for children who receive services under the
same eligibility category. For example, in the Supreme Court's
first IDEA case, *Board of Education of Hendrick Hudson Central
School District v. Rowley*, a deaf kindergarten student had
demonstrated the ability to lipread 60 percent of the words
spoken to her in an evaluation and the ability to pass easily from
kindergarten to first grade. Her parents asserted that the services
the school district had provided (i.e., speech therapy and some

tutoring) were not enough; she needed a sign language interpreter to access the general curriculum. The Supreme Court sided with the school district, noting the student's progress without an interpreter in place.[18] Even with this precedent, however, many deaf and hard of hearing students receive sign language interpreters because they cannot benefit from the curriculum without one.

The determination of what services a school must provide hinges almost exclusively on a student's need for the services. The school district must provide not only the educational services at no cost to the parents but also any ancillary services necessary for the student to access its education, such as tuition for private schools; tuition, room, and board for residential schools; and transportation to and from any school that a student must attend for educational reasons. Although some jurisdictions permit courts to consider the cost of the requested educational services, this is not the case in the majority of jurisdictions.[19] Further, the Supreme Court has twice ruled that the cost of providing services that enable a student with health conditions to attend school is not a valid defense of the school's refusal to provide the services.[20]

Least Restrictive Environment

The free, appropriate public education determined by the IEP must be implemented in "the least restrictive environment." The IDEA defines "least restrictive environment" in terms of the presence of students who do not have a disability, requiring that, to the maximum extent possible, students with disabilities must be educated in the same classroom, program, or building as students without disabilities. At the same time, states are required to maintain a continuum of alternative placements to meet the needs of children with disabilities. Such placements include mainstream classes, special classes, special schools, residential schools, and combinations of different types of programs.[21] According to the statute, special classes and separate school placements are appropriate only when the disability is of a nature or severity that placement in regular classes with the use of supplementary aids and services will not meet that child's educational needs.[22]

Procedural Rights

A set of procedures of escalating formality governs the process by which schools and parents determine what constitutes a free, appropriate education and the least restrictive environment for a student.[23] The initial determination of placement and services is made by an IEP. The IDEA outlines the specific individuals who must attend the meeting, the topics they must discuss, and the elements that must appear in the IEP itself.[24] These details are outlined in the next section.

Parents have a right to meaningfully participate in the development of the IEP. To facilitate participation, parents are entitled to review their student's educational records, to make a recording of any IEP meeting, to receive IEP notes and submit addenda to be included in their child's IEP or educational record, and to receive prior written notice of the school's reason to provide or refuse any service, evaluation, or placement. Schools are required to inform parents of these rights at critical junctures in the IEP process and must do so in a language and communication mode that the parents understand. Additionally, schools must provide interpreting services or other accommodations where necessary to enable the parents to participate fully in the meeting. Although these procedural rights may not manifest as a substantive service to the student, they can be used to create a record of the parents' requests and the schools' response to them, which can be beneficial in later dispute-resolution proceedings.

The Individualized Educational Program

At the crux of the free, appropriate public education guaranteed to each student lies an individualized determination of the student's potential for educational progress and the services and accommodations necessary to enable the student to make this progress. As mentioned earlier, the student's goals, services, and placement are outlined in an individualized education program. The IEP is a written report that identifies and assesses the child's disability, establishes long- and short-term learning goals, and lists the services the school must provide to help the child achieve these goals. Special education and related services are then provided in accordance with the terms of the IEP.[25]

As the school is legally required to provide the services that are written into the IEP, parents should leverage their procedural rights to ensure that the IEP includes every special service their child needs. They should not sign an IEP that lacks these services in order to benefit from a special education.

The IDEA sets certain requirements for IEPs and IEP team meetings. As mentioned earlier, it specifies which personnel must attend the meeting and what this team must consider in developing the IEP, and it dictates which elements the IEP itself must include. By design, the IDEA does not require that the school provide a given curriculum or set of accommodations. Rather, the team must design a program of goals and supports around the student's unique needs.

The goals and objectives that are written into the IEP are not limited to academic performance but should also relate to social, psychomotor, communicative, and emotional needs as well as to conventional academic goals. The IEP team must consider the child's strengths and the results of the child's evaluations before determining the appropriate placement and services. Evaluations and tests used to assess a child must not be discriminatory on a racial or cultural basis and must be performed in the child's native language or other mode of communication.[26]

The 1997 IDEA reauthorization added a list of special factors to be considered in developing the IEP of a deaf or hard of hearing child. Pursuant to this provision, the IEP team must consider the communication needs of the child, including the child's academic level, language and communication needs, and opportunities for direct communication with peers and professional personnel in the child's language and communication mode.[27] To communicate directly means to do so without any third-party involvement (i.e., interpreters). The child's language and communication mode refers to how the child communicates, such as American Sign Language (ASL), Signing Exact English (SEE), or oral communication. If the child is in an environment where direct communication with everyone is not available, an alternative placement such as a special program or school may be more appropriate. These vital aspects of IDEA must be considered to ensure that the deaf or hard of hearing child receives an appropriate education.

In addition, the IEP should also describe the amount, kind, and frequency of any specialized instruction time the child will receive as well as any auxiliary aids and services or other accommodations. It is especially important to identify specialized equipment and services early enough so that the school system will have these services in place at the beginning of a school year.

The school has certain obligations toward the parents in developing the IEP. Most important, the school cannot simply draw up an IEP and present it to the parents for their signature. Rather, it must give them an opportunity to be included in the meeting in which the IEP is being developed, including providing interpreters where necessary to ensure full parental participation. This obligation does not require schools to defer to parents' wishes but does require them to include parents' concerns in the IEP record, grant parents access to students' educational records, and permit parents to bring advocates and other knowledgeable people to IEP meetings. The school must also obtain parental consent before starting an IEP for a student and before changing the services, placement, or certain other elements of the IEP.

Parents have certain rights with respect to the IEP. Because schools must consider parents' concerns, parents may draft a letter articulating their concerns and have it included in their child's educational file. Parents also have rights with regard to the evaluation of their child. Even though schools do not need parental consent to evaluate a child in an area of suspected disability, they must conduct such an evaluation at the parent's request. Parents also have a right to have an independent entity conduct an evaluation at public expense, and the IEP team must consider, although it is not required to defer to, the results of such evaluations.

Furthermore, IEPs must be reviewed at least once a year, and they should be written in the spring or early summer so they can be implemented when school starts in the fall. Although a single student's failure to made adequate yearly process on state assessments does not establish conclusively that the services in the IEP are insufficient, special education students' widespread failure to make progress can carry implications for the school district, according to the 2004 IDEA reauthorization. Parents should ask for and keep a copy of their child's IEP so they can remember what was agreed on and hold the school to its promises. If they later have to go to court to obtain the services, the IEP will be the primary item of evidence.

Contents of the IEP

The IEP must include the following:

- a statement of the child's present levels of educational performance
- a statement of measurable annual goals, including benchmarks or short-term objectives
- a statement of the special education and related services and supplementary aids and services to be provided to or on behalf of the child and a statement of the program modifications or supports for school personnel that will be provided for the child
- an explanation of the extent, if any, to which the children will not participate with children without disabilities in the regular class and in other activities
- a statement of any individual modifications in the administration of state- or districtwide assessment of student achievement that are needed in order for the child to participate in the assessment
- the projected dates for the beginning of the services modifications described and the anticipated frequency, location, and duration of those services and modifications
- a statement of how the child's progress toward annual goals will be measured and how the child's parents will be informed of the evaluation.[28]

In developing the IEP, the IEP team must consider the following:

- the child's strengths
- the parents' concerns for enhancing their child's education
- the results of the child's initial or most recent evaluation

+ the child's academic, developmental, and functional needs
+ certain special factors, including the following:
  ⋄ for students with behavioral issues, the use of positive behavioral interventions and supports
  ⋄ for students with limited English proficiency, the child's language needs
  ⋄ for students who are blind or have some other visual impairment, instruction in Braille
  ⋄ for students who are deaf or hard of hearing, the child's language and communication needs, opportunities for direct communications with peers and professional personnel in the child's language and communication mode, academic level, and full range of needs, including opportunities for direct instruction in the child's language and communication mode
  ⋄ a determination of whether the child needs assistive technology devices and services.

Required Attendees at an IEP Meeting

The following individuals must attend the IEP meeting unless the parties agree that their attendance is not necessary:

+ the parents of a child with a disability
+ not less than one regular education teacher of such child (if the child is, or may be, participating in the regular education environment)
+ not less than one special education teacher or, where appropriate, not less than one special education provider of such child
+ a representative of the local educational agency who (1) is qualified to provide, or supervise the provision of, specially designed instruction to meet the unique needs of children with disabilities; (2) is knowledgeable about the general education curriculum; and (3) is knowledgeable about the availability of the local educational agency's resources
+ an individual who can interpret the instructional implications of evaluations
+ at the discretion of the parent or the agency, other individuals who have knowledge or special expertise regarding the child
+ whenever appropriate, the child with a disability

Parents' Procedural Rights

Schools are required to adhere to parents' procedural rights, including their right:

+ To participate in the development of the IEP
+ To review their child's educational records prior to the IEP meeting or at any point thereafter
+ To record the IEP team meeting
+ To have an interpreter to enable them to participate in the meeting
+ To receive prior written notice whenever the local education agency proposes or refuses to initiate or change the identification, evaluation, or educational placement of the child or the provision of a free appropriate public education to the child
+ To receive an independent educational evaluation, at public expense, whose results are considered by the IEP team
+ To refuse the implementation of an IEP in total or in part
+ To initiate an independent review of the parents' dispute with the school, including filing a state complaint, entering into mediation, or initiating administrative proceedings against the school
+ To receive an explanation of the procedural safeguards available to them, written in the parents' native language and in an easily understandable manner

Even though these procedural rights may not manifest as a substantive service to the student, they can be used to create a record of the parents' requests and the schools' response to them, which can be beneficial in later dispute-resolution proceedings.

Important Considerations in Developing an IEP

The unique needs of deaf and hard of hearing students pose challenges for the development of an educational program that will truly benefit them. Factors such as the chosen language medium or the placement can have unanticipated consequences as these students grow and develop. Parents should take these consequences into account when making their initial selection and, whenever possible, should educate the school on these issues. In addition, the availability of assistive technology and qualified service providers can also influence the degree of benefit the students derive from their program.

Appropriate Language Medium

In determining the proper educational program and writing an IEP, the critical first step is to identify the language medium appropriate for a particular child. What is best varies from child to child, depending on that child's native language, the amount and type of residual hearing (if any), the level of the child's communication skills, the child's exposure to manual communication methods, age of onset of deafness, the primary language used by the child's family, and other conditions. What is found to be appropriate should be noted in the IEP. If interpreters or teachers will be using sign language, the IEP should also identify the minimum skill level or competence these professionals should have. In a few states, such as Texas, efforts have been made to identify levels of sign language or interpreter competence using state tests.[29] Whenever possible, such criteria should be included in an IEP in order to ensure that teachers and interpreters working with children who are deaf or hard of hearing will be able to communicate effectively.

Controversy over language methods has raged in deaf education programs for years. The original debate centered on the efficacy of oral versus sign language. Any consideration of educational methods using manual components is complicated by the existence of sign language variants and by the number of different systems for using manual language with children in a learning environment. "Sign language" is a continuum of language systems that can be differentiated by the types of visual components used (signs, fingerspelling, body movement, and facial expression) and by the degree to which a particular system parallels formal English syntax and vocabulary or comprises its own distinct linguistic elements.

American Sign Language is a language that is linguistically distinct from English and has its own formal syntax, lexicon, and idioms. Many schools for deaf children have adopted the bilingual approach, which emphasizes American Sign Language and English as separate languages and expects the students to become fluent in both. Other schools and programs rely on sign language variants that are closely related to English. Some of these are pidgin signed English systems that use signs in a rough approximation of English word order. Other systems have been devised to make English "visible" by providing word-for-word translation of English through signs and fingerspelling, with additional signs to represent word endings and other grammatical components. Cued speech is another method that has been introduced in some school systems. Cued speech is not a language but a system of specific handshapes placed at specific locations around the head; the combination of handshapes and locations represents English sounds. The children speechread while simultaneously reading the manual cues. Finally, some programs for deaf children are purely oral and emphasize the use of residual hearing and speechreading.

Selecting the proper communication medium is important because it makes instruction both possible and meaningful. All educators of deaf children endeavor to maximize children's use and understanding of the English language. A related but more immediate goal is to make what happens in the classroom accessible to those children. With some youngsters, this might mean providing only a hearing aid; others will require both an aid and a sign language interpreter; and still others will need a special teacher, a modified curriculum, and a range of support services. The IEP should spell out the individual child's communication requirements.

Appropriate Placement

Although mainstreaming can reduce stigma and isolation for many children with disabilities, it is not always appropriate for children who are deaf or hard of hearing. In 1988 the Commission on Education of the Deaf (COED) report warned that mainstreaming has been more detrimental than beneficial to many deaf children.[30] Without substantial support systems and services, placement in a mainstream classroom often constitutes a more socially and educationally restrictive environment for a deaf child than a setting in which the students and the teachers have a shared language.

Legally, the services required to provide an appropriate education determine which setting is least restrictive for the child. Thus, if the IEP team agrees that the student requires direct access to instruction in ASL, the team members must determine whether direct access can be provided in the general education setting. If it cannot, they must decide on the "least restrictive" environment where such instruction can be provided. In reality, many schools view the least restrictive environment as the initial consideration; however, this approach ignores the actual needs of most deaf and hard of hearing students. At the meeting, the school's representatives may argue that direct communication is not available in the child's current placement and resist changing the placement due to the least-restrictive environment requirement.

In recent years, the special factors provision has encouraged some courts to rule in favor of placing deaf or hard of hearing children in a school for deaf students, although these cases uniformly involve deaf or hard of hearing students with co-occurring disabilities, such as autism spectrum disorder or Down syndrome.[31] Despite this provision, the overall trend toward placing deaf and hard of hearing students in mainstream environments appears to have continued.[32]

An individual child's specific needs must govern any decision about that child's program. Education consists of more than listening to a teacher. Education also involves small group discussions, formal and informal interactions with peers and teachers, physical and recreational education, extracurricular activities, and social aspects of learning. No one type of placement is appropriate for all deaf or hard of hearing children. Parents need to be fully involved in determining both the placement that will allow their child to achieve the full range of educational goals and the full range of support services that will make that placement successful.

Assistive Technology and Related Services

The IEP must be worded to ensure that the deaf child has access to related services and communication technology in the classroom. As mentioned earlier, the IDEA specifically mentions speech-language and audiology services, psychological and counseling services, physical and occupational therapy, recreation, early identification, orientation and mobility services, school health services, social work services, and parent counseling and training.[33] However, because this list is not exhaustive, other services can and should be included in the IEP. Typical related services for deaf and hard of hearing children include amplifiers (e.g., hearing aids and/or assistive listening systems), computer-assisted real-time transcription (CART) services, computer software and hardware, and interpreters. Some deaf children benefit from having supplementary hearing devices that range from conventional hearing aids to specialized auditory training devices and amplification equipment. In addition to these services and technologies, a child often requires further services to complement the child's use of residual hearing. This assistance should be specified in the IEP and provided as part of the child's program.

For example, it may be essential to control background noise if a child is to receive the full benefit of a hearing aid. If so, this need should be identified so the school can take appropriate steps to improve acoustics in the rooms the child will be using. The United States Access Board, in conjunction with the American National Standards Institute (ANSI) and the Acoustical Society of America, has developed acoustic standards for classrooms, the ANSI/ASA S12.60-2002. These standards were revised in 2010 to separately address permanent schools and relocatable classrooms. They address acoustic performance criteria and design requirements for classrooms and similar environments. Importantly, the ANSI-ASA S12.60-2002 standards are not legal standards unless specifically addressed by state law. However, parents may find them useful in developing their child's IEP.

Improved lighting may also be necessary to ensure that information presented visually is clear and understandable. Speech therapy, auditory training, and media support services (such as captions for any videos) are other types of assistance that a deaf child might need; if so, these should be written into the IEP. Related forms of aid include audiology services, interpreters, counseling for parents and the child, and parental training to help parents acquire the necessary skills that will allow them to support the implementation of the child's IEP. The school may have to provide sign language education and training for parents and families to ensure that the child continues language development and educational progress at home.

The school must ensure that the child's hearing aids and other assistive technology devices are functioning properly and are available at no cost if the IEP determines that those devices are necessary. If the IEP also determines that the use of those devices is required in a child's home or in other settings so that the child can continue to have access to an appropriate education, the school must allow the child or the parents to take those devices outside the school environment.[34]

Qualified Professionals

Being deaf during childhood is a low-incidence disability. Most school systems have relatively few deaf children in each age group, a factor that increases the difficulty of providing properly trained teachers and highly specialized, related services to ensure an appropriate education in mainstream classes.

A position paper by the International Association of Parents of the Deaf (now the American Society for Deaf Children) noted the following:

> Currently, many local and public schools lack qualified
> diagnostic staff for making the placement, lack supportive
> services, lack trained personnel, lack necessary amplifica-
> tion equipment and a desirable visual environment, lack
> an understanding of total communication which may be
> essential for communication with students, and in many
> cases, lack financial resources required for the education
> of deaf children and lack commitment.[35]

Although this statement was made in 1976, these problems still exist. School systems are required by law to evaluate children to determine whether they are deaf or hard of hearing, to create special programs to provide hearing assistance, and to provide counseling and guidance to students, parents, and teachers on issues related to being deaf or hard of hearing. They are responsible for determining a child's need for amplification, for selecting and fitting an appropriate aid, and for evaluating the effectiveness of the amplification. These responsibilities can overwhelm teachers and administrators who lack special training. Opportunities for such training must be made available to school staff so they may become more knowledgeable about deaf and hard of hearing children with or without other disabilities, the range of possible solutions and accommodations, and how they may best fulfill their responsibilities under the law. It may be appropriate for a school system to require in-service training, special certification, and fluency in sign language for teachers who will be working with deaf and hard of hearing students.

In 2004 the IDEA was amended to give all students with disabilities the right to highly qualified teachers in a manner similar to the No Child Left Behind Act of 2002. Teachers working with special education students are now required to be fully certified in special education or pass state special education licensure exams, hold a bachelor's degree, and demonstrate subject knowledge. In addition, states are now required to develop a plan outlining the provision of special education services within the state, including targets for providing a free, appropriate public education and the disproportionate representation of minorities in certain disability categories.

Personnel providing special education or related services must meet the state educational agency's recognized certification, licensing, registration, or other comparable requirements. This could mean the requirement of certified educators of deaf and hard of hearing children, certified sign language interpreters, and licensed audiologists.

Deaf and Hard of Hearing Children's Bills of Rights

In a growing trend, states have passed laws specifically addressing the unique educational needs of deaf and hard of hearing students, often called a deaf and hard of hearing children's bill of rights. As of the publishing of this book, fourteen states had passed a DCBR. In addition, one state had passed a portion of the traditional DCBR and another had passed a DCBR as a House Resolution, which does not have the force of law.

Common Elements

Although DCBRs vary in content and in strength, they have the following elements in common.

An emphasis on communication. These bills stress the basic human need for a child to be able to communicate freely with others. The bills usually state that their purpose is to promote understanding of communication needs and not to favor any one particular communication mode or language over another.

The availability of qualified and certified personnel who can communicate directly with deaf and hard of hearing children. In order for an educational placement to be appropriate, the child must be provided, when appropriate, qualified and certified teachers, psychologists, speech therapists, assessors, administrators, interpreters, and other personnel who understand the unique nature of deafness and are specifically trained to work with deaf and hard of hearing children. These personnel should be proficient in the primary communication and language mode of deaf and hard of hearing children.

The availability of same language mode peers who are of the same age and ability level. This is designed to ensure a "critical mass" where there is a sufficient number of peers of the approximate age and ability level with whom deaf and hard of hearing children can communicate directly in the same language.

Opportunities to interact with deaf and hard of hearing adult role models. Parents and educators should be informed of the benefits of an education in which deaf and hard of hearing students have deaf and hard of hearing role models or adult mentors available as part of the student's education experience in school and during extracurricular activities. Children should be provided access to deaf and hard of hearing adults as teachers, mentors, and advocates.

Equal opportunity to benefit from all services and programs at their schools. Deaf and hard of hearing children must have direct and appropriate access to all components of the education, including recess, lunch, extracurricular, social, and athletic activities.

Appropriate assessments. Language, communication, academic, and social development should be assessed at an early age and throughout the child's educational experience. Qualified and certified individuals proficient in the language(s) of the child should perform the assessments.

Unique Provisions

Beyond these common elements, some legislative bills offer unique provisions for particular issues.

Communication. To protect deaf and hard of hearing children's linguistic abilities and to meet their needs, some DCBRs provide for early intervention services using a consistent communication system during the child's critical language-learning years. That system may be ASL, speech, cued speech, sign language, another method, or a combination of methods. The DCBRs also require that the child's communication mode must be respected, utilized, and developed to an appropriate level of proficiency and vocabulary equivalent to that of hearing students of similar age. They further require that opportunities be made available for interactions that enhance the child's intellectual, social, emotional, and cultural development. In addition, they require schools to equip deaf and hard of hearing children with a full spectrum of appropriate assistive technology.

With respect to the selection of a language medium, a DCBR may prohibit IEP and IFSP teams from denying a deaf or hard of hearing student an opportunity for instruction in a particular communication mode or language solely because of the child's remaining hearing, the fact that the child's parents are not fluent in the communication mode or language being taught, or the fact that the child has previous experience with some other communication mode or language. Rather, the child's *preferred* mode should be respected in order to attain the highest level of education possible for that individual in an appropriate environment. In addition, some DCBRs require teachers to demonstrate competence in American Sign Language in addition to English language and communication proficiency in order to obtain any certification required to teach deaf and hard of hearing students.

Placement, curriculum, and program development.   Some DCBRs require IEP teams to consider that the state school for deaf or hard of hearing students may be the least restrictive environment for them. The DCBRs grant these students the right to have ASL as one of the academic subjects in their educational curriculum when their primary language is ASL. They also require that the extent, content, and purpose of programs and services for these children be developed with the involvement and assistance of deaf and hard of hearing people, parents of deaf and hard of hearing students, and qualified and certified teachers and professionals trained in the education of this population of students.

Implementation and Outreach.   Some DCBRs look to parental involvement and state outreach. These provisions require states to ensure that parents are enabled to make informed decisions about which educational options are best suited to their child. To do so, they need to receive and review information about all of the school district's educational options available to the child, as well as about those not provided by the school district. These DCBRs establish an outreach program that provides sign language training and assistance and other support services to the parents of a deaf or hard of hearing child. Finally, some DCBRs require states to take steps to implement the bill of rights by developing materials, disseminating information, and providing workshops, symposia, and other gatherings to ensure that decision makers understand and implement the act. Even in states that do not have a DCBR, the provisions provide useful guidance in articulating the educational needs of deaf and hard of hearing students. Parents are encouraged to bring them to schools' attention and to use them wherever possible.

Procedural Safeguards

The IDEA provides procedural safeguards by which parents can be assured of both their own participation in the decision-making process and an appropriate education for their child.[36] A school system must give written notice to parents when it wishes to initiate or change the identification, evaluation, or placement of a child with a disability. The notice must describe procedural protections, the action that the school system proposes or refuses to take, and its reasons. The notice must also describe any options the school system considered and explain why those options were rejected, and describe each evaluation procedure, test, record, report, or other relevant factor the school system used as a basis for the proposed change.

The notice must be written in language understandable to the general public and provided in the parents' native language(s) or any other form of communication used by the parents.[37] If the native language is not a written language, the school system has to translate the notice and ensure that the parents understand it. For example, a qualified sign language interpreter must translate and explain the notice to deaf parents who communicate in sign language.

If the parents do not accept the school system's evaluation and proposed placement or if they are not confident that the school system has the resources to provide an appropriate education, they can request a due process hearing.[38] To accomplish this, the parents need to notify the school officials that they are dissatisfied, state their reasons, and ask for a hearing. Within fifteen days, the school must meet with the parents for an early resolution session or go through mediation. If the early resolution session does not satisfy the parents' concerns, a due process hearing must commence within thirty days of the resolution session. This hearing is intended to be an informal dispute-resolution process during which both the parents and the school can present their grievances to a neutral hearing officer. Parents should be aware that this process utilizes formal procedural elements and strict deadlines. As a practical matter, both parents and school systems are often represented by attorneys. A neutral hearing officer is appointed according to procedures established by the state. Public agencies must keep a list of hearing officers and their qualifications.

Preparation for the Hearing

Preparation for a due process hearing begins at the IEP. It is highly advisable to record the IEP, request independent evaluations, and submit any parental concerns in writing. Another essential step is to find experts in education who can testify in support of the parents' position that the current placement or services are inappropriate and the desired placement or services are appropriate. The expert should visit the proposed and current placements before the hearing in order to testify whether the proposed placement can meet the specific needs of that individual child. The parents themselves should visit the proposed placement and see how the IEP could be implemented with that school's resources.

The parents also should examine all school records relevant to their child's placement. Under IDEA, the school system must comply with any reasonable request by the parents to inspect and receive an explanation of their child's records before any hearing. If the parents believe that information in the file is incorrect, they can request amendment of the record. If the parents disagree with a school evaluation of their child, they have the right to an independent evaluation; the school system is required to take this evaluation into account in deciding the child's placement. Well before the hearing date, the parents should request a list of witnesses who will be testifying for the school.

The key issue at the hearing is whether the proposed placement or service is appropriate to meet the individual needs of the child. At the hearing, the parents can have a lawyer and can call witnesses who are experts in educating children with disabilities. They also have the right to present evidence and to confront and cross-examine any of the witnesses.

Parents can obtain a written or an electronic verbatim record of the hearing, which is important in an appeal. The hearing officer must provide written findings of fact explaining his or her decision. Until a decision is rendered, the child must remain in the present educational placement unless the school and the parents agree otherwise. If, however, the complaint involves an application for initial admission to public school, the child must be placed in the public school program until completion of all proceedings.

Decisions and Appeals

The hearing officer has the authority to determine the appropriate placement for the child and is not restricted to merely accepting or rejecting the school's program. The hearing officer can order services that are necessary to provide a free, appropriate education for the child. The decision of the hearing officer is final and must be obeyed by the school system unless it is appealed to the state department of education or the courts. If an appeal is made to the state education agency, the agency must conduct an impartial review of the decision. The official who conducts the review must:

+ examine the entire hearing record
+ ensure that the procedures at the hearing were consistent with the due process requirements of the law
+ seek additional evidence if necessary
+ afford the parties an opportunity for oral or written argument or both
+ make an independent decision on completion of the review
+ give the parties a copy of the written findings and the decision

If still dissatisfied, the parents may file a civil lawsuit in state or federal court to challenge the decision of the state agency.

GENERAL ACCESSIBILITY ISSUES: SECTION 504 AND THE ADA

Both public and private schools are subject to the civil rights mandates of the ADA and, if they receive any federal funding, to Section 504 of the Rehabilitation Act. Therefore, schools have the duty to be accessible to people with disabilities. The ADA and Section 504 apply to all programs and activities offered by a private school or a public school system, including school board meetings, extracurricular programs, teacher conferences, recreational activities, social and cultural activities, adult education, summer school or hobby classes, and children's educational programs. Title II of the ADA applies to public school systems. Title III of the ADA applies to all types of private schools and educational programs for children and adults. Section 504 of the Rehabilitation Act of 1973 applies to school systems and educational agencies (public and private) that receive federal financial assistance, including the federally subsidized school lunch program.

In the Department of Education's Section 504 regulation, public elementary and secondary schools are required to provide a "free, appropriate public education" to qualified children with disabilities regardless of the nature of their disability.[39] This means that any children with disabilities must be able to participate in a curriculum designed to meet their unique needs at no cost. If the school system refuses to provide an appropriate education, the Department of Education can cut off federal funds.

The Ninth Circuit recently determined that the ADA and Section 504 provide rights in addition to the IDEA. In *K.M. v. Tustin Unified School District* the court held that two students who did not require CART to achieve the educational benefit required by the IDEA nonetheless may require CART to achieve the effective communication required by the ADA. Thus, the hearing officer's determination that the school district had satisfied its IDEA obligation without providing CART for the students did not establish that the school had satisfied its ADA obligation.[40] Because of this ruling, a school's obligation toward deaf and hard of hearing students may no longer stop at the *Rowley* question of whether a student is making educational progress. It may extend to whether the school has provided auxiliary aids and services to access the classroom at a level *equal to* that of their hearing peers. It remains to be seen, however, whether this standard will be adopted by other circuits or even upheld by the Supreme Court.

Section 504 and the ADA also provide additional protection in the context of private schools, architectural accessibility, extracurricular activities, summer programs, adult education, and services for parents, school personnel, and other adults. The ADA regulations specifically address a school's obligation to remove communication barriers for deaf individuals by providing "appropriate auxiliary aids and services" so that they can participate in school programs.[41] The appropriate auxiliary aids depend on the context of the communication and the needs of the individuals. For example, in a school auditorium or a school board meeting, some deaf people may need a sign language interpreter to follow and participate in the proceedings. Other people may need CART or an assistive listening device in order to understand

and participate in the same activity. If the school has videotapes or films or if it broadcasts on cable television, captions are the most appropriate way to give access to deaf viewers. The primary focus is whether or not the auxiliary aid or service is effective and gives the concerned persons an opportunity to participate effectively.

Public school systems must comply with the ADA in all of their services, programs, and activities, including those that are open to parents or to the public. For instance, for parents and guardians with disabilities, public school systems must provide program accessibility to these programs, activities, and services and appropriate auxiliary aids and services whenever necessary to ensure effective communication, as long as the provision of such auxiliary aids or services is not an undue burden or a fundamental alteration of the program.[42] A federal court has ruled that school systems must provide interpreters when deaf parents meet with teachers or attend school functions such as orientation programs.[43] The Department of Education's Office for Civil Rights has held that parent teacher association (PTA) programs and activities are covered by the ADA because the school district provides significant indirect assistance to the PTA.[44]

In order to ensure that deaf individuals are alerted to a fire or other emergency, school systems should install visual (flashing) fire alarms in areas used by deaf students. Examples of additional accommodations include amplification systems that are compatible with hearing aids and entry systems that do not depend on a student's ability to use an intercom or respond to a buzzer or other auditory device. Some form of telecommunications access such as a videophone or a TTY (as long as it is effective for the particular deaf or hard of hearing individual) may also be necessary, so that the school and the parents can communicate directly about illnesses, schedules, discipline of a child, and other problems.

Any time a school building is altered or constructed, the building must meet the minimum standards in the ADA accessibility guidelines (ADAAG) or the Uniform Federal Accessibility Standards. These architectural accessibility standards may require a school to make structural changes to provide equal access to everyone.

NOTES

1. 20 U.S.C. §1400.
2. 20 U.S.C. §1401 et seq.
3. P.L. 105-17, Title I, §101, 111 Stat. 37.
4. P.L. 108-446, Title I, §101, 118 Stat. 2647.
5. 34 C.F.R. §300.1.
6. *Mich. Admin. R. Special Educ. R.* 340.1701c.
7. See, for example, Cal. Educ. Code §56000.5; O.C.G.A. §20-2-152.1; Va. Code §22.1-217.02.
8. See 20 U.S.C. §1431 et seq.
9. 20 U.S.C. §1434.
10. 20 U.S.C. §1432(5).
11. 20 U.S.C. §1436.
12. 20 U.S.C. §1436(b).
13. 20 U.S.C. §1436(d).
14. 20 U.S.C. §1411-19.
15. 20 U.S.C. §1401(3).
16. 20 U.S.C. §1401(9).
17. *Board of Education of Hendrick Hudson Central School District v. Rowley,* 458 U.S. 176, 203 (1982).
18. Ibid., 209–10.
19. Cf. *Daniel R.R. v. State Bd. of Educ.,* 874 F.3d 1036 (5th Cir. 1989) (omitting cost of services from the factors to be considered under the IDEA); *Sacramento City Sch. Dist. v. Rachel H.,* 14 F.3d 1398 (9th Cir. 1994) (including the cost of service provision among the factors to be considered under the IDEA).
20. See *Cedar Rapids Community Sch. Dist. v. Garret F.,* 526 U.S. 66 (1999); *Irving Indep. Sch. Dist. v. Tatro,* 468 U.S. 883 (1984).
21. 34 C.F.R. §300.115.
22. 20 U.S.C. §1412(a)(5)(A).
23. See generally 20 U.S.C. §1415.
24. See generally 20 U.S.C. §1414(d).
25. See 20 U.S.C. §1414(d).
26. 34 C.F.R. §300.346.
27. 20 U.S.C. §1414(d)(3)(B)(iv).
28. 20 U.S.C. §1411–19.
29. Texas Hum. Res. §81.007 (1997).
30. Commission on Education of the Deaf, *Toward Equality: Education of the Deaf: A Report to the President and the Congress of the United States* (Washington, DC, 1998), 30–34.
31. *S.F. v. McKinney Indep. Sch. Dist.,* No. 4:10-CV-323-RAS-DDB, 2012 U.S. Dist. LEXIS 29584 (E.D. Tex. 2012) (a deaf education classroom with deaf peers is the least restrictive environment for

deaf students with autism spectrum disorder); *J.S. v. Department of Education,* No. 10-00022 DAE-LEK, 2010 U.S. Dist. LEXIS 85656 (D. Haw. 2010) (a Total Communication program is the least restrictive environment for deaf students with Down syndrome).

32. See Caroline Jackson, "The Individuals with Disabilities Education Act and Its Impact on The Deaf Community," *Stanford Journal of Civil Rights and Civil Liberties* 6, no. 2 (2010): 355.
33. 34 C.F.R. §300.24.
34. 34 C.F.R. §300.308.
35. International Association of Parents of the Deaf, October 1976, position statement.
36. 34 C.F.R. Part 303.
37. 20 U.S.C. §1415(d).
38. 20 U.S.C. §1415(b)(6).
39. 34 C.F.R. §104.33
40. *K.M. v. Tustin Unified Sch. Dist.* F.3d, 2013 U.S. App. LEXIS 16228, at *31–32 (9th Cir. 2013).
41. 28 C.F.R. §35.104; 28 C.F.R. §36.303.
42. *56 Fed. Reg.* 35,696 (July 26, 1991) (analyzing the ADA's Title II regulations).
43. *Rothschild v. Grottenthaler,* 907 F 2d. 886 (2d. Cir. 1990).
44. Irvine Unified School District, 19 IDELR 883 (OCR 1993).

Chapter 5

Postsecondary and Continuing Education

Since 1973 Congress has required that postsecondary education and professional development opportunities be made accessible to people with disabilities.[1] At that time, the Rehabilitation Act of 1973, specifically Section 504, opened doors to educational institutions, including vocational and commercial schools, that receive federal money. Section 504 prohibited such institutions from discriminating against students with disabilities in recruitment, admissions, and programs and services. The Americans with Disabilities Act (1990) has expanded this requirement to all postsecondary educational institutions, regardless of whether they receive federal financial assistance, as well as to examinations and courses related to education and to professional advancement.[2] To accommodate a person with a disability, a college or university is not obligated to make substantial changes to the requirements of its academic program, but it must afford equal opportunity to the person to benefit from the program, without segregation from the other students or limits on participation. The ADA and Section 504 both mandate auxiliary aids and services, and methods of evaluation are required to measure a student's actual achievement and not the accessibility or inaccessibility of the tests.

RECRUITMENT, ADMISSIONS, AND MATRICULATION

Educational institutions may not refuse to admit applicants because of their disabilities or subject them to any form of discrimination in admissions or recruitment procedures.[3] If a college or university requires preadmission interviews for applicants, then it must conduct an interview with a deaf applicant, too, and provide interpreters or other auxiliary aids and services when required for effective communication. If there are tours or orientation meetings, the deaf applicant must be able to participate with effective communication provided. The institution cannot place a limit or quota on the number or proportion of students with disabilities admitted.

In general, colleges and universities may not make preadmission inquiries about students' disabilities except when the intent is to recruit students with disabilities. Such specialized recruitment efforts are allowed under two conditions: (a) when the school is taking remedial action to overcome the effects of past discrimination or (b) when it is taking voluntary action to overcome the effects of conditions in the past that limited the participation of persons with disabilities.[4] In either of these circumstances, the school must clearly state that the information sought is intended for use only in connection with remedial or voluntary action.

Educational institutions must ensure that admissions tests are selected and administered in a manner that measures applicants' actual aptitude or achievement level and not the effects of being deaf or hard of hearing.[5] For example, oral instructions during examinations should be made accessible to deaf and hard of hearing test takers by translating them into sign language or putting them in writing. Oral examinations should be conducted with a qualified sign language interpreter or other appropriate aid. If a test is designed to measure some area other than English language skills, then it should be modified for a deaf applicant who does not have standard English skills. In addition, the college should allow a student to take more time on a test or to take a test that is less reliant on English competence.

Once students with disabilities have matriculated at a given college or university, they must be treated the same as students without disabilities.[6] All programs and services of the college or university must be conducted in an integrated setting. With rare exceptions, separate facilities and programs for students with disabilities are not permitted.[7] Postsecondary institutions must also ensure that other programs in which students with disabilities participate do not discriminate.[8] Examples are internships, clinical placement programs, student teaching assignments, or course work at other schools in a consortium. Postsecondary institutions may not continue relationships with any program that in any way discriminates against students with disabilities.

Colleges and universities must make adjustments to academic requirements that discriminate against a student with a disability.[9] For example, where the degree sought is not in music, the college or university must permit a deaf student to substitute a music history or art appreciation course for a required course in music appreciation. Some schools waive foreign language requirements for deaf students or allow them to substitute sign language courses. The individual capabilities and needs of each student must be considered and academic adjustments made as appropriate. Similarly, where a college or university requires that students acquire a specific technological device, such as a laptop, tablet, or e-reader, it has an equivalent obligation to make accommodations to ensure that such devices are accessible to the students with disabilities.

However, a college or university is not required to make substantial modifications in its program in order to accommodate students with disabilities. In addition, they are not compelled to change academic requirements that they can prove are essential either to the program of instruction or for a particular degree.[10]

Example Cases

The contours of colleges' and universities' obligations to accommodate students with disabilities have been outlined in two landmark decisions, one by the Supreme Court of the United States and the other by the United States Court of Appeals for the Fifth Circuit.

Southeastern Community College v. Davis

In *Southeastern Community College v. Davis,* the Supreme Court defined the outer bounds of preadmission inquiries regarding students' disabilities and the extent of affirmative relief required by Section 504 of the Rehabilitation Act. In its first ruling on the merits of a case brought under Section 504, the Supreme Court held that a nursing school could require "reasonable physical qualifications for admission to a clinical training program" and reject a student whose disability would require substantial modifications of the program.[11]

Frances Davis, a licensed practical nurse who was hard of hearing, sought to enroll in a nursing school program to become a registered nurse. Despite evidence that she could perform well in this program, Southeastern Community College rejected Davis's application due to her hearing disability. A federal district court in North Carolina upheld the college's decision, noting that in settings such as an operating room, intensive care unit, or postnatal care unit, wearing a surgical mask would prevent Davis from speechreading to understand what was happening. The court concluded that Davis's "handicap actually prevents her from safely performing in both her training program and her proposed profession."[12] Although the United States Court of Appeals for the Fourth Circuit reversed this decision, the Supreme Court reinstated the district court's ruling, finding unanimously that the college had not violated Section 504:

> Nothing in the language or history of §504 reflects the intention to limit the freedom of an educational institution to require reasonable physical qualifications for admission to a clinical training program. Nor has there been any showing in this case that any action short of a substantial change in Southeastern's program would render unreasonable the qualifications it imposed.[13]

Writing for the Supreme Court, Justice Lewis Powell found that Section 504 does not compel schools to disregard an applicant's disabilities "or to make *substantial* modifications in their programs to allow disabled persons to participate" (emphasis added).[14] Instead, the Court interpreted Section 504 to mean that mere possession of a disability is not a permissible ground for assuming an inability to function in a particular context.[15]

The Supreme Court also found that, under Section 504, an "otherwise handicapped person" is "one who is able to meet all of a program's requirements in spite of his handicap."[16] Davis was considered unable to meet those requirements since "the ability to understand speech without reliance on lipreading is necessary for patient safety during the clinical phase of the program."[17] The Court stated that on the basis of meager evidence contained in the trial record, it was unlikely that Davis could successfully participate in the clinical program with any of the accommodations the regulation requires. The Court concluded that either close individual supervision or changing the curriculum to limit her participation to academic classes exceeded the "modification" required by the regulation.

The Supreme Court noted, however, that continuing some requirements may wrongly exclude qualified people with disabilities from participating in programs: "Thus situations may arise where a refusal to modify an existing program might become unreasonable and discriminatory. Identification of these instances where a refusal to accommodate the needs of a disabled person amounts to discrimination against the handicapped continues to be an important responsibility of HEW."[18]

Grantham v. Moffett

In *Grantham v. Moffett,* one of the first ADA cases to go to a jury trial, a federal appellate court further elucidated a university's obligations toward deaf and hard of hearing students when disability had a more tenuous relationship to a student's chosen course of study.[19] Nadelle Grantham was a deaf student who communicated via speechreading, sign language, and speaking, and she used a sign language interpreter for her academic classes. Her career goal was to teach English to deaf children in a public school setting. Her plan was to receive a degree in elementary education from Southeastern Louisiana University (SLU) in Hammond, Louisiana, and then acquire an "add-on" certification for teaching deaf children.

In 1990 Grantham began taking pre-education courses at SLU. On her application Grantham stated that she intended to major in elementary education. The Louisiana Division of Rehabilitation Services listed Grantham's career goal as "Teacher of the Deaf (specifically, teaching English to deaf students)" and her major as elementary education. That Louisiana agency provided sign language interpreter services and notetakers while Grantham was enrolled at SLU.

After being accepted into the SLU teacher education program, Grantham wrote to the department chairperson, asking to substitute another class for a music class, but SLU denied the request. Subsequently, the dean of the College of Education advised Grantham that she was expelled from the teacher education program based on "concerns about [your] profound hearing impairment, . . . concerns about [your] ability to perform the essential functions of a lower elementary teacher in a regular, multidisciplinary classroom setting," and "concerns over the health and safety of students under [your] supervision in the pre-teaching experience."

Grantham filed a lawsuit under Title II of the ADA. She was represented by the NAD Law Center and the Advocacy Center for the Elderly and Disabled in New Orleans. At the time of the trial, nine witnesses testified for Grantham, including experts from Gallaudet University and Lamar University, who stated that Grantham was qualified for the elementary education program based on her academic performance, as well as the following facts:

+ The few accommodations she required were not difficult or burdensome.
+ SLU would not have to lower its academic standards or substantially modify its elementary education program.
+ Grantham could perform student teaching in an elementary classroom safely and competently.

Despite SLU raising the *Davis* standard as a defense, a jury found that SLU's decision to expel Grantham from the lower education program because of her deafness violated the ADA. The jury awarded Grantham $181,000 in damages.[20] The United States Court of Appeals for the Fifth Circuit affirmed the jury verdict.[21] The case demonstrates that professional educators may not rely on stereotypical assumptions that are not truly indicative of a deaf individual's ability to participate in a college program.

AUXILIARY AIDS AND SERVICES

Postsecondary institutions' obligations to be accessible to students with disabilities arise under three specific sections of federal laws: Section 504 of the Rehabilitation Act, for educational institutions receiving federal financial assistance; Title II of the ADA, for public colleges and universities; and Title III of the ADA, for private colleges and universities. Under Titles II and III of the ADA, state, community, and private colleges and universities must provide auxiliary aids and services to ensure effective communication with deaf and hard of hearing people.[22] The ADA also requires the removal of structural communication barriers that are in existing facilities.[23] The Department of Education has determined that Section 504 likewise requires colleges and universities to provide necessary auxiliary aids and services, including interpreter services for deaf students.[24] The department's analysis to the Section 504 regulation notes the following:

> Under §104.44(d), a recipient must ensure that no handicapped student is subject to discrimination in the recipient's program because of the absence of necessary auxiliary educational aids. Colleges and universities expressed concern about the costs of compliance with this provision. The Department emphasizes that recipients can usually meet this obligation by assisting students in using existing resources for auxiliary aids, such as state vocational rehabilitation agencies and private charitable organizations. Indeed, the Department anticipates that the bulk of auxiliary aids will be paid for by private agencies, not by colleges and universities.[25]

The requirement to provide auxiliary aids and services extends to all required and optional elements of courses even if an element does not take place in the classroom. For example, if a program of study requires that all students acquire a tablet computer, the institution must ensure that deaf and hard of hearing students have access to a tablet computer that supports captioning, or any other accommodation that the student requires, at no added cost to the student. If a professor requires that students work in groups to complete a given project, the institution must provide interpreters or captioners to allow the student to participate in this group work. Likewise, if a professor assigns a particular video for students to watch, the university must either find a captioned version of the video or provide captions in time for the student to complete the assignment. Pursuant to the Twenty-First Century Communications and Video Accessibility Act of 2010 (CVAA), all videos that have aired on television as of 2012 or 2013 (depending on the nature of the video) and are later shown on the Internet in their entirety must be captioned[26] (see chapter 10 for more information about this law). In addition, many major providers of online videos have committed to captioning their entire library within the next few years.

Selecting the Auxiliary Aid or Service

As explained in chapter 1, the wide variation in communication methods used by deaf and hard of hearing individuals means that no one set of auxiliary aids or services can be considered per se effective in providing the communication access required by the ADA and the Rehabilitation Act. While some deaf or hard of hearing students can access classroom communication through sign language interpreters, others require assistive listening devices or captioning services.

In *Alexander v. Choate* the Supreme Court specified that, to meet the Rehabilitation Act standard, accommodations "are not required to produce the identical result or level of achievement for handicapped and nonhandicapped persons but must afford handicapped persons equal opportunity to obtain the same result, to gain the same benefit, or to reach the same level of achievement."[27] Therefore, the analysis must focus on the opportunity created for the student by virtue of the provision of interpreters, captioners, or assistive listening devices. Under the

ADA's implementing regulations, the DOJ established that the auxiliary aid or service must provide the individual with "effective communication."[28]

The standard for which auxiliary aids and services are necessary to achieve effective communication differs slightly between Title II and Title III of the ADA. While the implementing regulations of Title II require the entity to "give primary consideration to the requests of individuals with disabilities,"[29] Title III allows the entity more latitude in selecting which auxiliary aid or service to furnish "provided that the method chosen results in effective communication."[30] In determining what constitutes "necessary auxiliary educational aids," the U.S. Department of Justice has explained that "the individual with a disability is most familiar with his or her disability and is in the best position to determine what type of aid or service will be effective."[31]

A comprehensive list of auxiliary aids and services is set forth in the Justice Department's ADA rule, discussed in chapter 2.[32] For many sign language users, the only effective way to achieve effective communication is usually through use of qualified interpreters.[33] In addition to a qualified interpreter, the student will often need a competent notetaker because it is impossible to simultaneously watch an interpreter and take notes.

For deaf and hard of hearing people who do not use sign language, a college or university can provide a computer-assisted, real-time transcript system. A trained stenographer types everything spoken during a class into a computer, which simultaneously converts these notes to a written English transcript on a computer screen. In some situations, this system is preferable to a sign language interpreter because it gives the student the exact language of the course. For people who do not use sign language, the CART system may be the best way to ensure effective communication.

Argenyi v. Creighton University

In *Argenyi v. Creighton University*, the United States Court of Appeals for the Eighth Circuit emphasized that a student's own testimony is often the most instructive piece of evidence as to

which auxiliary aid or service will meet the student's needs.[34]
Michael Argenyi sued Creighton University's medical school for
refusing to provide the captioning services he had requested for
lectures and the sign-supported oral interpreters that he had
requested for labs and discussion groups. Instead, for Argenyi's
first year of medical school, Creighton provided an FM system,
which only amplifies sound without providing any visual cues.
Creighton added sign-supported oral interpreters for the lecture
portions of Argenyi's second-year classes. These arrangements
were not what Argenyi had requested (i.e., captioning for lectures
and sign-supported oral interpreters for labs and discussion
groups). Due to Creighton's refusal to provide the necessary auxiliary aids, Argenyi had paid out of pocket for these aids so that
he could understand the content of the courses, labs, and discussion groups and remain in school.

The district court initially ruled against Argenyi, finding that
Argenyi's affidavit, along with letters from his audiologists
explaining that he required captioning to understand the complex terminology used in medical school lectures, was "self-serv-
ing" and did not constitute sufficient evidence to establish his
case.[35] The United States Court of Appeals for the Eighth Circuit
reversed this decision and held that Argenyi had put forth sufficient evidence to proceed to trial. The court followed the DOJ's
standard and cautioned that "In a case such as this, it is especially
important to consider the complainant's testimony carefully
because 'the individual with a disability is most familiar with his
or her disability and is in the best position to determine what type
of aid or service will be effective.'"[36] In the Appeals Court's view,
the numerous letters written on Argenyi's behalf, coupled with
Argenyi's own description of the barriers he faced without the
requested accommodations, "provide[d] strong evidence that
Creighton's accommodations were inadequate."[37]

With remand from the Appeals Court, the District Court conducted a trial. The trial jury found that Creighton University had
not provided Argenyi with the necessary auxiliary aids and services, tacitly ruling that sign-supported oral interpreters do not
achieve effective communication, nor do they provide equal
access to a medical school education for a deaf student who relies

on CART. The jury found that Argenyi was not able to follow a medical school education by lipreading complex medical terminology and that CART was the means for effective communication for Argenyi in this setting.

Obligation of Colleges and Universities to Pay for Auxiliary Aids and Services

As in all other settings in which auxiliary aids and services are provided, higher education institutions may not pass on the cost of the these types of assistance to the student requesting them.[38] In a case that the Department of Justice brought against the University of Alabama, the U.S. Court of Appeals for the Eleventh Circuit held in 1977 that the university must provide qualified interpreters for deaf students even if the students do not have financial need and even if they are in part-time or other special noncredit categories.[39] The court held that Congress intended colleges and universities to provide free auxiliary aids for these students because, without this assistance, they are denied meaningful access to an opportunity to learn.

In *Camenisch v. University of Texas,* a district court issued a preliminary injunction in 1977 requiring the University of Texas to provide interpreters for a deaf graduate student. As part of the legal basis for issuing the preliminary injunction, the court noted that "[t]here is a substantial likelihood that Plaintiff will ultimately prevail on the merits."[40] The U.S. Court of Appeals for the Fifth Circuit affirmed this decision.[41] As an additional issue in the case, both the district court and the Fifth Circuit held that people with disabilities have a right to sue in federal court to enforce their rights under Section 504 and are not required to first exhaust administrative remedies.

Under the ADA and Section 504, covered entities that are responsible for providing auxiliary aids and services have two defenses: fundamental alteration and undue burden. The fundamental alteration defense is rarely invoked because a covered entity would have to demonstrate that providing the auxiliary aid or service would drastically change the entity's programs or services. This is a difficult standard, and covered entities are more likely to argue that the provision of auxiliary aids and services would result in an undue burden in light of the overall resources of the site providing the services and the entity as a whole.

Although the courts have not articulated a threshold for what constitutes an undue burden, *Argenyi v. Creighton University* is instructive on this point. In *Argenyi,* a deaf student attending medical school at a private university requested auxiliary aids and services that would cost between $50,000 and $75,000 per year for the medical school to provide. The school charged between $46,000 and $49,000 per year in tuition and did not receive state funding. Nevertheless, a jury determined that providing the auxiliary aids and services the student requested would not result in an undue burden for Creighton University. This case indicates that a student's auxiliary aids and services may cost significantly more than that student's tuition without resulting in an undue burden for the entity charged with providing the services.

Responsibility of Vocational Rehabilitation Agencies to Provide Services

In *Schornstein v. N.J. Division of Vocational Rehabilitation Services*[42] and *Jones v. Illinois Department of Rehabilitation Services,*[43] two federal courts held that state vocational rehabilitation (VR) agencies are expected to provide auxiliary aids and services to deaf students who are VR clients as part of the students' individual plan for employment (IPE, formerly called an individual written rehabilitation plan). Since 1977 the U.S. Department of Education has assumed that the bulk of auxiliary aids for college students will be paid for by state VR agencies and private charitable organizations.[44] If a student is not eligible for VR services or if a VR agency fails to provide funding for the services a student needs, then the college or university remains responsible for ensuring that its program is accessible to that student.

In 1998 Congress amended the Rehabilitation Act to instruct state VR agencies to enter into interagency agreements with other public entities, including public colleges and universities operated by state and local governments. These agreements spell out which entity (the state rehabilitation agency and/or the public institution of higher education) will finance which communication services. The agreements can call for shared costs, formulas for the provision of services, or decisions on a school-by-school basis. The agreements should divide responsibilities clearly and do so in advance of demand from any given student so that services for that student will not be delayed or denied unnecessarily while the various agencies argue over who will pay for what. Thus, with respect to public (state, county, and local government) colleges, universities, and vocational, technical, or trade schools, some or all communication services may be financed by state rehabilitation agencies on behalf of deaf or hard of hearing clients of those agencies who attend these postsecondary institutions.

Students at private postsecondary institutions may also receive VR support for tuition and other educational expenses, including interpreter and communication services. Especially where private institutions are the most appropriate source of the kind of training an individual client requires, the VR agency must provide necessary services or monitor the situation to ensure that the private program provides appropriate services. However, if the student is not a VR client or if the student is not eligible for VR services under VR policies or the interagency agreement, public and private colleges are required by federal law to make their programs accessible, which includes paying for interpreters, CART, or other necessary accommodations.

CAMPUS LIFE

The obligation of colleges and universities to provide accommodations for students with disabilities does not stop at the classroom door. Students with disabilities have a right to the full and equal enjoyment of all programs, services, and activities of both public and private colleges and universities. This includes the right to accommodations in dormitories and extracurricular activities. For deaf and hard of hearing students, common auxiliary aids and services that provide equal access to dormitories and campus in general include but are not limited to the following:

+ flashers for fire alarms both in students' rooms and all areas of residential access, such as hallways, common rooms, lobbies, and shared bathrooms
+ flashers for door knockers in students' rooms, common rooms, and shared bathrooms
+ flashers for fire alarms in classrooms and all areas of educational and general access, such as hallways, lounges, libraries, the offices of student organizations, and the offices of university staff with frequent student visitors
+ the capacity to display captions on any public-use TV, such as a TV in a common room or lobby
+ a system for sending emergency alerts via text message if the university has an emergency alert system
+ visual displays of any announcements made through a public address system, likely through an LED ribbon board, including at campus arenas and stadiums
+ accessible telephones (if telephones are otherwise provided to students), such as a videophone or captioned telephone, depending on students' needs. Please note that TTYs are no longer commonly used by deaf or hard of hearing people; every effort should be made to provide a device in common usage

CONTINUING EDUCATION COURSES AND PROFESSIONAL EXAMINATIONS

In addition to the ADA's requirement that colleges and universities be accessible to students with disabilities, Title III establishes that "[a]ny person that offers examinations or courses related to applications, licensing, certification, or credentialing for secondary or post-secondary education, professional, or trade purposes shall offer such examinations or courses in a place and manner accessible to persons with disabilities or offer alternative accessible arrangements for such individuals."[45] This language specifies that the requirement to provide accommodations under Title III extends to online colleges and universities, as well as to providers of continuing education units (CEUs), test preparation courses, and other examinations or coursework relating to ongoing education or professional development. Under this section, the fact that an organization is privately run or provides exclusively online materials does not exempt it from the obligation to make its offerings accessible to people with disabilities.

It is important to understand that the ADA and Section 504 do not recognize cost as an undue burden when the expense of a requested auxiliary aid or service is greater than the revenue generated by the deaf or hard of hearing participant or even by the workshop as a whole. The Department of Justice has clarified that the undue burden analysis is not limited in scope to a single workshop. Rather, the analysis must take into account the "overall financial resources" of the provider and must be measured with respect to the specific accommodations request at hand,[46] not the hypothetical burden of providing accommodations for individuals who have not yet requested them. Consequently, a provider cannot argue that it would be an undue burden to have to provide an auxiliary aid or service at every workshop.

Providers of covered courses also may not satisfy their obligations under Title III by providing a captioned video of similar material in lieu of making available auxiliary aids or services for workshops. This alternative approach runs afoul of the ADA when: (1) the certification at issue requires that a certain number of CEUs be taken face-to-face and *not* via videos; (2) the captioned video offered presents material that differs from that of the chosen course or workshop; or (3) the entity advertises its on-site and online workshops as different services even if the same material is covered in both sets of courses.

In 1996 the Department of Justice issued a consent order against Testmasters, an LSAT prep company, for its failure to provide auxiliary aids and services to ensure effective communication for a deaf student enrolled in its LSAT preparatory course.[47] The Department of Justice has also entered into a settlement agreement with the National Board of Medical Examiners, requiring that it provide auxiliary aids and services to ensure effective communication for all students during the United States Medical Licensing Examination.[48]

NOTES

1. 29 U.S.C. §794.
2. 42 U.S.C. §§12131, 181, 189.
3. 28 C.F.R. §36.301; 34 C.F.R. §104.42.
4. 34 C.F.R. §104.42(c).
5. 28 C.F.R. §36.309; 34 C.F.R. §104.35.
6. 28 C.F.R. §§36.201, 36.202; 34 C.F.R. §104.43.
7. 28 C.F.R. §36.203; 34 C.F.R. §104.43(c), (d).
8. 34 C.F.R. §104.43(b).
9. 34 C.F.R. §104.44(a).
10. 42 *Fed. Reg.* 22,692 (May 4, 1977).
11. *Southeastern Community College v. Davis*, 442 U.S. 397 (1979).
12. 424 F.Supp. 1341, 1345 (E.D.N.C. 1976).
13. 442 U.S. 397 at 414.
14. 442 U.S. 397 at 405.
15. Ibid.
16. 442 U.S. 397 at 406.
17. 442 U.S. 397 at 407.
18. 442 U.S. 397 at 412–13.
19. *Grantham v. Moffett,* 1996 U.S. Dist. LEXIS 102, Civ. A. No. 93-4007(N)3 (E.D. La. May 23, 1995).
20. Ibid., at *2.
21. *Grantham v. Moffett,* 101 F.3d 698 (5th Cir. 1998).
22. 28 C.F.R. §§35.160, 36.303.
23. 28 C.F.R. §§35.150, 36.304.
24. 34 C.F.R. §104,44(d).
25. 45 *Fed. Reg.* 30,954 (May 9, 1980).
26. 47 U.S.C. §613, 47 C.F.R. §79.4.
27. *Alexander v. Choate,* 469 US 287, 305 (1985) (citing 45 C.F.R. §84.4(b)(2)).
28. 28 C.F.R. §36.303(c)(1) ("A public accommodation shall furnish appropriate auxiliary aids and services where necessary to ensure effective communication with individuals with disabilities."). See 28 C.F.R. §35.160 (a)(1) ("A public entity shall take appropriate steps to ensure that communications with applicants, participants, members of the public, and companions with disabilities are as effective as communications with others.").
29. 28 C.F.R. §35.160(b)(2).
30. 28 C.F.R. §36.303(c)(1)(ii).
31. U.S. Department of Justice, "Americans with Disabilities Act, Title II Technical Assistance Manual," http://www.ada.gov/taman2.html.

32. 28 C.F.R. §36.104.
33. *Schornstein v. N.J. Div. of Voc. Rehab. Serv.*, 519 F. Supp. 773 (D.N.J. 1982), *aff'd* 688 F.2d 824 (3d Cir. 1982).
34. *Argenyi v. Creighton University,* 703 F. 3d 441 (8th Cir. 2013).
35. *Argenyi v. Creighton University,* 2011 U.S. Dist. LEXIS 108764, no. 8:09CV341, at *31–32 (September 22, 2011).
36. 703 F.3d at 446 (quoting U.S. Department of Justice, "Americans with Disabilities Act Title II Technical Assistance Manual," at II-7.1100 [1993]).
37. Ibid., at 447.
38. See, for example, *Crawford v. Univ. of N.C.*, 440 F. Supp. 1047 (M.D.N.C. 1977); *Barnes v. Converse College*, 436 F. Supp. 635 (D.S.C. 1977).
39. *United States v. Bd. of Trustees for the Univ. of Ala.*, 908 F. 2d 740 (11th Cir. 1990).
40. 1978 U.S. Dist. LEXIS 17728, Civ. A. No. A-78-CA-061, at *5 (W.D. Tex. May 17, 1978).
41. *Camenisch v. Univ. of Tex.*, 616 F.2d 127 (5th Cir. 1980).
42. 519 F. Supp. 773 (D.N.J. 1982), *aff'd* 688 F. 2d 824 (3d Cir. 1982).
43. 504 F. Supp. 1244 (N.D. Ill. 1981), *aff'd* 689 F. 2d 724 (7th Cir. 1982).
44. 42 *Fed. Reg.* 22692-93 (May 4, 1977).
45. 42 U.S.C. §12189.
46. 28 C.F.R. §36.104.
47. *Consent Order Between the U.S. at Robin Singh Educ. Serv., Inc., d/b/a Testmasters*, Consent Order No. CV06-3466 ABC (2006).
48. *Settlement Agr. Between U.S. and Nat'l Bd. of Medical Examiners*, DJ# 202-16-181 (February 23, 2011).

Chapter 6

Health Care and Social Services

Federal law ensures meaningful access to the complicated web of public and private health care and social services available in most communities. Many healthcare providers and social services receive significant federal assistance and must therefore comply with Section 504 of the Rehabilitation Act of 1973. In addition to Section 504 obligations, public and private healthcare providers must also comply with the Americans with Disabilities Act of 1990. Together, these federal laws require public and private agencies to provide auxiliary aids and services to people with disabilities. Providers are not allowed to discriminate against people with disabilities. Federal law requires them to ensure that their deaf and hard of hearing clients, customers, patients, and loved ones receive effective communication.

This does not mean that deaf and hard of hearing people find it easy to get the services to which they are entitled. They are sometimes turned away from a program simply because no one on the staff can communicate with them or understand what they need. Deaf and hard of hearing people often get little or no service in situations where hearing people receive good service. A hearing person may get answers to questions about food stamp eligibility, for example, or advice on how to complete an application, or information on the details of a program. But a deaf or hard of hearing person may be handed a standard written form with cursory explanations of office and program procedures. As a result, this individual might misunderstand the form and lose benefits.

The sections that follow describe the federal laws that govern how healthcare facilities treat patients who are deaf and hard of hearing. Other considerations include court rulings and state civil rights and disability laws.

FEDERAL DISABILITY RIGHTS LAWS

Federal disability rights laws include Section 504 of the Rehabilitation Act, the Americans with Disabilities Act, Justice Department guidelines, and standards set by individual agencies. These federal laws require effective communication from private doctors,[1] private and public hospitals, and federally funded agencies.[2] Further, agencies that provides information or services by telephone must ensure that telecommunications relay services are used to provide equally effective services to deaf and hard of hearing individuals.[3]

Section 504 of the Rehabilitation Act of 1973

Section 504 of the Rehabilitation Act of 1973 (discussed in chapter 3) requires any program that receives federal financial assistance and has fifteen or more employees to be accessible to people with disabilities. A hospital or doctor's office that takes Medicare payments receives federal financial assistance; a social service agency that receives federal grant money is receiving federal financial assistance; and healthcare or social services agencies operated by state and local government agencies usually receive federal financial assistance.

An agency covered by Section 504 must provide appropriate "auxiliary aids" to people with disabilities when these aids are necessary to afford them an equal opportunity to benefit from the service in question.[4] Auxiliary aids are specifically defined to include interpreters, Braille, taped material, and other aids.[5] Smaller agencies may also be required to provide auxiliary aids when doing so would not impair the agency's ability to provide its normal benefits or services.[6] Interpreters can be hired for a reasonable hourly fee for occasional deaf clients. Videophones and other accessible devices can be acquired for a one-time investment of a few hundred dollars. These expenses are not unduly burdensome for most agencies.

Section 504 applies to many public and nonprofit agencies. For example, food stamp offices must provide a sign language interpreter to assist in explaining the application procedure, eligibility criteria, and benefits available to deaf applicants who rely on sign language to understand this information. Social Security offices must provide auxiliary aids and services, including qualified interpreters. In addition, such offices are required to accept relay calls so that deaf people can telephone for information, schedule appointments, or consult with caseworkers (see chapter 1).

Although such an agency is not required to have an interpreter on staff at all times, deaf people should be able to request an interpreter and be scheduled for an appointment in a timely manner. This appointment procedure is a reasonable method of providing equivalent services even if applications are ordinarily handled on a first-come, first-served basis. The agency should also post a notice clearly explaining that interpreters are available on request and the process for requesting one.

Unfortunately, some healthcare providers or social service agencies have denied these communications accommodations and even denied any services to deaf and hard of hearing individuals. In one case, a deaf woman who was pregnant went to a gynecologist's office with her mother. When the doctor walked into the examining room and discovered that the woman was deaf, he refused to treat her and said that, because she was deaf, she must go to a center for high-risk pregnancies. The woman filed suit against the doctor, who received federal financial assistance in the form of Medicaid payments. The court awarded the woman $10,000, finding that the doctor had discriminated against the woman in violation of the Rehabilitation Act.[7]

The Americans with Disabilities Act of 1990

Under the Americans with Disabilities Act, deaf people have the right to equal access to and participation in healthcare and social services. They also have the right to effective communication with their healthcare providers and social service agencies.[8] The ADA prohibits discrimination by public and private agencies regardless of the agency's size or receipt of federal financial assistance. In this way, the ADA is much broader than Section 504. The ADA obligates hospitals, physicians, social service agencies, and public and private healthcare providers, among others, to provide auxiliary aids and services to individuals with disabilities.[9]

Title II of the ADA prohibits discrimination by state and local governments. This means that public agencies, such as welfare offices and state hospitals, must allow deaf people equal access to their services and programs. For example, the local welfare office must provide interpreters to deaf clients when needed for effective communication. Title II also protects deaf and hard of hearing prisoners seeking healthcare or social services from discrimination.[10] State and local prisons violate the law if they discourage or prevent deaf prisoners from participating in group therapy or counseling programs because of their disability. When a deaf prisoner needs an interpreter for effective communication, Title II of the ADA directs that a qualified interpreter be provided.

Private healthcare providers, such as private hospitals, doctors, and mental health counselors, are governed by Title III of the ADA. Under Title III, private healthcare providers must provide auxiliary aids and services so that people with disabilities can benefit from their services.[11] For deaf and hard of hearing people, this means that their doctors, mental health counselors, training programs, and nursing homes may not discriminate. In fact, any place of public accommodation must provide necessary auxiliary aids and services.

One key element of the ADA is that places of public accommodation may not charge the deaf person for the cost of these auxiliary aids and services. "A public accommodation may not impose a surcharge on a particular individual with a disability or any group of individuals with disabilities to cover the costs of measures, such as the provision of auxiliary aids . . . that are required to provide that individual . . . with the nondiscriminatory treatment required by the Act."[12]

Despite the clarity of this ADA mandate, deaf people continue to be billed and surcharged for the cost of auxiliary aids in violation of law. Some providers attempt to circumvent the legal mandate for auxiliary aids by asking a family member or friend to interpret for the deaf person. Such practice is not permitted. Furthermore, such practice violates the more general legal requirement that an interpreter interpret information "effectively," "accurately," and "impartially."[13]

Generally, a doctor who has a deaf patient's family member interpret for the deaf patient has not provided effective communication. Under the law, family members do not meet the strict standards of a "qualified interpreter," who must be able to interpret information "effectively, accurately, and impartially." First of all, most family members are not trained as sign language interpreters and are not able to interpret effectively or accurately. Additionally, most family members would not be able to interpret "impartially" in medical situations involving their own family. The family member may fail to communicate necessary information in a misguided effort to shield the deaf patient. Moreover, the deaf person may not ask certain questions in the presence of a family member or friend. In addition, the family member or friend may be too emotionally upset by the situation to interpret correctly. Therefore, friends or family members should not interpret unless the deaf person specifically requests they do so and only if the person is competent to provide the service.

The right to effective communication is not limited to the patient who is deaf or hard of hearing but also includes any family members or loved ones who typically get services or information.[14] In other words, medical care providers must provide effective communication to the following: deaf parents whose hearing children are receiving services, deaf spouses whose hearing spouses are receiving services, deaf siblings and cousins and partners who are supporting hearing patients, and the like. These deaf family members and loved ones must be able to receive the same information that they would if they were hearing.

Some healthcare providers covered by the ADA have argued that it is too costly to pay for auxiliary aids and services. For example, a doctor might argue that it would be an undue burden to pay for an interpreter. However, a public accommodation such as a doctor's office may not deny an auxiliary aid unless it can demonstrate that providing that aid would fundamentally alter the nature of the service or would constitute an undue burden or expense.[15] Whether or not a particular auxiliary aid constitutes an "undue burden" is difficult to decide. It depends on a variety of factors, including the nature and cost of the auxiliary aid or service and the business's overall financial and other resources.[16] The undue burden standard is intended to be applied on a case-by-case basis. Undue burden is not measured by the amount of income the business is receiving from a deaf client, patient, or customer. Instead, it is measured by the financial impact on the whole entity.[17]

Therefore, it is possible for a business to be responsible for providing auxiliary aids even if it does not make a sale or receive income from a deaf patient or customer—as long as the cost of the auxiliary aid would not be an undue burden on its overall operation. Even if a public accommodation is able to demonstrate that a fundamental alteration would be necessitated or an undue burden would arise, it must be prepared to provide an alternative auxiliary aid if one exists.[18] For example, a doctor who refuses to provide interpreting services will be obligated to show that effective communication can be achieved by other means.

The cost of auxiliary aids is slight when compared to the overall budget of most healthcare providers. Effective communication is vital for deaf and hard of hearing consumers, but it is also important for healthcare providers because it protects them from malpractice claims when a medicine is prescribed or a treatment given without knowing the deaf person's medical history or without obtaining informed consent. Healthcare providers benefit when they communicate effectively with their patients. Under the Revenue Reconciliation Act of 1990, some providers may even be eligible for tax credits for expenses incurred in the course of accommodating patients with disabilities.[19]

AGENCY RESPONSIBILITIES

Some service agencies attempt to evade their legal responsibilities for effective communications. Small agencies may claim that providing auxiliary aids is beyond their financial means. They may seek a waiver of the requirement to provide auxiliary aids on the basis of their small size and budget. However, some auxiliary aids are critical, and most are not excessive in cost. Deaf consumers are entitled by law to receive such auxiliary aids free of charge. Under Section 504 of the Rehabilitation Act, the cost is the responsibility of the agency receiving and making use of the federal money. Under the ADA, the cost is the responsibility of the healthcare or other service provider that is covered under Titles II and III.

Agency Rules and State Laws

In addition to the requirements of Section 504 and the ADA, most federal agencies have specific rules that prohibit discrimination against people with disabilities in the services they support.[20] Some states have adopted laws that prohibit discrimination against people with disabilities by government and private social service agencies. Others have laws specifically requiring certain services for deaf people. For example, in New York State, the New York Hospital Codes, Rules, and Regulations require hospitals to produce a sign language interpreter for deaf emergency room patients within ten minutes of the patient's request.[21]

Most states have civil rights laws prohibiting discrimination by facilities open to the public. Traditionally, these laws have dealt only with racial or religious discrimination. More recently, many of these state laws were amended to now also prohibit discrimination based on disability. In addition to commercial enterprises, such as restaurants, hotels, and stores, these state laws apply to service agencies that are open to the public.[22]

HOSPITAL COMMUNICATION BARRIERS

It is not possible to have equal access to services without communication. Communication is perhaps the most important element of health care. Without it, patients cannot explain the symptoms of their illness to the medical staff. Without communication, patients cannot comprehend the routines of treatment or preventive medicine. If all medical patients were treated like this, the general population would be outraged. Yet deaf people face these circumstances daily.

Before the passage of Section 504 and the ADA, deaf and hard of hearing people had virtually no right to effective communication in hospitals. When deaf people entered a hospital, they had to take what was offered them, sometimes settling for ineffective or even life-threatening health care because they and or the healthcare provider did not understand what was being said. Through written notes or lipreading, complicated medical terms were used regardless of whether the deaf patient understood them. Drugs were prescribed without any explanation of what they were for or how to take them. Sometimes deaf people took these drugs with other medicines, not knowing the possible reactions. Hospital admissions procedures were rarely explained. If they wanted assistance from the nursing staff, they could not use the intercom. If a pregnant woman went into the labor room, she did not receive an interpreter to assist with communications, and she could not understand what her doctor wanted her to do because the doctor's surgical mask made lipreading impossible. Under current federal law, these kinds of discriminatory conduct are no longer legal. However, deaf and hard of hearing people continue to fight to ensure that hospitals are accessible to them.

Compounding the Stress

A person in a medical situation may be apprehensive, nervous, confused, and in pain. When these feelings are compounded by the stress of trying to understand what a health provider is saying, the experience can be traumatic. In the past, many hospitals have relied on the exchange of written notes, lipreading, or other means of communicating with deaf and hard of hearing patients, and usually those efforts were ineffective. For a person with limited English skills, written English can be unproductive, frustrating, and even dangerous. Written communication also tends to be a very concise summary of a discussion rather than effective communication with all the nuances and contextual clues that are so important in medical situations. Writing usually takes considerably more time than speaking, and very often medical professionals who are already under time constraints do not write down anywhere near as much information as they would speak to hearing individuals. Likewise, deaf and hard of hearing patients may not be given time to write down all of their information, concerns, and/or questions. Understanding is further hampered by unfamiliar medical terms and the need for fast, efficient communication during a medical emergency.

Some hospitals have attempted to get by with a staff member who has some knowledge of sign language instead of bringing in a skilled interpreter from outside the hospital. This might be acceptable if the staff member is qualified as a skilled sign language interpreter, but this is rarely the case. More often, the staff member's limited proficiency in sign language creates serious misunderstandings, leading to ineffective treatment and even misdiagnosis.

Planning for Deaf and Hard of Hearing Patients

Federal law requires healthcare providers to offer a full range of communication options (auxiliary aids) so that deaf and hard of hearing persons receive effective healthcare services. For more than twenty years, the government has required providers to prepare in advance for the reality that deaf and hard of hearing patients will at some time need to use their services. In order to be ready to give these patients the access required by law, the government asks providers to be equipped to offer various communication options and to do so by consulting with deaf persons and organizations advocating for the rights of deaf persons. The auxiliary aids and services options that must be provided, at no cost to the deaf patient, include but are not limited to the following:

+ formal arrangements with qualified interpreters who can accurately, effectively, and impartially interpret fluently in sign language, both expressively and receptively
+ supplemental hearing devices such as amplified telephones, telecommunications devices such as videophones, televisions equipped with captioning equipment, and loop systems
+ written communication (with the understanding that this option may not be effective for many individuals and situations)
+ staff training in identifying communication access challenges, cultural differences, and basic sign language[23]

These guidelines mean that each healthcare provider must make its staff aware of local interpreters and/or interpreting agencies, including their names, addresses, phone numbers, and hours of availability. In addition, healthcare providers must accept relay calls so that deaf patients can make appointments, notify providers that they will be needing auxiliary aids, and communicate with deaf family and friends to the same extent as hearing patients. They also have a responsibility to make sure that deaf people seeking treatment are given advance notice of the various communication options, typically through signage in the hospital or medical care center. Advance planning makes it possible for deaf patients to access the auxiliary aids that will enable them to communicate with providers.

Communication that is "effective" and aids that are "appropriate"—two terms used in federal regulations—are best determined by the deaf patient. Title II of the ADA requires that primary consideration be accorded to the deaf patients' request for their own communication needs.[24] Hospital personnel often assume that they are better able than deaf patients to decide how to communicate with these patients. For example, hospital staff might insist that because they think they can understand the deaf person, the patient can therefore understand them. Hospitals might assume that communication by pen and paper is adequate and that the decision to use an interpreter is up to the doctor. A hospital may claim to have an interpreter on its staff, yet the staff member has studied sign language for only a few months and cannot understand most signs. In most circumstances, deaf people are in the best position to judge what is needed so that they have equal access to health care. The government has repeatedly stressed that when choosing methods for effective communication, patients' judgments must be considered to be of the utmost importance.[25]

Deaf patients have nothing to gain by requesting an inappropriate auxiliary aid. The risks for both the patient and the provider are too serious. Even in those rare circumstances when an emergency facility is unable to immediately provide a specific type of communication, providers are still obligated to provide the most effective communication in view of the limits of time in the emergency situation.

Advance Preparation for Emergency Care

Emergency healthcare regulations are especially important. Hospitals are required to establish a special emergency healthcare procedure for effective communication with deaf people in emergency rooms. Hospitals should be able to locate qualified sign language interpreters on very short notice. They should also accept relay calls in the same manner as they accept any other calls so that deaf people can alert the hospital that a deaf patient is coming in and will need an interpreter or other special services. Hospitals should also provide equal access to telecommunications through videophones and other devices to enable deaf individuals to call out of the hospital or get a medical professional's attention. Emergency room staff should be trained to use and recognize basic sign language necessary for emergency care. They should be trained to quickly recognize that a person is deaf and should know how to find appropriate auxiliary aids.

Hospital Compliance

Services must be equivalent for both hearing and deaf patients and companions. There are many ways a hospital or health center may accommodate deaf patients and companions. For example, one that ordinarily allows only one person to accompany a woman through natural childbirth may have to alter its delivery room rules to allow both the husband and an interpreter to be present during the delivery. A hospital that prohibits the admission of deaf people to its psychiatric unit unless they lip-read will have to change its policy to comply with Section 504 and the ADA.

Patients in a hospital room have many devices to make the hospital stay more bearable. Yet many of these devices are useless for deaf patients without modification. For example, if a deaf patient presses the intercom button, the nurse at the station will answer by speaking through the intercom, but this is not effective for the deaf patient. The deaf patient would naturally assume that the nurse knows that the patient is deaf, but too often the nurse may be unaware of this. After repeated attempts to contact each other, the nurse and the deaf patient may become exasperated with one another, resulting in a hostile relationship that may affect the quality of the deaf patient's care. This typical problem can be avoided by flagging deaf patients' charts and intercom buttons so that all pertinent hospital personnel know to respond in intercom situations. Deaf patients should also have a telecommunications device such as a videophone and televisions that have the captions activated.

Hospitals must also provide ongoing staff training to sensitize personnel to other special needs of deaf and hard of hearing people: adequate, glare-free lighting; control of background noise for all hearing-aid wearers; modifications to auditory fire alarm systems; and changes in oral evaluation procedures. Freedom of movement, especially for hands and arms, is crucial in allowing a deaf patient to sign and/or gesture.

Healthcare facilities should take special steps to make sure that deaf people know about services the hospital normally offers and about any special services to which they may be entitled because of their disabilities. For example, many hospitals provide new patients with an orientation to the hospital, its personnel, and its services. All such information should be available in writing at a level of English that most people can understand. It should include an easy-to-read notice about the availability of sign language interpreters, telecommunications devices such as videophones, and other special services. If a facility gives information by telephone, it must accept relay services' calls and treat them just like any other calls.

Some deaf people do not know about hospitals' legal obligations. They may not know how to request an interpreter. It is the hospital's responsibility to provide this information. Hospitals also should have easy-to-read notices posted in the emergency room, outpatient clinic, and all admitting areas to inform deaf people of how they can obtain interpreter services or other assistance.

Hospitals often ask patients to sign a written consent to treatment or legal waivers of rights before they will treat them. Federal laws require hospitals to take any necessary steps to ensure that deaf people understand these rights prior to signing these consents. It may be necessary for a qualified sign language interpreter to be present when doctors discuss consent papers with the deaf patient. In addition, it is helpful if the consent and waiver papers are written in language that the deaf patient can understand.

There are many ways an agency, health center, or hospital can make its services available and useful to deaf people. In 2010 the National Association of the Deaf Law Center and a private law firm filed an ADA and a Section 504 complaint against a hospital on behalf of deaf parents in Virginia.[26] The hospital denied the parents interpreter services in a hospital during the course of the care of their newborn son, who had a life-threatening heart condition. The Justice Department also filed suit against the hospital. The result of this case was a policy to provide deaf and hard of hearing people with an equal opportunity to receive and benefit from hospital services and to facilitate accurate, effective, timely, and dignified communication between hospital personnel and people who are deaf or hard of hearing.

The policy describes a model system where deaf patients receive qualified interpreters; telecommunication devices such as videophones; captioned televisions; assistive listening devices; trained notetakers; computer-assisted real-time transcription services; telephone flashers to indicate incoming calls; and other aids and services. Additional important elements of the policy include signage explaining the rights of deaf patients, training for hospital staff, and initial patient surveys that would notify hospital staff that a patient is deaf or hard of hearing.

Other hospitals are discovering that not complying with federal civil rights laws can be very costly. One New Jersey hospital recently agreed to pay $700,000 to four deaf residents for failure to provide interpreters, closed captioning, and telecommunication devices over a ten-year period.[27] In Connecticut, deaf and hard of hearing people, along with the Connecticut Association of the Deaf, sued ten acute-care hospitals for failing to provide effective communication. The lawsuit settled for approximately $350,000, along with an agreement to remove barriers that prevent effective communication in hospitals.[28] As a result, Connecticut will have a comprehensive, on-call system for obtaining interpreters that will be the first cooperative, hospital-sponsored system in the country. In New York, a jury awarded $250,000 to a deaf woman who was denied interpreter services in the hospital.[29]

Guidelines for Hospitals

The following NAD guidelines help hospital administrators develop procedures for serving the needs of their deaf and hard of hearing patients and comply with federal regulations:

1. A central office should be designated to supervise services to deaf and hard of hearing patients. This office should establish a system to obtain qualified sign language and oral interpreters on short notice twenty-four hours a day.
2. The unit to which a deaf or hard of hearing patient is admitted should immediately notify the designated office when that patient is admitted.
3. A staff person responsible for assessing communication needs should be sent to the patient immediately to consult with the patient as to the appropriate method of communication, which may include the following:
   a. use of a qualified sign language and/or oral interpreter
   b. lipreading

c. handwritten notes

d. supplemental hearing devices

e. any combination of the above

The responsible staff person should give the patient notice of the right to a qualified sign language and/or oral interpreter to be provided by the hospital without charge to the patient. If no interpreter is available within the hospital, the patient should be given written notice of these rights.

4. The interpreter facilitates communication between the patient and the staff to ensure that the deaf or hard of hearing patient is receiving equal services and equal opportunity to participate in and benefit from hospital services. These situations include but are not limited to the following:

a. obtaining the patient's medical history

b. obtaining informed consent or permission for treatment

c. diagnosis of the ailment or injury

d. explanations of medical procedures to be used

e. treatment or surgery if the patient is conscious or to determine whether the patient is conscious

f. those times the patient is in intensive care or in the recovery room after surgery

g. emergency situations that arise

h. explanations of the medications prescribed, how and when they are to be taken, and possible side effects

i. assisting at the request of the doctor or other hospital staff

j. discharge of the patient

5. Friends or relatives of deaf or hard of hearing patients cannot be used as interpreters unless those patients specifically request that they interpret and the friends or relatives are qualified to interpret. Deaf and hard of hearing patients, their friends, and their families should be told that a professional interpreter will be provided at no cost where needed for effective communication.

6. The deaf patient should be informed that another interpreter will be obtained if the patient is unable to communicate with a particular interpreter.

7. Any written notices of rights or services and written consent forms should be written at no higher than a fifth-grade reading level to ensure access for everyone. An interpreter should be provided if the deaf or hard of hearing patient is unable to understand such written notices.

8. Relay services should be used when communicating with deaf and hard of hearing individuals over the telephone for making appointments, giving out information, and assisting in emergency situations. Portable telecommunication devices such as videophones should be available on request for deaf and hard of hearing patients. Telephone amplifiers should be provided for patients who are hard of hearing. All telephones should be hearing-aid compatible.

9. Visual access to information made available over auditory intercom systems, paging systems, and alarm systems should be provided for all deaf and hard of hearing patients.

10. Ongoing efforts should be made by the hospital to sensitize staff to the various special needs of deaf and hard of hearing patients.

11. Contact with local deaf and hard of hearing people, organizations for and of these individuals, and the community agencies serving them should be maintained for assistance in drawing up a list of qualified interpreters and in developing a program of hospital services that is responsive to the needs of this group of patients.

12. A video remote interpreting system may be used in the place of in-person sign language interpreters, but specific steps must be taken to ensure the VRI system meets the needs of the deaf or hard of hearing patient or family members.

Video Remote Interpreting Systems in the Health Care Setting

Video remote interpreting systems are one of the auxiliary aids and services enumerated in the ADA regulations and are defined as "an interpreting service that uses video conference technology over dedicated lines or wireless technology offering high-speed, wide-bandwidth video connection that delivers high-quality video images."[30] The regulations go on to spell out the standards for VRI as follows:

1. Real-time, full-motion video and audio over a dedicated high-speed, wide-bandwidth video connection or wireless connection that delivers high-quality video images that do not produce lags, choppy, blurry, or grainy images, or irregular pauses in communication
2. A sharply delineated image that is large enough to display the interpreter's face, arms, hands, and fingers, as well as the participating individual's face, arms, hands, and fingers, regardless of the person's body position
3. A clear, audible transmission of voices
4. Adequate training to users of the technology and other involved individuals so that they may quickly and efficiently set up and operate the VRI[31]

However, it is critically important that hospital staff be mindful that VRI is not always appropriate in every situation that involves deaf or hard of hearing patients or companions. Hospitals, medical care providers, and other ADA-covered entities that choose to obtain VRI should not use this service exclusively but should use in-person interpreters whenever possible, particularly when these patients are in pain or otherwise not able to focus on the VRI screen.

In addition, care must be taken to ensure that the VRI system is in good working order and well maintained by knowledgeable hospital staff on a 24/7 basis. Whenever a hospital provides a VRI system for communication access, the failure to maintain it in good working order can have legal consequences for the hospital. This was the case in *Gillespie v. Dimensions Health Corporation*, in which a hospital attempted to use its VRI system but was unable to provide effective interpreting services for its deaf patients, resulting in no communication access for them.[32]

Direct Care Staff

Hospital staff can do many things to enable communication with deaf or hard of hearing patients and to make them more comfortable with the hospital environment, thereby providing better service. Common sense and basic information about deafness will help hospital staff provide good health care. As mentioned before, deaf patients know their preferred mode of communication and should be consulted about it and about any problems that arise. The isolation of deaf people can be overcome to a great extent by explaining what is happening and answering any questions the patients might have.

The importance of using a qualified interpreter to ensure effective communication cannot be overemphasized. However, in many routine situations (such as bringing meals or taking temperatures) an interpreter may not be necessary. The following guidelines on working with deaf patients will help in such situations. These recommendations, if implemented, will also improve the quality of care provided:

A. Make added efforts to communicate in such a way that the patient understands what is happening.
   1. Allow more time for every communication, and do not rush through what is said. To make sure the patient understands, some thoughts should be repeated using different phrases.
   2. Lip movements should not be exaggerated. Speak at a normal rate of speed and separate words. This is recommended with deaf individuals are comfortable with lipreading.
   3. Patients' arms should not be restricted; they should be free to write and sign.
   4. Make cards or posters of typical questions and responses that can be pointed to quickly.
   5. Keep paper and pen handy, but be sensitive to the patient's level of English language fluency and writing skills.
B. Be sensitive to the visual environment of deaf patients by adjusting lighting and using visual rather than auditory cues and reassurances.
   1. Use charts, pictures, and/or three-dimensional models when explaining information and procedures to deaf patients.
   2. Do not remove a deaf patient's glasses or leave a deaf patient in total darkness.

3. Remove any bright lights in front of the deaf person when communicating; glare makes it difficult to read signs or lips.
4. Face the patient when speaking, and do not cover your face or mouth.
5. Keep facial expressions pleasant and unworried so as not to alarm the patient.

C. Alert all staff to the presence and needs of the deaf patient, and be sensitive to those needs.

1. Flag the intercom button so that workers will know the patient is deaf and requires a personal visit rather than a response over the intercom.
2. Flag the patient's charts, room, and bed to alert staff to use appropriate means of communication.

D. Inform hospital personnel of the special needs of people with hearing aids or cochlear implants.

1. Allow these patients to wear their hearing aids or cochlear implants.
2. Do not shout at the patient.
3. Be sure that the patient has fully understood what is said.

MENTAL HEALTH ISSUES

Section 504 of the Rehabilitation Act and the Americans with Disabilities Act both mandate that mental health services for deaf and hard of hearing individuals be accessible in terms of effective communications, but quality mental health services for deaf and hard of hearing individuals require specialized care. Very few deaf or hard of hearing individuals have access to appropriate mental health services provided by qualified therapists who are knowledgeable about deafness and are able to communicate effectively with deaf individuals.[33] Progressive programs exist in some parts of the country, but there are few mental health facilities functioning specifically for deaf and hard of hearing patients.[34] Also, few regular facilities are even adequately staffed and equipped to help this group of patients despite the relative ease and modest expense of these services.

The primary problem is the lack of mental health professionals who have experience working with deaf and hard of hearing people. Even with an interpreter present, the mental health professional must be empathetic to this population and fully aware of their culture if therapy is to be effective. Additionally, communication is a huge issue. There is a gross shortage of psychologists, therapists, clinical social workers, and other mental health professionals who are able to provide counseling and psychotherapy services in sign language.[35]

The most extreme result of lack of communication is misdiagnosing a patient's deafness and speech as psychopathology or mental retardation. Such misdiagnoses result in improper placement, mistaken treatment, misguided case management, and unjustified exclusion of the patient from hospital programs and activities, as well as inappropriate aftercare. The result is the patient's isolation, bewilderment, and even rage, all of which run counter to the purposes of mental health treatment.

Surveys of psychiatric hospitals and institutions for people with mental retardation frequently reveal that a disproportionate number of patients are deaf. Dr. McCay Vernon, a psychologist noted for his work with deaf people, has observed, "It has been established that IQ is essentially normally distributed in the deaf population. Obviously gross error had been made in the fundamental but relatively easy-to-make diagnosis of mental retardation."[36]

Misdiagnosis can result in a deaf patient being inappropriately assigned and confined to an institution for many years before the mistake is discovered. There are numerous accounts of inappropriate institutionalization. Vernon, for example, reported the case of a patient who spent thirty-five years at Idaho's state school and hospital for those with mental retardation when the patient's primary disability was being deaf, and similar cases have been reported in the District of Columbia and in North Carolina.[37]

Increased attention to the needs of deaf and hard of hearing patients has resulted in vastly improved knowledge of effective mental health services. Research, training, and clinical service models are now available. The NAD has developed a model plan known as *Standards of Care for the Delivery of Mental Health Services to Deaf and Hard of Hearing People*.[38] These standards identify guidelines for resources, criteria, and methods of administration and financing for statewide systems of mental health service delivery. They also identify the specialized demands for appropriate mental health services in diagnosis, treatment modalities, treatment personnel, treatment settings, access to care, and organization and financing of services. Using the legal tools described in the following section and the professional standards being developed by knowledgeable clinicians, deaf people can have access to public and private mental health services. In addition, the NAD put forth its Position Statement on Mental Health Services (2003),[39] as well as its Supplement on Culturally Affirmative and Linguistically Accessible Services in 2008,[40] and its Position Statement on Mental Health Interpreting Services with People Who Are Deaf (2012).[41]

Specialized Mental Health Programs for Deaf People

Treatment methods and modalities for deaf patients require special interventions, communication methods, and equipment. Few mental health professionals have experience treating deaf patients. As a result, these patients often do not receive appropriate care in mental health facilities.[42] Deaf and deaf-blind patients are sometimes the target of abuse or hostility in mental health institutions. Unable to summon help or to identify attackers, they and their food and property are easy targets for more aggressive patients. Even in well-managed facilities where these abuses are rare, deaf people may find the very process of institutionalization difficult to cope with given their lack of communication with others. Deaf-blind patients may be particularly isolated, frustrated, and unable to understand what is happening.

Responding to these problems, some hospitals and mental health administrations have begun to develop specific programs for deaf people. Such programs are usually characterized by an intake system that permits deaf patients to be consolidated in one unit. The unit is staffed with mental health professionals who know sign language and have knowledge of the cultural and psychosocial implications of deafness and the common dynamics within families with deaf members. Sign language interpreters are provided for staff members who do not have sign language skills. The units are equipped with telecommunication devices such as videophones, captioned television, and necessary assistive listening devices. Patients in the deaf unit may be taught sign language if they have not developed language. Often these units incorporate a treatment philosophy that recognizes the impact of deafness and communication on personality development and mental health. Some units provide education, consultation, diagnostic, and evaluation services to other community mental health programs. They may offer outreach or consultation services to other mental health facilities and outpatient clinics.[43]

Some states fund deaf units through their departments of mental health; others channel such funding to departments of vocational rehabilitation. Some deaf units have a mix of federal and state grants to pursue their work. Because such grants are temporary, though, new ones must be sought constantly.

When no leadership exists in a state mental health system or vocational rehabilitation department, or when the legislature is indifferent, alternate methods for improving treatment of deaf patients with mental illness must be found. Courts are increasingly recognizing that mentally ill patients have legal rights, so legal action may serve to improve mental health services for deaf patients.

Legal Action for Mental Health Services

Because of the difficulty in bringing individual suits and the limitation of the remedy only to the patient who brought the suit, class action lawsuits have been more effective means of achieving institutional change. A class action suit is filed by a patient who claims to represent all people similarly situated. Because the remedy resulting from the action applies to all such people, some class action litigation has resulted in the definition and articulation of rights of patients with mental illness, minimum standards for care and treatment, and responsibilities and liabilities of the treating staff.

A seminal class action suit, *Wyatt v. Stickney,* later called *Wyatt v. Aderholt,* resulted in the recognition and establishment of the constitutional right of a patient with mental illness to be treated and not merely held in custodial care.[44] The court issued a far-reaching and effective decision, ruling specifically that patients involuntarily committed through noncriminal procedures to a state mental hospital have a constitutional right to receive such individual treatment as will give them an opportunity to improve or cure their mental condition. The court decreed minimal constitutional standards for adequate treatment, including an individual treatment plan that provides a statement of the least restrictive treatment conditions necessary to achieve the purposes of commitment. The decision recognized a mental health patient's rights to a humane psychological and physical environment, privacy, dignity, and freedom from isolation. The court also established a human rights committee to investigate violations of patients' rights and to oversee implementation of the plan. It also ordered a minimum number of treatment personnel per 250 patients and other changes to ensure more humane living conditions.

Under the *Wyatt* decision, an individualized treatment plan for a deaf person could potentially include programs such as a specialized deaf unit with qualified clinicians knowledgeable about deafness and sign language. By including training and therapy in sign language, the program would allow the patient to participate fully in therapy and to interact with staff and other deaf patients, who themselves would know or be learning sign language. The emphasis on communication skills would be a central aspect of therapy and rehabilitation, allowing the patient an opportunity for social adjustment and eventual integration into society.

Mental health service providers thus bear the responsibility of providing interpreters and specialized personnel to deaf patients. Facilities that refuse to provide them risk a private lawsuit or having HHS cut off their federal funds. The Office for Civil Rights (OCR) of HHS has investigated complaints against several mental health facilities for failure to provide appropriate services. As a result of a complaint brought by the North Carolina Association of the Deaf, a comprehensive, long-range plan has been developed and is being implemented by the North Carolina Department of Human Services.[45]

In a complaint brought by the NAD against the Ohio Department of Mental Health, the Office for Civil Rights (OCR) of HHS found that sixteen psychiatric hospitals did not have appropriate policies for serving deaf patients.[46] The OCR found that deaf patients not assigned to the existing deaf unit were maintained in a state of social isolation and sensory deprivation. Treatment team members routinely attempted to communicate with deaf patients by exchanging notes. Even when arrangements were made for securing qualified interpreters, the treatment team staff generally did not possess training on the psychosocial issues pertaining to deaf people who have a mental illness. In the course of the investigation, the agency implemented procedures for securing qualified interpreters, established TTY services, and trained staff about deafness and the use of auxiliary aids. The Ohio Department of Mental Health was ordered to establish comprehensive service planning on a statewide basis, with adequate availability of specialized deaf units staffed by mental health professionals with sign language competence and training in the psychosocial issues of deafness.[47]

Section 504 generally prohibits hospitals or other agencies from establishing different or separate facilities for people with disabilities. In the context of mental health services for deaf individuals, however, OCR found that the treatment needs of deaf individuals justify separate units staffed by professionals with appropriate communication skills and expertise:

> It is the opinion of Deaf Unit staff, corroborated by research conducted by experts in the field, that such units are the only way most deaf patients can receive an equal opportunity to participate in and benefit from services. This is due to lack of understanding by most people in the field of mental health of the unique communication and psychosocial problems of the deaf and misinterpretation of their use of gestures and nonstandard written English.[48]

Another class action, *Tugg v. Towey,* was a victory for mental health services for deaf and hard of hearing patients on a therapy level.[49] Prior to the lawsuit, Florida state services offered deaf and hard of hearing individuals mental health counselors along with sign language interpreters. Finding this unacceptable, deaf individuals and their families brought a lawsuit to require the state to provide mental health counselors who could sign and who understood the deaf community. The court sided with the deaf patients and their families, finding evidence of denial of benefits of mental health services provided by the state to other patients who were not deaf.[50]

In addition to the *Tugg v. Towey* case, deaf individuals have achieved victories in several important lawsuits. A deaf woman committed to a Maryland mental hospital received no treatment for more than twenty years. In *Doe v. Wilzack,* brought on her behalf by the NAD Legal Defense Fund, the woman won individual relief, and the state of Maryland agreed to establish an inpatient treatment unit for her and other deaf inpatients in state facilities.[51] In a similar case in Minnesota, brought by the Legal Advocacy Project for Hearing Impaired People, the state agreed to establish comprehensive treatment programs for deaf mental health patients, with services for the four plaintiffs, as well as staffing, program services, and obligation to secure funding in state facilities for the state's other deaf patients.[52] In New York, a deaf child won $1.5 million dollars when he proved that it was medical malpractice to diagnose him as mentally retarded when he was a normal, bright, deaf child.[53] In Alabama, a deaf individual and his mother filed a lawsuit against the state for failure to have proper mental health services, and the state agreed in settlement to set up a state mental health system for deaf and hard of hearing individuals.[54]

More recently, the state of Georgia was found to be liable for discrimination against deaf mental health patients by denying them access to services.[55] The court found that the lack of accommodations, including not providing counselors who could communicate in ASL, denied deaf patients meaningful access to the state's mental health services. Furthermore, the state also lacked group homes for deaf patients who had developmental disabilities. As a result of this case, Georgia was given a detailed order with specific instructions on overhauling the state's provision of deaf mental health services, starting with the creation of the Office of Deaf Services. The director of such services must be fluent in ASL and have experience with deaf culture. The following additional positions and offices were created:

+ community service coordinator: responsible for the state-wide coordination of all services provided to persons who are deaf
+ communication access/sign language interpreter coordinator: coordinates interpreter services statewide in all mental health services
+ regional offices: oversee six regional deaf services offices

In addition, the order requires the state to complete a communication assessment of all deaf clients, establish a communications database that lists each known deaf patient's communication preference, and create accessible group homes. The order also aims to have 80 percent of noncrisis outpatient mental health counseling for deaf people be provided by a counselor who is fluent in ASL.[56]

One of the most comprehensive court judgments was handed down in *DeVinney v. Maine Medical Center,* a case that was brought by a deaf patient who sought emergency psychiatric services.[57] The hospital was unable to treat the patient because it failed to provide an interpreter. The patient was left without treatment, isolated and alone. Another federal district court in Maine had previously approved a consent decree that established detailed standards for the care and treatment of people with mental retardation who are placed in community settings.[58] Maine recognized that, regardless of their age and degree of retardation or other disability, people released from institutions into the community have the right to receive "habilitation." Habilitation specifically includes the right to an individualized plan of care, education, and training and to services, including physical therapy, psychotherapy, speech therapy, and medical and dental attention.

The Maine Medical Center consent decree was the first one that obligated a state to consider specifically what was required in order for deaf people to benefit from state services. These requirements included the following: (1) outpatients with a hearing impairment who could not acquire speech would be taught sign language, (2) the state would provide sign language training to staff and others working with deaf citizens, (3) screening for hearing ability would be conducted with each patient, (4) treatment and further evaluation would be provided by qualified speech and hearing professionals, and (5) hearing aids, when needed, would be provided and maintained in good working order. The court appointed a master to monitor implementation of the agreement.[59]

NOTES

1. 28 C.F.R. §36.303(c).
2. 45 C.F.R. §84.52(a).
3. 45 C.F.R. §84.21(f).
4. 45 C.F.R. §84.52(d)(1).
5. 45 C.F.R. §84.52(d)(3).
6. 45 C.F.R. §84.52(d)(2).
7. *Sumes v. Andres,* 938 F. Supp. 9 (D.D.C. 1996).
8. 28 C.F.R. §35.160; 28 C.F.R. §36.303(b)(1).
9. 42 U.S.C. §12142 et seq.; 42 U.S.C. §12181 et seq.
10. See *Pennsylvania Department of Corrections v. Yeskey,* 118 U.S. 1952 (1998), *National Disability Law Reporter* 12: 195.
11. 42 U.S.C. §§12182, 12183.
12. 28 C.F.R. §36.301(c).
13. 28 C.F.R. §35.160(c); 28 C.F.R. §36.303(c)(2)–(4).
14. 28 C.F.R. §35.160(a); 28 C.F.R. §36.303(c)(1).
15. 28 C.F.R. §35.164; 28 C.F.R. §36.303(a).
16. 28 C.F.R. §35.164; C.F.R. §36.104.
17. C.F.R. §36.104.
18. 28 C.F.R. §35.164; C.F.R. §36.303(g).
19. See IRS publications 535 and 334 and IRS form 8826.
20. In the HHS Section 504 regulations, these rules are in Subpart F; 45 C.F.R. §84.51 et seq.
21. 10 New York Hospital Codes, Rules, and Regulations §405.7(a) (7)(ix)(a).
22. See, for example, State Government Article, Section 20-304, Annotated Code of Maryland; Maine Rev. Stat. Title 5 §4591; California Civil Code section 51.

23. "Position on the Provision of Auxiliary Aids for Hearing-Impaired Patients in Inpatient, Outpatient, and Emergency Treatment Settings," memorandum from Roma J. Stewart (director, Office for Civil Rights, Department of Health, Education, and Welfare) to OCR regional directors, April 21, 1980.

24. 28 C.F.R. §35.160(b)(2).

25. Ibid.

26. *Heisley v. Inova Health System,* Case No. 1:10-cv-714-LMB/IDD (2011), settled through consent decree, http://www.ada.gov/inova.htm.

27. *Williams v. Jersey City Medical Center,* Sup. Ct. of New Jersey, Hudson County Law Division, No. HUD-L-5059-95 (1998).

28. *Connecticut Association of the Deaf v. Middlesex Memorial Hospital,* No. 395-CV02408 (AHN) D. Conn. (1998).

29. "Deaf Woman Wins Suit Against Two Hospitals," *New York Times,* August 22, 1997.

30. 28 C.F.R. §35.104; 28 C.F.R. §36.104.

31. 28 C.F.R. §36.303(f).

32. *Gillespie v. Dimensions Health Corporation,* No. DKC-05-CV-73 (D. MD) (2005), settled in consent decree, http://www.ada.gov/laurelco.htm.

33. It is estimated that only 2 percent of more than five million deaf individuals in the United States who need mental health treatment every year actually receive appropriate treatment. See Western Interstate Commission for Higher Education Mental Health Program, *Information Gaps on the Deaf and Hard of Hearing Population: A Background Paper* (May 2006). It is also estimated that approximately 130,000 deaf people will require mental health services in ASL. See Michael J. Gournaris, Steve Hamerdinger, and Roger C. Williams, "Creating a Culturally Affirmative Continuum of Mental Health Services: The Experiences of Three States," in Neil S. Glickman, *Deaf Mental Health Care* (New York: Routledge, 2013), 138–80.

34. National Information Center on Deafness, "Residential Facilities for Deaf Adults" (Washington, DC: Gallaudet University, 1993); National Information Center on Deafness, "Residential Programs for Deaf/Emotionally Disturbed Children and Adolescents" (Washington, DC: Gallaudet University, 1993).

35. Lawrence J. Raifman and McCay Vernon, "Important Implications for Psychologists of the Americans with Disabilities Act: Case in Point, the Patient Who Is Deaf," *Professional Psychology: Research and Practice* 27 (372): 376; Michael J. Gournaris, Steve Hamerdinger, and Roger C. Williams, "Creating

a Culturally Affirmative Continuum of Mental Health Services: The Experiences of Three States," in Neil S. Glickman, *Deaf Mental Health Care* (New York: Routledge, 2013).

36. McCay Vernon, "Techniques of Screening for Mental Illness among Deaf Clients," *Journal of Rehabilitation of the Deaf* 2 (1969): 24.

37. Saundra Saperstein, "Deaf Woman Confined Wrongly, Suit Claims: Held 55 Years at D.C. Home for Retarded," *Washington Post*, September 14, 1985, B1.

38. Randall R. Myers, ed., *Standards of Care for the Delivery of Mental Health Services to Deaf and Hard of Hearing Persons* (Silver Spring, MD: National Association of the Deaf, 1995), 11.

39. NAD, "Position Statement on Mental Health Services for People who are Deaf and Hard of Hearing," 2003, http://nad.org/issues/health-care/mental-health-services/position-statement.

40. NAD, "Position Statement Supplement: Culturally Affirmative and Linguistically Accessible Mental Health Services," 2008, http://nad.org/issues/health-care/mental-health-services/access.

41. NAD, "Position Statement on Mental Health Interpreting Services with People who are Deaf," n.d., http://nad.org/issues/health-care/mental-health-services/position-statement-mental-health-interpreting-services-peo.

42. Irene W. Leigh, ed., *Psychotherapy with Deaf Clients from Diverse Groups* (Washington, DC: Gallaudet University Press, 1999); Michael J. Gournaris, Steve Hamerdinger, and Roger C. Williams, "Creating a Culturally Affirmative Continuum of Mental Health Services: The Experiences of Three States," in Neil S. Glickman, *Deaf Mental Health Care* (New York: Routledge, 2013).

43. Irene W. Leigh, ed., *Psychotherapy with Deaf Clients from Diverse Groups* (Washington, DC: Gallaudet University Press, 1999); Michael J. Gournaris, Steve Hamerdinger, and Roger C. Williams, "Creating a Culturally Affirmative Continuum of Mental Health Services: The Experiences of Three States," in Neil S. Glickman, *Deaf Mental Health Care* (New York: Routledge, 2013).

44. *Wyatt v. Stickney*, 325 F. Supp. 781 (M.D. Ala. 1970), 344 F. Supp. 373 (1972); *aff'd. sub. nom. Wyatt v. Aderholt*, 503 F. 2d 1305 (5th Cir. 1974).

45. *North Carolina Association of the Deaf v. N.C. Department of Human Resources, U.S. Department of Health and Human Services, Office of Civil Rights* (OCR), Complaint No. 04-92-3150 (1992), Settlement Agreement and Release (December 31, 1992).

46. *National Association of the Deaf Legal Defense Fund v. Ohio Department of Mental Health,* OCR Docket No. 05883054 (1990).
47. Ibid., 2–3.
48. Ibid.
49. *Tugg v. Towey,* 864 F. Supp. 1201, 5 NDLR 311 (S.D. Fla. 1994).
50. Ibid.
51. *Doe v. Wilzack,* Civ. No. HAR 83-2409 (D. Md. 1986), stipulated judgment order.
52. *Handel v. Levine,* Ramsey County District Court File 468475 (1984, Minn.).
53. *Snow v. State,* 469 N.Y.S., 2d 959 (A.D.2 Dept. 1983), *aff'd* 485 N.Y.S. 2d 987 (1984).
54. *Bailey v. Sawyer,* No. 99-cv-1321 (M.D. Ala. 1999).
55. *Belton v. Georgia,* 2012 WL 1080304, No. 10-cv-0583 (N.D. Ga. 2010).
56. Ibid., order entered June 18, 2013.
57. *DeVinney v. Maine,* No. 97-276-P-C (D. Maine, 1997), consent decree, http://www.ada.gov/devin.htm.
58. *Wouri v. Zitnay,* No. 75-80-SD (D. Maine, 1978).
59. *DeVinney v. Maine.*

Chapter 7

Employment

Employer attitudes are the greatest barrier to employment opportunities for deaf and hard of hearing people. Employers often harbor stereotypical assumptions that underestimate the capabilities of these individuals. One early study indicated that people with disabilities must generally be more qualified or competent than individuals without disabilities in order to overcome negative attitudes and assumptions.[1] Employers often refuse to hire people with disabilities because of unjustified fears that they cannot perform a job safely. However, other studies on the safety of people with mental and physical disabilities in the employment setting indicate that these fears are groundless.[2]

Employers have used communication barriers as a reason for limiting job opportunities for deaf applicants and employees. Such difficulties, however, are "often exaggerated, and fairly effective substitutes for oral communication have been disregarded."[3] Employers often cite the inability to use the telephone as a reason not to consider a deaf applicant even when the use of a telephone is not an integral part of the job. While deaf and hard of hearing individuals are capable of making and receiving telephone calls through the use of relay systems as well as other forms of communications such as fax, email, and other forms of electronic communication, there are additional alternative ways to handle job duties. In jobs requiring only occasional telephone communication, minor changes in job responsibilities can accommodate the deaf worker. For example, a deaf worker could assume some of a hearing coworker's responsibilities while the hearing person answers the phones. If a job requires significant telephone contact with another office, the use of electronic communications or relay systems will allow the deaf employee to perform all job duties.

Employers also cite the requirement of attendance at various meetings or conferences as a reason not to consider deaf applicants. However, reasonable accommodations such as interpreters or computer-assisted, real-time transcription services enable deaf workers to participate fully in group meetings and training sessions.

Today a variety of federal statutory remedies are available to combat employment discrimination. Those solutions are found in Title I of the ADA and in Sections 501, 503, and 504 of the Rehabilitation Act of 1973. Title I of the ADA, which covers private employers with fifteen or more employees, mandates the removal of barriers that prevent qualified individuals with disabilities from enjoying the same employment opportunities that are available to people without disabilities. It also covers employment agencies, unions, and joint labor/management committees.

The ADA applies to employment practices such as recruitment, hiring, job assignments, firing, promotions, pay, layoffs, benefits, leave, training, and all other employment-related activities. Under the ADA, it is also unlawful for an employer to retaliate against individuals who assert their rights under the statute. Likewise, the act also protects an individual who is a victim of discrimination because of family, business, social, or other relationships with someone with a disability. Pursuit of a complaint under Title I of the ADA requires the person who experienced discrimination to first file with an administrative agency, such as the Equal Employment Opportunity Commission, before pursuing action in a federal court.

The remedies available to employees with disabilities in Sections 501, 503, and 504 of the Rehabilitation Act are similar in many respects. These three sections, however, differ somewhat in application, scope, and quality. Each applies to different types of employers:

+ Section 501 applies to federal government agencies that employ people.
+ Section 503 applies to companies that do business with the federal government (federal contractors).
+ Section 504 applies to recipients of federal financial assistance.

Each section imposes varying levels of responsibility on each set of employers. Sections 501 and 503 require affirmative action, while Section 504 imposes a duty of nondiscrimination. Section 504 allows aggrieved individuals to go directly to federal court to enforce their statutory rights. Section 501 requires individuals to first file an administrative complaint before seeking relief in court. By contrast, Section 503 permits only an administrative remedy. The sections also differ in the procedures to be followed when filing an administrative complaint. When faced with disability employment discrimination pursuant to the Rehabilitation Act, one must determine which of the three sections applies.

QUALIFIED INDIVIDUALS WITH A DISABILITY

The ADA and the Rehabilitation Act do not guarantee jobs for people with disabilities. Instead, these federal laws prohibit discrimination in employment against individuals with disabilities who are "qualified" for a job. The ADA defines a qualified individual with a disability as someone who has a physical or mental impairment that substantially limits a major life activity but who can perform the essential functions of a job with or without reasonable accommodation.[4] Major life activities include but are not limited to "caring for oneself, performing manual tasks, seeing, hearing, eating, sleeping, walking, standing, lifting, bending, speaking, breathing, learning, reading, concentrating, thinking, communicating, and working."[5] The Americans with Disabilities Amendments Act of 2008 (ADAAA) significantly broadened the scope of the ADA to ensure protection for individuals with disabilities. The ADAAA changed the definition of "disability" so that individuals who meet the definition of disability under the ADA but use assistive devices, medications, reasonable accommodations, or auxiliary aids and services that mitigate the substantial impairment of major life activities are nevertheless still covered by the ADA.[6] With this definition change provided by the ADAAA, deaf individuals who use hearing aids, cochlear implants, or other hearing devices are still protected by the ADA.[7]

The ADA also defines individuals with disabilities as those who are "regarded as having . . . an impairment" that substantially affects major life activities; these individuals are covered by the statute regardless of whether the impairment exists.[8] If a person is disqualified for a job on the basis of an actual or a perceived condition, and the employer cannot articulate a legitimate job-related reason for the rejection, then a perceived concern about employment of an individual with disabilities could be inferred, and the plaintiff would qualify for coverage under the ADA.[9] In addition, individuals who have a record of having a disability are also protected under the ADA.[10]

Although the Rehabilitation Act originally had a different definition for an individual with a disability, the regulations for the Rehabilitation Act were amended to refer to those under the ADA.[11] Section 503 and 504 regulations define a "qualified individual with a disability" as one who is capable of performing a particular job with reasonable accommodation to the individual's disability.[12]

In all of these definitions, the three central questions in determining whether an individual with a disability is qualified for a specific position are as follows: (1) What are the essential functions of the job? (2) Does the individual with the disability require reasonable accommodations to perform the job's essential functions? If so, (3) what are those reasonable accommodations?

ESSENTIAL FUNCTIONS

The regulations of the ADA (and, by reference, the Rehabilitation Act) provide guidance on the determination of the "essential functions" of a job:

(2) A job function may be considered essential for any of several reasons, including but not limited to the following:

   (i) The function may be essential because the reason the position exists is to perform that function;

   (ii) The function may be essential because of the limited number of employees available among whom the performance of that job function can be distributed; and/or

   (iii) The function may be highly specialized so that the incumbent in the position is hired for his or her expertise or ability to perform the particular function.

(3) Evidence of whether a particular function is essential includes, but is not limited to:

   (i) The contractor's judgment as to which functions are essential;

   (ii) Written job descriptions prepared before advertising or interviewing applicants for the job;

   (iii) The amount of time spent on the job performing the function;

   (iv) The consequences of not requiring the incumbent to perform the function;

   (v) The terms of a collective bargaining agreement;

   (vi) The work experience of past incumbents in the job; and/or

   (vii) The current work experience of incumbents in similar jobs.[13]

In other words, employers are required to consider whether employees in the position are actually required to perform each of the job functions and, if so, whether the removal or modification of the function fundamentally changes the job. A function may be considered essential if any of the following conditions are met: It is a necessary part of the job; a limited number of other employees are available to perform the function; or it is a highly specialized function and the person in the position is hired for special expertise or ability to perform this function.

An assessment of the job's "essential functions" is critical in making certain that employers do not disqualify people with disabilities just because they have difficulty with a task that is only marginally related to the job. For example, a deaf person considered for a word-processing position should not be disqualified because the person may have difficulty using a conventional telephone. In practice, the essential functions of each job must be determined on a case-by-case basis. The employer has a duty to restructure the job, including rewriting job descriptions, if necessary, to eliminate nonessential tasks that are barriers for workers with disabilities. It is part of the employer's duty to make reasonable accommodations to meet the needs of workers with disabilities. In judicial or administrative proceedings, the burden of showing the essential functions of a job rests with the employer. And, as mentioned earlier, a determination of whether an individual can perform those essential functions must include ascertaining whether a reasonable accommodation exists that would allow the individual to do so.

REASONABLE ACCOMMODATIONS

Failure to make "reasonable accommodations to the known physical or mental limitations of an otherwise qualified individual with a disability who is an applicant or employee" is considered discrimination under both the ADA and the Rehabilitation Act.[14] Under these laws, an employer must provide an employee with reasonable accommodations that will allow the individual to perform the essential functions of the job as long as doing so does not create an undue burden for the employer.[15]

Reasonable accommodation includes modifications or adjustments to a job, the work environment, or the manner in which the job is usually handled that enable a qualified individual with a disability to perform the essential functions of a position.[16]

According to the ADA and the Rehabilitation Act, reasonable accommodations may include the following:

+ making existing employee facilities readily accessible to and usable by individuals with disabilities
+ restructuring the job (e.g., creating part-time or modified work schedules)
+ reassigning an individual to a vacant position
+ acquiring or modifying equipment or devices
+ appropriately adjusting or modifying examinations, training materials, or policies
+ providing qualified readers or interpreters[17]

Some specific examples of reasonable accommodations that deaf or hard of hearing employees may request include any combinations of the following:

+ videophones, captioned telephones, amplified telephones, and TTYs
+ instant messaging and email systems
+ assistive listening systems and devices
+ visual alerts for audible alarms and messages
+ modifications to reduce ambient noise levels
+ captioned audiovisual information
+ permission to bring service animals into the workplace
+ modification of intercom entry systems for secured areas or buildings
+ policies and procedures for procuring necessary, qualified interpreter services and/or real-time captioning (CART) services.[18]

The Equal Employment Opportunity Commission (EEOC) Interpretive Guidance[19] separates reasonable accommodations into three general categories:

1. those that are required to ensure equal opportunity in the application process
2. those that enable employees with disabilities to perform the essential functions of the job
3. those that enable employees with disabilities to enjoy the same benefits and privileges of employment as are enjoyed by employees without disabilities

Accommodations may include making sure a benefit provided for the convenience of the employees is accessible to individuals with disabilities or that employees with disabilities have access to the same insurance coverage as employees without disabilities.[20]

The regulations also require that the employer conduct an informal, interactive discussion with the applicant or employee who is in need of an accommodation.[21] "This process should identify the precise limitations resulting from the disability and potential reasonable accommodations that could overcome those limitations."[22]

Reasonable accommodations are often a matter of common sense. For example, a deaf welder worked in an outdoor yard where trucks delivered fruit bins. His supervisor fired him because he believed the man could not work there safely as a result of the trucks coming and going in the yard. Later the supervisor realized that it was possible to station the deaf employee where he could see any danger from the trucks. With this accommodation and with the other employees informed of his being deaf, the man could safely perform his job in a fully satisfactory manner.

Another situation involved a bookkeeper who was hard of hearing and had difficulty working in one part of her office because background noise interfered with her hearing aid. When she was moved to a quieter part of the office, her difficulty was reduced, and her productivity increased.

Reasonable accommodations can also include modifications of policy to suit the needs of a deaf employee. In a 2009 case, *Howard v. Alabama Board of Pharmacy,* a pharmacist was unable to receive prescription orders made by telephone because she was denied the use of a telecommunications relay service (TRS), and she brought a lawsuit to remedy this denial.[23] As a result of the suit, the Alabama Board of Pharmacy drafted a new policy to allow the use of a TRS by deaf and hard of hearing pharmacists in Alabama so that they may effectively communicate with healthcare professionals and patients.[24]

Employers also should not attempt to claim that deaf workers will not be able to hear fire alarms and warning devices on machinery. These audible devices can simply be fitted with a visual alarm system.

In *Bryant v. Better Business Bureau of Greater Maryland,* a hard of hearing employee who worked in the membership department brought an ADA claim alleging that her employer denied her a reasonable accommodation. The employer had transferred the employee to a different position instead of providing her with a better amplification device or a TTY, which would have enabled her to complete her telecommunication duties. The court held that the reasonable accommodation question asks whether "the accommodation (1) would be effective, i.e., would it address the job-related difficulties presented by the employee's disability; and (2) would allow the employee to attain an equal level of achievement, opportunity and participation, that a non-disabled individual in the same position would be able to achieve."[25]

In another case, *EEOC v. Pinnacle Holdings, Inc.,* the employer failed to provide or consider possible accommodations for an employee who was hard of hearing and could not hear the intercom. The employer subsequently fired the individual for this reason. The jury found the employer's actions violated the ADA and awarded compensatory damages to the individual.[26]

Moreover, federal employment guidelines also play a factor in the accommodations to be provided to employees. A federal employee won a lawsuit when the judge found that his supervisors had not considered the Office of Personnel Management's guidelines on reasonable modifications.[27]

EMPLOYER DEFENSES AND EXEMPTIONS

If an employer can demonstrate that an individual with a disability poses a direct threat to his or her health or safety or to others in the workplace, or if the employer can demonstrate that the reasonable accommodation is an undue hardship, then the employer may have a defense against liability under the ADA.

Direct Threat

An employer can sometimes defend against a charge of discrimination by showing that individuals pose a direct threat to their own health or safety or to that of others in the workplace.

However, the ADA has a strict definition of "direct threat," which states that such a determination must be based on an individualized assessment of the person's present ability to safely perform the essential functions of the job. If a person poses a direct threat, the employer must see whether a reasonable accommodation would either eliminate or reduce the risk to an acceptable level. In determining a direct threat, decisions must be made on a case-by-case basis based on objective, factual evidence rather than on fears or stereotypes.

The ADA legislative history and the EEOC refer to a federal case involving a hard of hearing person, *Strathie v. Department of Transportation,* as an example of the requirement that decisions on safety must be based on actual facts of risk. In *Strathie,* the state of Pennsylvania had enacted a rule prohibiting hearing aid users from obtaining licenses to drive school buses. A Pennsylvania federal court had supported the ban on issuing such licenses to hearing aid users on the basis of general safety concerns. The federal appeals court reversed the lower court, finding evidence in the record rebutting the state's safety concerns and showing that an appropriate hearing aid would enable a hard of hearing person to drive a school bus without appreciable risk to passenger safety. This evidence had to be considered in determining whether a driver wearing a hearing aid would actually present a risk to the safety of school bus passengers.[28]

In another case, *Rizzo v. Children's World Learning Center,* a woman who was hard of hearing and used hearing aids was removed from her position as the driver of a van for a children's educational center because her employer was afraid that she would not be able to "hear a child choking in the back of the van."[29] The employer contended that the employee posed a direct threat to the children. A jury awarded the woman $100,000 in her ADA discrimination claim. The court of appeals affirmed the ruling, stating that the woman was qualified for her position and that there was no evidence that an essential element of the job was the ability to hear a choking child. The court said that the relevant inquiry was whether the person is able to safely drive the van and not present a direct threat to the children's safety.

Undue Hardship

Undue hardship means significant difficulty or expense for a business. In deciding whether an accommodation would be an undue hardship to a business, the following conditions should be considered:

1. The nature and net cost of the accommodation needed under this part, taking into consideration the availability of tax credits and deductions and/or outside funding
2. The overall financial resources of the facility or facilities involved in the provision of the reasonable accommodation, the number of persons employed at such facility, and the effect on expenses and resources
3. The overall financial resources of the covered entity, the overall size of the business of the covered entity with respect to the number of its employees, and the number, type, and location of its facilities
4. The type of operation or operations of the covered entity, including the composition, structure, and functions of the workforce of such entity, and the geographic separateness and administrative or fiscal relationship of the facility or facilities in question to the covered entity
5. The impact of the accommodation on the operation of the facility, including the impact on the ability of other employees to perform their duties and the impact on the facility's ability to conduct business[30]

The analysis to the EEOC regulations gives the following example involving a deaf applicant. An independently owned fast-food franchise receives no money from the parent company that gives out the franchises. The franchise refuses to hire a deaf person because it says it would be an undue hardship to provide an interpreter for monthly staff meetings. Since the financial relationship between the local franchise and the parent company is only a franchise fee, only the financial resources of the local franchise would be considered in deciding whether providing the accommodation would be an undue hardship. However, a different fast-food chain might be organized in another way. If a factual determination shows that a financial or an administrative relationship exists between the parent company and the local site providing the accommodation, then the parent company's resources should be considered in determining whether the hardship is undue.[31]

QUALIFICATION STANDARDS, TESTS, AND OTHER CRITERIA

It is unlawful under the ADA for an employer to use qualification standards, employment tests, or other selection criteria that screen out or tend to screen out individuals with disabilities.[32] Tests may be given if they are job related and required by business necessity. It would be discriminatory, for example, for an employer to require every applicant to pass a written test that measures language skills when the essential functions of the job in question do not require those skills. Such tests have excluded some deaf and hard of hearing people from being hired or promoted. In certain situations, an appropriate accommodation would be to waive parts of written tests for a deaf person where the test is not an accurate test of ability to perform the essential functions of the job. Under the ADA, an employer must select and administer tests to a person with a sensory, manual, or speech impairment that accurately reflect the test taker's skills or aptitude rather than the person's impairment.[33] For example, it would be illegal to require an oral test for a person who does not have the ability to speak.

In Texas, an employer refused to hire an individual who had hearing and vision impairments on the basis of his disabilities. The employer had posed a disability-related inquiry to the applicant during the interview process. The jury awarded both compensatory and punitive damages to the individual because of the unlawful pre-offer inquiries about the nature and severity of the applicant's disability.[34]

Medical Examinations

Deaf people are sometimes denied particular jobs on the basis of medical criteria that disqualify any person who does not pass a hearing test. Deaf people have been medically disqualified as bus mechanics or geologists solely on the basis of their hearing loss. These blanket medical exclusions can be challenged if they are not job related. Under ADA and Rehabilitation Act regulations, an employer may make offers of employment dependent on the results of medical examinations only if these are administered confidentially and in a nondiscriminatory manner to all employees.[35]

Prior to a job offer, an employer cannot conduct medical examinations or ask about an applicant's disability. However, an employer can ask about the person's ability to perform specific essential job functions with or without reasonable accommodation. An employer can also require a medical examination *after* an offer of employment has been made and before the start of employment. The employer may make the offer of employment contingent on the results of the examination if all entering employees take the examination and the information obtained during the examination is kept confidential.

However, supervisors and managers may be informed of necessary restrictions or accommodations to the work of the employee, and first-aid and safety personnel may be informed that the disability might require emergency treatment. Government officials investigating ADA compliance may also be informed of the examination results. The employer cannot discriminate against an individual with a disability on the basis of the examination unless the reasons for rejection are job related and necessary for the conduct of the employer's business. The employer also cannot refuse to hire an individual because of a disability if that person can perform the essential functions of the job with or without an accommodation. Deaf and hard of hearing applicants have been excluded from consideration for jobs on the basis of medical examinations before jobs have been offered. This section of ADA prohibits such practices. Moreover, once an employee has been hired and started work, an employer cannot require that the employee take a medical examination or answer questions about his or her disability unless the questions are related to the job and necessary for the conduct of the employer's business.

The EEOC has issued guidance on preemployment inquiries under the ADA.[36] This guidance offers examples of permissible and impermissible questions and examinations. For example, an employer may ask about an applicant's ability to perform the physical requirements of a job, such as lifting a certain amount of weight or climbing ladders. Employers may ask applicants to demonstrate or describe how they would perform job tasks. The EEOC guidelines also discuss what constitutes a medical examination and the permissible types of procedures and tests. An employer may ask applicants to perform physical agility or fitness tests in which the applicant demonstrates ability to perform actual or simulated job tasks.

One recurring issue with medical examinations has to do with hearing tests used for qualification as a commercial truck driver. This was an issue first in *Morton v. UPS* and later in a class action, *Bates v. UPS,* when deaf employees sued the United Parcel Service (UPS) because the company would not allow deaf employees to drive the package delivery trucks. In both cases, the company precluded deaf employees from driving positions even when these vehicles weighed less than ten thousand pounds. At the time, the Department of Transportation (DOT) required drivers of trucks weighing ten thousand pounds or more to be certified by a hearing test. In *Morton,* the court found that UPS could not apply a broad DOT rule to a nonregulated class of vehicles.[37] Years later in *Bates,* the court overruled *Morton,* arguing that a qualification test could be used when it was job related and consistent with business necessity and when the performance could not be achieved by reasonable accommodation.[38]

After the *Bates* decision, UPS settled with the plaintiffs for $5.8 million to cover the costs of interpreters and reasonable accommodations denied to plaintiffs and implemented a hearing test protocol to test deaf drivers individually. Today UPS allows candidates who can "demonstrate, at either 1 kHz or 2 kHz, a binaural sound field threshold of 45 dB . . . or better . . . with or without hearing aids" to drive UPS vehicles weighing less than ten thousand pounds.[39] The Department of Transportation currently requires that commercial drivers be able to hear a "forced whisper at not less than 5 feet in the better ear with or without a hearing aid, or . . . [do] not have an average hearing loss in the better ear greater than 40 decibels at 500 Hz, 1,000 Hz, and

2,000 Hz with or without a hearing aid."[40] However, after extensive advocacy by the NAD, the DOT granted forty exemptions to these qualifications to deaf drivers in 2013, and safe drivers who are deaf may apply for an exemption by contacting the Federal Motor Carrier Safety Administration.[41]

AFFIRMATIVE ACTION

A substantive difference between the ADA and the three employment sections of the Rehabilitation Act is their mandate for affirmative action hiring policies. Affirmative action characteristically means special programs to actively recruit, hire, train, accommodate, and promote qualified people with disabilities. Nondiscrimination, on the other hand, usually means an obligation to treat employees with disabilities in the same manner as other employees and to provide reasonable accommodations. Nondiscrimination does not require affirmative action, although affirmative action has the potential to ensure the increased hiring of people with disabilities.

The ADA contains no affirmative action hiring provisions. Sections 501 and 503 of the Rehabilitation Act require the federal government and federal contractors to take affirmative action to hire, promote, and retain qualified people with disabilities.[42] Section 504, however, does not require affirmative action; it simply requires nondiscrimination.[43]

With regard to disabilities, however, identical treatment without accommodation can be discriminatory. An employer who holds a staff meeting for all employees has effectively excluded a deaf employee from participating if no interpreter is provided. The same is true of an employer who hires a person in a wheelchair to work in a building that does not have ramps. By treating the employee who has a disability precisely the same as the employee without a disability, the employer has acted unfairly. In all situations in which identical treatment constitutes discrimination against employees with disabilities, the ADA and the Rehabilitation Act both require specific steps to provide equal opportunity and *equally effective* means of taking advantage of those opportunities.

Federal Obligations

The federal government has established several policies and programs designed to fulfill its affirmative action obligations under Section 501. For example, it will make special arrangements for applicants taking the Civil Service examination when applicants' disabilities prevent them from competing equally. These include providing a waiver of certain verbal tests for deaf applicants; readers for blind applicants; interpreters for deaf applicants; enlarged answer blocks for applicants with poor manual dexterity or motor coordination; taped or Braille tests; and extended time limits for taking the tests.

The government has also designed special hiring programs to facilitate the appointment of employees with disabilities. A program used to hire individuals with disabilities is known as an "excepted" or "Schedule A" appointment.[44] It is available to applicants with disabilities. Under the excepted appointment program, people with disabilities can be hired for permanent jobs by federal agencies without having to take the Civil Service examination. The purpose of the program is to avoid the discriminatory effects of the examination.

Following its obligations under Section 501 and the Civil Service Reform Act of 1978, the federal government has authorized several methods of hiring interpreters for deaf employees in various work situations. Each federal agency has the option of either (1) hiring full-time interpreters, (2) using other employees who can interpret competently, or (3) contracting out with individual interpreters or interpreter referral agencies on an as-needed basis.[45] The best method depends on the work situation involved. If a particular deaf employee's job requires frequent use of an interpreter, or if there are several deaf employees in one agency whose combined needs require frequent service, then a full-time interpreter on staff would be the best solution. If an interpreter is needed for an occasional or a regular office meeting, it might be best to contract with a private interpreter for services.

Moreover, it is highly recommended that federal agencies implement "funding mechanisms that will avoid charging individual offices for the cost of accommodations, such as a full or partial centralized agency fund for accommodation costs."[46] Through a centralized agency fund, deaf and hard of hearing employees can request communication accommodations without their division or office having to take funds from its operating costs, which can adversely affect the employment opportunities of the deaf and hard of hearing employees.

FURTHER ASSISTANCE

More detailed information on the procedures for taking advantage of all of these special federal programs and services can be obtained by contacting federal job information centers throughout the country. Also, the personnel office of each federal agency has a selective placement coordinator who is responsible for implementing these programs. These coordinators want advice and need assistance from vocational rehabilitation counselors on all issues and problems involving recruiting, hiring, and providing accommodations for employees with disabilities. Rehabilitation counselors should develop contacts with federal personnel offices and be thoroughly familiar with federal hiring practices and job application procedures. Continuing interaction among counselors, selective placement coordinators, managers, and supervisors is essential.

Guidance for Rehabilitation Counselors

The federal government has suggested measures that rehabilitation counselors can take to ensure that affirmative action is implemented:

+ Survey federal agencies to determine what types of jobs are likely to be available and which of these are likely to be in demand by individuals with disabilities.
+ Work with other counselors and organizations to establish referral systems.
+ Provide follow-up assistance to agency supervisors after a person with a disability has been hired.

+ Arrange for selective placement coordinators, managers, and supervisors to tour rehabilitation and independent living centers and attend workshops and consciousness-raising programs.
+ Give recognition awards and publicity to agencies that actively participate in employment programs for individuals with disabilities.
+ Share information about federal job vacancies and personnel needs with rehabilitation counselors in the area.
+ Involve selective placement coordinators in the activities of rehabilitation agencies.[47]

REMEDIES

Individuals with disabilities have the same remedies available to all other protected groups under Title VII of the Civil Rights Act of 1964, as amended by the Civil Rights Act of 1991.[48] The latter act provides the same remedies as those under both Title I of the ADA and Section 501 of the Rehabilitation Act. Before an individual files a discrimination complaint, the Civil Rights Act stipulates that the individual must exhaust administrative remedies. Thus, before an individual can get into court, he or she must first file a complaint with the EEOC or the appropriate state or local fair employment practice agency.

An employer found in violation of the employment section of the ADA may be ordered to discontinue discriminatory practices, to correct policies and practices, hire a qualified individual with a disability, or rehire the person with back pay and/or provide the person with a reasonable accommodation. In addition, an employer may be required to provide compensatory and punitive damages for intentional discrimination.[49] Damages may not be awarded where the employer demonstrates "good faith efforts" to identify and make reasonable accommodations.[50] Employers who lose a specific case will be required to pay attorney's fees and costs incurred by the complainant with a disability.

Various remedies are available under Section 503 of the Rehabilitation Act, including injunctive relief, withholding progress payments, terminating the federal contract, and precluding the violator from receiving future government contracts.[51] A court may impose sanctions for an employer's noncompliance with affirmative action mandates, failure to ensure protection for individuals filing complaints, or failure to comply with Section 503.[52]

ENFORCEMENT PROCEDURES

Procedures under the Americans with Disabilities Act

As mentioned earlier, the EEOC enforces Title I of the ADA. An individual who believes that he or she has been the victim of employment discrimination can file a complaint with the EEOC district office that services the area. A discrimination charge must be filed within 180 days of the alleged discriminatory act. If a state or local law provides relief for discrimination on the basis of a disability, an individual may have up to three hundred days to file a charge. It is best, however, to contact the local EEOC office promptly if discrimination is suspected.

Once the EEOC receives a complaint, it will offer mediation as an option in an effort to resolve the dispute. Both parties would need to agree to the mediation for it to take place. If mediation does not resolve the dispute, the EEOC launches an investigation. At its conclusion the EEOC will either offer to conciliate, issue a notice of a "right to sue" letter to the individual alleging discrimination, or take legal action on behalf of the United States and the individual alleging discrimination. If the individual has received the "right to sue" letter from the EEOC, the individual may file a complaint in federal or state court. This complaint must be filed within ninety days of receiving the notice.

Procedures under the Rehabilitation Act

Section 501: Federal Employees

A federal employee or an applicant with a disability who believes he or she has been discriminated against by a federal agency can file an administrative complaint with that agency's equal employment opportunity (EEO) office pursuant to Section 501. Each step of the procedure must be carried out within strict time limits. Although a waiver of the time limits is sometimes allowed for good cause, a complaint can be rejected for failure to meet the deadline. The person with a disability has the right to be represented by an attorney at all stages of the complaint process. If interpreters are necessary to ensure effective communication at any stage of the proceedings, the agency is required to provide the interpreters. The process includes the following steps:

A. Informal Precomplaint Counseling
1. An employee or an applicant for employment must contact the agency's EEO office. The contact may be made in person or by letter. No form is required.
2. The EEO office will assign an EEO counselor to the case. The person bringing the complaint (complainant) must provide all of the information about the discriminatory policy or action to the EEO counselor.
3. The role of the EEO counselor is to:
    a. make inquiries about the complaint and discuss it with everyone involved;
    b. attempt an informal resolution within twenty-one days;
    c. not discourage the complainant from filing a formal complaint;
    d. not reveal the identity of the complainant unless authorized to do so.
4. If informal resolution cannot be achieved, the EEO counselor will send the complainant a "notice of final interview" informing the individual of the right to file a formal complaint with the agency.
B. Formal Complaint
1. If informed counseling is not successful, the complainant has a right to file a formal complaint with the agency's EEO office.
    a. The formal complaint is written on a form provided by the agency's EEO office and is filed with that office.
    b. The written complaint should discuss in detail all of the facts involved and include copies of letters and other documents substantiating those facts.

    c. If a pattern or policy of discrimination continues, the complainant should describe the discriminatory activity as "continuing" in order to avoid any time/deadline problems.

2. Rejection of complaint

    a. The agency may reject the entire complaint or some of the issues raised if it is not filed on time, the complaint raises matters identical to those in another complaint made by the employee, the complainant is not an employee of or an applicant for employment at the agency, or the complaint is not based on disability discrimination.

    b. If the agency rejects the complaint, the complainant must be notified in writing. The employee may then appeal to the Equal Employment Opportunity Commission or file suit in federal district court.

3. Investigation of complaint

    a. If the agency accepts the complaint, it will appoint an EEO investigator, a person other than the EEO counselor.

    b. The investigator will conduct an in-depth inquiry, take sworn affidavits from the people involved, and gather documents and statistics.

    c. If the complainant believes that important witnesses have not been interviewed or that important evidence has not been explored, he or she should notify the investigator in writing.

4. Adjustment of complaint

When the investigation is completed, the investigator writes a report. The EEO office sends copies of the report to both the complainant and the employer and provides them an opportunity to informally adjust (settle) the matter on the basis of the results of the investigation. If the complaint is informally adjusted, the terms of the adjustment must be in writing.

Proposed disposition

    a. If the complaint cannot be adjusted, the agency will issue a proposed disposition (decision).

    b. If the complainant is satisfied with the proposed disposition, the agency must then implement the terms of the disposition.

    c. If the complainant is dissatisfied with the proposed disposition, he or she may request a hearing before the EEOC in writing or file suit in federal district court of receipt of the proposed disposition.

  5. EEOC hearing

    a. At the hearing, as at all other stages in the process, the complainant has the right to be represented by an attorney and to have a qualified interpreter.

    b. On the basis of evidence submitted at the hearing, the examiner (judge) will issue a recommended decision that the agency can reverse.

    c. If the complainant is dissatisfied with the decision, he or she may appeal to the EEOC Office of Review and Appeals or file suit in federal court.

C. Right to Sue in Federal Court

  1. The complainant can file suit in federal district court at any time after 180 days from the date the formal EEO complaint was filed if the agency has not yet issued a final decision.

  2. In addition, as noted earlier, the complainant can file suit within thirty days after the completion of other stages of the administrative process (e.g., after receipt either of the notice of proposed disposition or of final agency action).[53]

Section 503: Federal Contractors

Section 503 of the Rehabilitation Act requires employers who have contracts with the federal government for more than $10,000 to take affirmative action to hire and promote qualified people with disabilities.[54] The work performed under these contracts includes construction of government buildings, repair of federal highways, and leasing of government buildings. In addition to primary contractors, Section 503 covers companies that have subcontracted for more than $10,000 of federal business from a primary contractor.

The administrative complaint procedure under Section 503 differs significantly from that in Section 501. Section 503 is enforced by the U.S. Department of Labor's Office of Federal Contract Compliance Programs (OFCCP). An applicant or employee who believes he or she has been discriminated against by a federal contractor can file a written complaint with the regional OFCCP office, which is directed to investigate promptly and attempt to resolve the complaint. If the regional office finds no violation of Section 503, then the complainant may appeal to the headquarters of the OFCCP in Washington, DC. If, however, the regional office finds that the employer has in fact violated Section 503, then an attempt is made to resolve the matter informally and provide the appropriate relief to the complainant.

If the employer has a federal contract subject to Section 503 and refuses to provide the appropriate relief, the OFCCP can then employ more formal enforcement mechanisms. These include bringing suit in federal court, withholding payments due on existing federal contracts, terminating existing federal contracts, and/or barring the contractor from receiving future federal contracts. If the OFCCP begins any of these measures, the employer can request a formal administrative hearing. Although the complainant can participate in the hearing, it is primarily a dispute between the OFCCP and the employer. The complainant is a witness but not a party to the enforcement action.[55]

In 2013 the OFCCP proposed a rule that made changes to the regulations implementing Section 503 of the Rehabilitation Act.[56] These changes, which became effective on March 24, 2014, serve to strengthen contractors' affirmative action and nondiscrimination responsibilities and update the language of the regulations in light of the Americans with Disabilities Act Amendments Act of 2008. Under the new regulations, employers are required to maintain quantitative measures of employees with disabilities in order to assess affirmative action efforts. Employers are invited to ask employees and applicants to self-identify as individuals with disabilities and are tasked with a 7 percent utilization goal, that is, for at least 7 percent of the employees to be individuals with disabilities. In addition, these regulations help to encourage awareness of and compliance with the Rehabilitation Act by requiring contractors to include mandated language about affirmative action and nondiscrimination responsibilities in contracts with subcontractors.

Section 504: Federal Financial Recipients

Unlike the ADA or the other sections of the Rehabilitation Act, individuals alleging a violation of Section 504 do not have to exhaust any administrative remedies before filing an action in court. Employers are required to adopt grievance procedures that will facilitate prompt complaint resolution.[57] The procedures for enforcing Section 504 are discussed in chapter 3. As noted there, Section 504 applies to all recipients of federal financial assistance. "Federal financial assistance" under Section 504 differs from a "federal contract" under Section 503. It can mean grants and loans of federal money, services of federal personnel, or the lease of federal buildings for less than fair market value. Because of widespread dependence on federal money, the recipients of federal financial assistance are many and varied.

Before receiving such assistance, all recipients must sign an "assurance of compliance" form agreeing to obey Section 504. The US government, as well as advocacy groups for people with disabilities, has always taken the position that Section 504 prohibits employment discrimination by all recipients of federal aid regardless of the purpose for which their federal funds are to be used. In other words, if a hospital received federal funds to buy medical equipment, Section 504 covers that hospital's employment practices.

State Statutes

State laws sometimes provide a remedy for employment discrimination when federal laws do not apply. A number of states have included a category such as "physical or mental disability" to the list of classes protected by traditional human rights and employment discrimination laws. These laws are useful because they often apply to all public and private employers, thereby prohibiting discrimination even by employers who do not have federal contracts or grants or those who have fewer than fifteen employees. In this sense, state laws sometimes help in cases of employment discrimination where neither the ADA nor the Rehabilitation Act is applicable.

There is no uniformity in state human rights laws. Some protect workers with physical disabilities but not those with mental disabilities. Some require reasonable accommodations for workers with disabilities, but some do not. Some allow private causes of action (i.e., the right of individuals to sue in state court), whereas others limit redress to administrative enforcement by state agencies. In most states, the agency charged with enforcement is the state civil rights commission or state employment agency. Enforcement procedures and remedies vary widely, as do the definitions of protected disabilities and of covered employers.

NOTES

1. Thomas E. Rickard, Harry C. Triandis, and C. H. Patterson, "Indices of Employer Prejudice toward Disabled Applicants," *Journal of Applied Psychology* 47, no. 1 (1963): 52–55.
2. See Joe Wolfe, "Disability Is No Handicap for Dupont," *Alliance Review* (Winter, 1973–1974): 13; Sandra Kalenick, "Myths about Hiring the Physically Handicapped," *Job Safety and Health* 2 (1974): 9.
3. Alan B. Crammatte, *The Formidable Peak: A Study of Deaf People in Professional Employment* (Washington, DC: Gallaudet College, 1965), 118.
4. 42 U.S.C. §12102(1) and §12111(8); 29 C.F.R. §1630.2(g) and §1630.2(m).
5. 42 U.S.C. §12101(4)(a)(ii)(A) (1990, amended 2008); 29 C.F.R. §1630.2(h)(2)(i).
6. 42 U.S.C. §12101 (1990, amended 2008); 29 C.F.R. §1630.2(j)(1)(vi).
7. See Marc Charmatz, Anna McClure, and Caroline Jackson, "Revitalizing the ADA: The Americans with Disabilities Amendments Act of 2008," in *Civil Rights Litigation and Attorney's Fees Annual Handbook*, National Lawyers Guild (2010).
8. 42 U.S.C. §12101; 29 C.F.R. §1630.2(g)(1)(iii).
9. 110 *H.R. Rept.* 730, 13.
10. 29 C.F.R. §1630.2(g)(1)(ii).
11. 29 U.S.C. §705(9); 29 C.F.R. §1614.203(b).
12. 41 C.F.R. §60.741.2(t), 29 C.F.R. §32.3.
13. 29 C.F.R. §1630.2(n)(2)–(3); 41 C.F.R. §60.741.2(i)(2)–(3).

14. 42 U.S.C. §12112(5)(a); 29 C.F.R. §1630.9(a); 41 C.F.R. §60–741.21(a)(6).
15. Ibid.
16. 42 U.S.C. §12111(9); 29 C.F.R. §1630.2(o)(1); 41 C.F.R. §60–741.21(s)(1)–(2).
17. 42 U.S.C. §12111(9); 29 C.F.R. §1630.2(o)(2).
18. National Association of the Deaf, "Discrimination and Reasonable Accommodations," 2014, http://nad.org/issues/employment/discrimination-and-reasonable-accommodations.
19. U.S. Equal Employment Opportunity Commission, "Enforcement Guidance: Reasonable Accommodation and Undue Hardship Under the Americans with Disabilities Act," October 17, 2002, http://www.eeoc.gov/policy/docs/accommodation.html#types.
20. 29 C.F.R. §1630.2(o)(3); 41 C.F.R. Part 60-741, App. A(3).
21. 29 C.F.R. §1630.3; 41 C.F.R. §60-741.21(s)(3).
22. 29 C.F.R. §1630.2.
23. *Howard v. Alabama Bd. of Pharm.,* 2009 WL 6906811 (N.D. Ala. 2009).
24. Alabama Board of Pharmacy, "Use of Telecommunications Relay Service (Policy #20100922)," September 22, 2010, http://www.albop.com/.
25. 923 F. Supp. 720 (D. Md. 1996).
26. No. CIV-95-0708 PHX RGS (D. Ariz).
27. *Crane v. Dole,* 617 F. Supp. 156 (D.D.C. 1985).
28. *Strathie v. Department of Transportation,* 716 F.2d 227 (3d Cir. 1983).
29. *Rizzo v. Children's World Learning Center,* 173 F.3d 254 (5th Cir. 1999).
30. 42 U.S.C. §12111(10); 29 C.F.R. §1630.2(p)(2); 41 C.F.R. §60-741.21(aa)(2).
31. *56 Fed. Reg.* 35,745 (July 26, 1991).
32. 29 C.F.R. §1630.10.
33. 42 U.S.C. §12112(7).
34. *EEOC v. Community Coffee Co.,* No. H-94-1061 (S.D. Tex. June 28, 1995).
35. 29 C.F.R. §1630.14; 45 C.F.R. §84.14(c) and (d).
36. See U.S. Equal Employment Opportunity Commission, "EEOC Notice 915.022: Enforcement Guidance on Pre-Employment Inquiries under the ADA," October 10, 1995, http://www.eeoc.gov/policy/docs/preemp.html.
37. See *Morton v. UPS,* 272 F.3d 1249 (9th Cir. 2001).
38. See *Bates v. UPS,* 511 F.3d 974, 995 (9th Cir. 2007).
39. *Bates v. UPS,* 511 F. 3d 974 (9th Cir. 2007), Settlement agreement reached, http://www.dralegal.org/impact/cases/bates-v-ups.

40. 49 C.F.R. §391.41(b)(11).
41. 78 *Fed. Reg.* 7,479 (Feb. 1, 2013).
42. 41 C.F.R. §60-741.40.
43. 29 U.S.C. §791(b) and §793.
44. See Office of Personnel Management explanation of Schedule A hiring: OPM, "Disability Employment Hiring," http://www.opm.gov/policy-data-oversight/disability-employment/hiring/.
45. See The U.S. Equal Employment Opportunity Commission, "Questions and Answers: Promoting Employment of Individuals with Disabilities in the Federal Workforce: Accommodation Requests," http://www.eeoc.gov/federal/qanda-employment-with-disabilities.cfm#request.
46. Ibid.
47. See Office of Personnel Management, "Handbook of Selective Placement of Persons with Physical and Mental Handicaps," OPM Doc. 125-11-3 (March 1979).
48. 42 U.S.C. §1981(a).
49. 42 U.S.C. §1981(b).
50. 42 U.S.C. §1981(a)(3).
51. 41 C.F.R. §60-741.
52. 41 C.F.R. §60-741.5(a)(3).
53. For more detailed information, see 29 C.F.R. §§1614.101–1614.110.
54. 29 U.S.C. §793(a).
55. For court rulings that there is no private right to sue under Section 503, see *Rogers v. Frito-Lay,* 611 P.2d 1074 (5th Cir. 1980); *Simpson v. Reynolds Metal Co.,* 629 P.2d 1226 (7th Cir. 1980); *Simon v. St. Louis County,* 656 P.2d 316 (8th Cir. 1981); and *Davis v. United Air Lines,* no. 81-7093 (2nd Cir. 1981). For court rulings that an individual may bring suit under Section 503, see *Hart v. County of Alameda,* 485 P. Supp. 66 (N.D. Cal. 1979), and *Chaplin v. Consolidated Edison of New York,* 482 P. Supp. 1165 (S.D. N.Y. 1980).
56. 78 *Fed. Reg.* 58,681 (Sept. 24, 2013).
57. 45 C.F.R. §84.7(b).

Chapter 8

Housing

In this country housing is generally recognized as a right that everyone should be able to enjoy. Every person should be able to live in housing that is both safe and within their financial means. However, legislation was necessary to promote fair housing, and laws were passed to protect certain classes of people from housing discrimination.

THE FAIR HOUSING ACT

The Fair Housing Act (FHA) was initially enacted through Title VIII of the Civil Rights Act of 1968.[1] President Lyndon B. Johnson promoted Title VIII as a response to the discrimination in housing that African Americans and Hispanics faced, which prevented them from purchasing or renting homes in certain areas.[2] Title VIII was amended by the Fair Housing Amendments Act of 1988 (FHAA).[3] The original FHA protects individuals from discrimination in housing on a number of bases.[4] The FHAA extended protections to individuals with disabilities, although the language of the FHAA uses the term *handicap*.[5] The Amendments Act also gave the Fair Housing Act enforcement authority.[6]

The FHAA defines *handicap* in the same way the Americans with Disabilities Act and the Rehabilitation Act define *disability:*

(1) a physical or mental impairment which substantially limits one or more of such person's major life activities
(2) a record of having such an impairment, or
(3) being regarded as having such an impairment[7]

The regulations of the FHAA define "physical impairments" as including "speech and hearing impairments" and "major life activities" as including hearing and speaking.[8] Pursuant to these definitions, deaf and hard of hearing individuals are covered by the FHAA.

Prohibited Discrimination

Several sections of the FHA spell out specific acts that are considered prohibited discrimination against people with handicaps. It is unlawful to make or publish notices, statements, or advertisements for the sale or rental of a dwelling that suggests discrimination based on handicap,[9] misrepresent a dwelling's availability because of a person's handicap,[10] and persuade a person to sell or rent a dwelling, for profit, by "representations regarding the entry or prospective entry into the neighborhood of a person or persons of a particular . . . handicap."[11] It is also discriminatory for anyone to refuse to sell or rent a dwelling to or to discriminate against anyone "in the terms, conditions, or privileges of a sale or rental . . . or in the provision of services or facilities in connection with such dwelling, because of a handicap of" (A) the buyer or renter, (B) the person who will live in the dwelling, or (C) anyone associated with the buyer or renter.[12]

The US Department of Housing and Urban Development (HUD) gives the following examples of (prohibited) unequal treatment that sometimes occur:

+ A landlord may give applicants with disabilities different information about the availability of advertised housing units than the landlord may give to persons without disabilities.

+ A housing provider may not offer persons with disabilities the same opportunities as persons without disabilities to inspect advertised or available units.
+ A rental agent may steer applicants with disabilities to different units, floors, or buildings than applicants without disabilities.
+ A housing provider may charge or require different rental rates, deposits, application fees, types of insurance, and credit check charges to persons with disabilities than the housing provider charges to persons without disabilities.
+ An agent discourages applicants with disabilities, by not returning telephone calls, making follow up contacts, inviting the applicants to complete an application, or offering waiting list opportunities while encouraging applicants without disabilities by these methods.[13]

The FHAA also prohibits the residential real estate–related transaction business to discriminate on the basis of handicap.[14] Brokerage service organizations may not deny or discriminate against a person on the basis of handicap.[15] Further, it is discriminatory for any person to coerce, intimidate, threaten, or interfere with a person exercising or enjoying the rights provided under the FHAA.[16] Discrimination includes refusing to make reasonable modifications or reasonable accommodations for a person with a handicap to live in the housing.[17]

Reasonable Modifications and Accommodations

It is unlawful for anyone to refuse reasonable modifications, done at the expense of the person with a handicap, if the modifications may be necessary to allow that person "full enjoyment" of the dwelling.[18] However, landlords of rented dwellings may, if reasonable, require the renter to restore the dwelling to its condition before the modification and/or "reasonable assurances that the work will be done in a workmanlike manner and that any required building permits will be obtained."[19] These landlords may not make the tenants with a handicap pay for costs exceeding the restoration.[20]

No one may refuse to make reasonable accommodations that may be necessary to allow an individual with a handicap an "equal opportunity to use and enjoy a dwelling unit, including public and common use areas."[21] Reasonable accommodations may include hearing dogs.[22] Both HUD and the Department of Justice (DOJ) have stated that, in order for an accommodation to be necessary, "there must be an identifiable relationship, or nexus" between the accommodation and the handicap.[23] An accommodation must also "affirmatively enhance" the life of a person with a handicap.[24] An accommodation is not reasonable if it would "impose an undue financial and administrative burden on the housing provider or would fundamentally alter the nature of the provider's operations."[25] Determining whether an accommodation is reasonable must be done on a case-by-case basis, balancing its necessity with its cost.[26]

Penalties

For intimidating a person with a handicap or preventing such person from exercising or enjoying his or her rights under the previous sections and for persuading others to withhold their aid or services to these individuals, a penalty of not more than $1,000 or imprisonment for not more than one year, or both, may be imposed.[27] If bodily injury results from the discrimination, the penalty can be up to $10,000 or any length of term of imprisonment.[28]

PUBLIC HOUSING REQUIREMENTS

Any recipient of federal funding that provides housing may not exclude from participation, deny benefits, or otherwise discriminate against persons with a handicap.[29] Those receiving federal funding have obligations to such individuals that are greater than those the FHAA requires of private entities that do not receive federal funds. Specifically, federally funded housing providers may not deny the opportunity to participate in or benefit from housing; give an opportunity not equal to what is offered to others that do not have a handicap; provide any housing or service that is not as effective as that offered to others; provide different or separate housing; aid or perpetuate discrimination in housing; deny the opportunity to participate on housing advisory boards; deny housing; or otherwise limit enjoyment of any housing benefits or services.[30]

The regulations for public housing contain specific requirements for communication access, including the provision of auxiliary aids.[31] When determining the type of auxiliary aids to provide, the recipient of federal funding is to give "primary consideration to the requests of the individual with handicaps."[32] Where the recipient communicates with applicants and beneficiaries by telephone, they must make it possible for deaf and hard of hearing individuals to obtain the same service, including through TTYs or "equally effective communication systems."[33] In addition, recipients of federal funding are to ensure that interested persons who are deaf or hard of hearing can obtain the same information provided to all others.[34]

Recipients of federal funding would not have to provide such auxiliary aids or effective communication systems if it would be a fundamental alteration of their programs or services or be an undue financial or administrative burden, but they must nevertheless provide benefits and services to individuals with handicaps to the maximum extent possible.[35]

STATE AND LOCAL HOUSING LAWS

In addition to the federal Fair Housing Amendments Act, some states and local municipalities also have housing discrimination laws.[36] Even though the FHAA sets the minimum requirements and standards for public housing as well as housing funded with federal monies, state and local housing laws can provide stronger protections for covered groups, including individuals with disabilities. In those states and municipalities with such statutes, generally an administrative entity is empowered to investigate violations of those laws and are an option for deaf and hard of hearing individuals to pursue their grievances against discriminatory providers.

Accessible Smoke Alarm Requirements

The Department of Housing and Urban Development has several types of funding for different forms of housing. For some of these types of housing, new homes receiving federal funds are required to provide smoke detectors equipped with an alarm system "designed for hearing-impaired persons, in each bedroom occupied by a hearing-impaired person."[37] In addition, those bedrooms "occupied by a hearing-impaired person must have an alarm system connected to the smoke detector installed in the hallway."[38]

In addition, some state and local laws require that accessible smoke alarms (with visual or tactile alerts) be provided to deaf and hard of hearing tenants, although some of these laws give the property owner flexibility with respect to the costs of such alarms.[39] Moreover, many fire departments throughout the country provide free smoke alarms that are designed for deaf and hard of hearing individuals.

The NAD believes that all smoke and carbon monoxide detectors should include auditory, visual, and tactile alerts to ensure that every person is warned of danger whether they are awake or asleep. There are too many stories of deaf and hard of hearing individuals perishing in fires where no visual or tactile alerts were installed, and probably those who could hear also were unaware of fires because they were sleeping and were not awakened by the auditory alert.[40]

Housing Discrimination Experienced by Deaf and Hard of Hearing People

Housing discrimination with respect to people with disabilities is usually perceived as one that affects persons who use wheelchairs, given the shortage of housing that provides accessible rooms, ramps instead of stairs for building entrances, elevators instead of stairs, and similar mobility access. However, deaf and hard of hearing individuals also experience housing discrimination in different ways.

Housing providers may not prohibit this population from having hearing dogs in their homes even if there is a "no pet" rule.[41] The Seventh Circuit Court of Appeals held in *Bronk v. Ineichen* that deaf individuals may have a hearing dog in their rental apartment even if there is a "no pet" rule as long as they are able to show that their dog is indeed trained as a hearing dog.[42] The court reversed the district court jury verdict that the dog in the case was not a hearing dog because the court gave the jury flawed instructions, which "may well have crystallized the jury's erroneous belief that if [the dog] had no schooling he could not as a matter of law have been a reasonable accommodation."[43] The appellate court remanded the case to the district court for a determination of whether the dog was sufficiently trained, even without formal schooling, to serve as a hearing dog.

In addition, homeowners' associations are required to ensure that their meetings are accessible to deaf and hard of hearing members, as long as the provision of communication access is reasonable and not an undue financial or administrative hardship.[44] Consequently, such associations must provide sign language interpreters or captioning services if they are necessary for these members to participate in meetings unless it can be shown that the cost of such services would be beyond the associations' ability to cover as part of their overall budget.

In 2007 a deaf man living in New York City sought to rent an apartment and asked the owner to provide a visual alarm to make it possible for him to know when someone was ringing the doorbell.[45] The owner not only refused to install the visual alarm but also refused to rent the apartment to the man because he was deaf. In 2009 the case settled with the owner agreeing to injunctive relief and $7,500 in damages.[46]

On January 9, 2014, the National Association of the Deaf, the National Fair Housing Alliance, and the Austin Tenants' Council filed eight HUD complaints against major apartment complex owners and management companies in Little Rock, Arkansas; Sacramento, California; Atlanta and Savannah, Georgia; Long Beach, Mississippi; Charleston, North Charleston, and Lexington, South Carolina; and Austin, Texas.[47] These complaints were filed after a year-long investigation involving "matched-pair testing" with a deaf tester and a hearing tester making calls to the same housing complexes. The investigation sought to determine whether differences occurred in the way housing complex staff responded to calls from the deaf tester and the hearing tester. The National Fair Housing Alliance compiled all of the results of this investigation in a report titled "Are You Listening Now? A National Investigation Uncovers Housing Discrimination against the Deaf and Hard of Hearing."[48] Examples of discriminatory conduct included the following:

+ a rental agent telling a deaf tester about two available units at a monthly rent of $725 while telling a hearing tester about a third available unit at a monthly rent of $675

+ a rental agent telling a deaf tester that no two-bedroom units were available while telling a hearing tester that two such units were ready to rent

+ a rental agent telling a hearing tester about three available units, with details about the amenities and the option of a nonrefundable deposit of $87.50 instead of the full $500 deposit, and telling a deaf tester about only two units, with none of the details and nothing about the special $87.50 deposit

+ a rental agent being patient with a hearing tester, giving details, and asking for a contact number while being abrupt with a deaf tester and not mentioning details or asking for any contact information

+ a rental agent hanging up on a deaf tester on the first call and telling the same tester some information on the second call, as well as requiring additional fees and background checks; the same agent immediately provided all information to the hearing tester and made no mention of additional fees or background checks

+ a rental agent asking for contact information and making a follow-up call with a hearing tester while not doing the same for a deaf tester

+ a rental agent hanging up repeatedly on a deaf tester while accepting the call from a hearing tester

+ a rental agent informing a deaf tester that the amount of the security deposit would depend on the credit check while not mentioning this requirement to a hearing tester

+ a rental agent hanging up on a deaf tester and sending subsequent calls to voice mail while accepting a call from a hearing tester[49]

More disturbing was the fact that the investigation showed that, at all of the tested housing complexes, 40 percent of the rental agents had hung up on deaf callers at least once; 86 percent had provided more information to hearing callers than to deaf callers; and 56 percent had indicated more requirements for background checks and financial qualifications to deaf callers than to hearing callers.[50]

Over the years, other housing access investigations like these have been carried out, and the results have invariably been bad. A housing provider in New York challenged the legality of such investigations, alleging that the government suborned perjury by having the deaf tester testify in court that he wanted to rent an apartment when in actuality he was only testing access issues.[51] The Second Circuit Court of Appeals upheld the federal district court's ruling that the testing was legal and that the housing provider was properly found to have violated the Fair Housing Act by refusing to rent an apartment to a deaf person and hanging up on the deaf person's relay call.[52]

Housing providers need to be prepared to accept all forms of calls, including relay calls from deaf and hard of hearing individuals seeking to rent apartments, and must provide the same information to all potential tenants rather than choosing to give less information to or impose more requirements on deaf and hard of hearing callers only.

Filing a Housing Complaint

Complaints under the Fair Housing Amendments Act can be filed at no cost with HUD by telephone or mail or via the Internet.[53] The complaint must be filed with HUD "not later than one year after an alleged discriminatory housing practice has occurred or terminated."[54] After the filing, HUD then investigates the complaint.[55] Once the investigation is completed, HUD can take action against the housing provider on behalf of the complainant, refer the matter to another agency, or decline to take any action.[56]

Individuals who have experienced discrimination under the Fair Housing Amendments Act can also pursue private action against the housing provider in either federal or state court but must do so "not later than 2 years after the occurrence or termination of an alleged discriminatory housing practice."[57]

NOTES

1. U.S. Department of Housing and Urban Development, "History of Fair Housing," http://portal.hud.gov/hudportal/HUD?src=/program_offices/fair_housing_equal_opp/aboutfheo/history.
2. Ibid.
3. Pub. L. No. 100-430 (HR 1158); Pub. L. No.100-430, (1988), 102 Stat. 1619.
4. 22 Causes of Action 2d 1 (2003) (stating that the bases were race, color, sex, national origin, handicap, and familial status); 42 U.S.C §§3604 et seq. (1988).
5. Pub. L. No. 100-430.
6. Ibid.
7. 42 U.S.C. §3602(h); 24 C.F.R. §100.201.
8. 24 C.F.R. §100.201.
9. 42 U.S.C. §3604(c).
10. 42 U.S.C. §3604(d).
11. 42 U.S.C. §3604(e).
12. 42 U.S.C. §3604(f)(1) and (2).
13. U.S. Department of Housing and Urban Development, *Discrimination against Persons with Disabilities: Testing Guidance for Practitioners, United States Department of Housing and Urban Development* (July 2005), 8, http://www.hud.gov/offices/fheo/library/dss-guidebook.pdf.
14. 42 U.S.C. §3605.
15. 42 U.S.C. §3606.
16. 42 U.S.C. §3617.
17. 42 U.S.C. §3604 (f)(3).
18. 24 C.F.R. §100.203.
19. 24 C.F.R. §100.203(a), (b).
20. 24 C.F.R. §100.203(a).
21. 24 C.F.R. §100.204(a).
22. See C.F.R. §100.204(b); U.S. Department of Housing and Urban Development and Department of Justice, *Reasonable Accommodations under the Fair Housing Act* (May 14, 2004), http://www.hud.gov/offices/fheo/library/huddojstatement.pdf (hereinafter *Joint Statement*).
23. *Joint Statement*.

24. 1 *Fed. Reg. Real Estate and Mortgage Lending* 12: 36 (4th ed.).
25. *Joint Statement.*
26. Ibid.
27. 42 U.S.C §3631.
28. Ibid.
29. 24 C.F.R. §8.4(a).
30. 24 C.F.R. §8.4(b).
31. 24 C.F.R. §8.6(a).
32. 24 C.F.R. §8.6(a)(1)(i).
33. 24 C.F.R. §8.6(a)(2).
34. 24 C.F.R. §8.6(b).
35. 24 C.F.R. §8.6(c).
36. Included in this group (not comprehensive) are the following:
    Alaska Statutes §18.80.210; California Government Code
    §12955; Connecticut General Statutes §§46a–64b; 6 Delaware
    Code Chapter 46; District of Columbia Code §2-1402.21; Florida
    Statutes §§760.20–760.60; Georgia Code §8-3-200 et seq.;
    Hawaii Revised Statutes §515-3; Idaho Statutes §67-5909; 775
    Illinois Compiled Statutes §§5/3-101 et seq.; Indiana Code
    §§22-9-6-1 et seq.; Iowa Code §§216.8–216.8A; Kansas Statutes
    §§44-1015 to 44-1031; Kentucky Revised Statutes §344.120,
    §§344.360 to §344.385; Maine Revised Statutes, Title 5, Part 12,
    Chapter 337, Subchapter 4; Maryland Code, State Government,
    §§20-701 to 20-710; Massachusetts General Law, Chapter 151B;
    Michigan Compiled Laws §§37.1501 to 37.1507; Minnesota
    Statutes §§363A.09 to 363A.10; Missouri Revised Statutes
    §§213.040 to 213.050; Montana Code §49-2-305; Nebraska
    Revised Statutes §§20-301 to 20-344; Nevada Revised Statutes
    §§118.010 et seq.; New Hampshire Revised Statutes §§354-A:8
    to 354-A:15; New Jersey Revised Statutes §§10:5-12.4 to 10:5-
    12.5; New York Consolidated Laws, Civil Rights §§18-A to 19-B;
    North Carolina General Statutes §§41A-1 et seq.; North Dakota
    Century Code §§14-02.5-01 et seq.; Ohio Revised Code
    §4112.02(H); Oregon Statutes §§659A.421; Rhode Island
    General Laws §§34-37-1 et seq.; South Carolina Code §§31-21-
    10 et seq.; South Dakota Codified Law §§20-13-20 to 20-13-
    23.7; Tennessee Code §§4-21-601 to 4-21-607; 9 Vermont
    Statutes §4503; Virginia Code §§36 36-96.1 et seq.; Revised Code
    of Washington §§49.60.222 to 49.60.225; West Virginia Code
    §§5-11A-1 et seq.; Wisconsin Statutes and Annotations §106.50.
37. 24 C.F.R. §880.207(g)(1); 24 C.F.R. §881.207(g)(1); 24 C.F.R.
    §883.310(c)(1); 24 C.F.R. §884.110(d)(1).
38. 24 C.F.R. §880.207(g)(2); 24 C.F.R. §881.207(g)(2); 24 C.F.R.
    §883.310(c)(2); 24 C.F.R. §884.110(d)(2).

39. List includes the following (not comprehensive): District of Columbia Code §6-751.01; Maine Revised Statutes §2464; Maryland Code, Public Safety §§9-102 and 9-105; Oregon Statutes §479.255; Code of Virginia §36-99.5; West Virginia Code §29-3-16a.

40. News stories of deaf people in fires: Maeve Reston, "Fire Deaths Shock Deaf Community," *Los Angeles Times*, December 04, 2007, http://articles.latimes.com/2007/dec/04/local/me-mobile4; Theresa Vargas, Susan Svrluga, and James Arkin, "Friends Recall Pair Killed in House Fire," *Washington Post*, January 24, 2013, http://www.washingtonpost.com/local/friends-recall-pair-killed-in-house-fire/2013/01/24/7af739f8-666b-11e2-85f5-a8a9228e55e7_story.html; Bill Spencer and Nakia Cooper, "Girl, Deaf Man Hospitalized After Fire Breaks Out in NW Harris County," KPRC 2 Houston, August 6, 2014, http://www.click2houston.com/news/2-hospitalized-when-teen-tries-to-rescue-deaf-father-from-house-fire/26845718.

41. *Joint Statement*, Question 6, example 3, http://www.justice.gov/crt/about/hce/jointstatement_ra.php.

42. *Bronk v. Ineichen*, Case No. 94-2882 (7th Cir., May 11, 1995).

43. Ibid.

44. "Frequently Asked Questions," webpage hosted by the Fair Housing Accessibility FIRST (an initiative sponsored by the United States Department of Housing and Urban Development), http://www.fairhousingfirst.org/faq/fha.html.

45. *King v. Meir Weiss and 2129 Cortelyou Road LLC*, Case No. 08-3047 (E.D. N.Y. 2009).

46. Fair Housing Justice Center, "Case Highlights," http://www.fairhousingjustice.org/resources/case-highlights/; Fair Housing Coach, *How to Comply With Fair Housing Law When Dealing With People Who Are Deaf or Hard of Hearing* (December 2012), http://918dac0aaf3565b9eeb2-8b29b0f5793c61c94be6939f37aeee4d.r65.cf2.rackcdn.com/FHC-DEC12.pdf.

47. Press statement of January 15, 2014, from the National Fair Housing Alliance, the National Association of the Deaf, and the Austin Tenants' Council (hereinafter NFHA Press Statement), http://www.nationalfairhousing.org/Portals/33/News%20Release%20deaf%20hh.pdf.

48. National Fair Housing Alliance Report, *Are You Listening Now? A National Investigation Uncovers Housing Discrimination against the Deaf and Hard of Hearing* (January 9, 2013), http://www.nationalfairhousing.org/Portals/33/2013-01-09%20Are%20You%20Listening%20Now%20-%20Housing%20Discrimination%20against%20the%20Deaf.PDF; National Fair

Housing Alliance, "Civil Rights Groups File Complaints Against Apartment Complex Owners and Managers for Discrimination Against the Deaf and Hard of Hearing," January 15, 2014, http://www.nationalfairhousing.org/Portals/33/News%20Release%20 deaf%20hh.pdf.

49. National Fair Housing Alliance, "Civil Rights Groups File Complaints Against Apartment Complex Owners and Managers for Discrimination Against the Deaf and Hard of Hearing."

50. Ibid.

51. *Space Kings, Inc. v. United States,* Case No. 11-3153-CV (2d Cir., Oct. 17, 2012).

52. Ibid.

53. Instructions for filing a complaint with the HUD are found at http://portal.hud.gov/hudportal/HUD?src=/program_offices/ fair_housing_equal_opp/complaint-process.

54. 42 U.S.C. §3610(a)(1)(A).

55. 42 U.S.C. §3610(a)(1)(B).

56. 42 U.S.C. §3610(f) and (g); 42 U.S.C. §3612; 42 U.S.C. §3613.

57. 42 U.S.C. §3613(a).

Chapter 9

The Legal System

In the absence of an interpreter, it would be a physical impossibility for the accused, a deaf [defendant] to know or understand the nature and cause of the accusation against him and . . . he could only stand by helplessly . . . without knowing or understand[ing], and all this in the teeth of the mandatory constitutional rights which apply. Mere confrontation would be useless.

ALABAMA COURT OF APPEALS IN *TERRY V. STATE* (1925)[1]

The incident described in the opening epigraph took place almost a century ago. Unfortunately, the legal system has not yet taken note of the court's opinion. Even with more legal protection in place today, deaf and hard of hearing people still face communication barriers in the legal system. They often cannot afford a lawyer; if they can, it may be difficult to locate one who is able to communicate with them and understand their needs. If they have to go to court, they often do not understand the proceedings and cannot adequately explain their side of the story. Encounters with the police are no better, and often misunderstandings due to lack of effective communication result in adverse outcomes for these individuals. Furthermore, other deaf and hard of hearing persons—lawyers, witnesses, and jurors—continue to fight to gain equal communication access to courts.

In recent years, considerable progress has been made at both federal and state levels to make courts more accessible to deaf people. The Americans with Disabilities Act requires all state and local courts to be accessible to deaf and hard of hearing individuals. Because virtually every state and local court receives federal funding, Section 504 of the Rehabilitation Act of 1973 also imposes the same requirements. Specifically, the ADA and Section 504 both require the provision of interpreters, transcriptions, or other appropriate auxiliary aids for deaf and hard of hearing people in court settings.[2] The ADA also prohibits charging deaf and hard of hearing litigants for the cost of these services.[3] State laws centering on interpreter services and qualifications for jury duty are slowly being rewritten to ensure the necessary access.

Despite these advances, today's courts still deny equal access and due process to deaf or hard of hearing people. Too many judges are unfamiliar with the federal civil rights laws. Some state laws centering on the provision of sign language interpreters are either inadequate or clash with the ADA and Section 504. State laws that permit judges to charge deaf or hard of hearing individuals for the cost of interpreters violate both the ADA and Section 504.

ACCESS TO COURTS

In the United States, each state has its own laws to regulate its own court system, and the federal court system has different rules and policies. Neither the Americans with Disabilities Act nor Section 504 applies to federal courts. In state and local courts, deaf and hard of hearing people enjoy rights to equal access under the ADA and Section 504 that are much broader than the protections available in federal courts. In federal courts, the Court Interpreter Act of 1979 largely governs the provision of an interpreter for a deaf defendant, party, or witness.[4]

State and Local Courts

Under the ADA and Section 504, deaf and hard of hearing people have the right to communicate effectively and to participate in proceedings conducted by all state and local courts.[5] Specifically, they are entitled to have courts provide auxiliary aids to enable them to understand the proceedings. These two federal laws protect *all* people participating in state and local court activities, including litigants, witnesses, jurors, spectators, and attorneys. They apply to proceedings in any state or local court, including civil, criminal, traffic, small claims, domestic relations, and juvenile courts.

The appropriate auxiliary aid depends on an individual's level of hearing, as well as the person's communication and literacy skills. For deaf and hard of hearing people who use sign language, the most effective auxiliary aid a court can provide is usually the service of qualified sign language interpreters trained in legal procedure and terminology. For deaf and hard of hearing people who do not use sign language and who have good levels of reading comprehension, the appropriate auxiliary aid may be the use of a computer-assisted, real-time transcription (CART) system. Through this system, a court reporter enters the words spoken during the proceeding into a computer, which simultaneously transcribes the words onto a computer screen to be read by the deaf or hard of hearing person. For other people, an oral interpreter may be needed to facilitate lipreading. For those who benefit from hearing aids, the appropriate auxiliary aid might be amplified or modified sound equipment or moving a trial to a small courtroom with good acoustics.

The U.S. Department of Justice has issued regulations explaining the requirements of both the ADA and Section 504.[6] In 1980 the Justice Department noted the following with respect to Section 504:

> Court systems receiving Federal financial assistance shall provide for the availability of qualified interpreters for civil and criminal court proceedings involving persons with hearing or speaking impairments. (Where a recipient has an obligation to provide qualified interpreters under this subpart, the recipient has the corresponding responsibility to pay for the services of the interpreters.)[7]

The Justice Department also noted that "court witnesses with hearing or speaking impairments have the right, independent of the right of defendants, to have interpreters available to them for their testimony."[8] Moreover, in its ADA regulations, the Justice Department requires state and local courts to provide auxiliary aids to ensure effective communication with deaf and hard of hearing individuals in all court proceedings:

(a) (1) A public entity shall take appropriate steps to ensure that communications with applicants, participants, members of the public, and companions with disabilities are as effective as communications with others.

(2) For purposes of this section, "companion" means a family member, friend, or associate of an individual seeking access to a service, program, or activity of a public entity, who, along with such individual, is an appropriate person with whom the public entity should communicate.

(b) (1) A public entity shall furnish appropriate auxiliary aids and services where necessary to afford individuals with disabilities, including applicants, participants, companions, and members of the public, an equal opportunity to participate in, and enjoy the benefits of, a service, program, or activity of a public entity.

(2) The type of auxiliary aid or service necessary to ensure effective communication will vary in accordance with the method of communication used by the individual; the nature, length, and complexity of the communication involved; and the context in which the communication is taking place. In determining what types of auxiliary aids and services are necessary, a public entity shall give primary consideration to the requests of individuals with disabilities. In order to be effective, auxiliary aids and services must be provided in accessible formats, in a timely manner, and in such a way as to protect the privacy and independence of the individual with a disability.[9]

The Justice Department regulation defines the term *auxiliary aids* for deaf and hard of hearing individuals as including qualified interpreters and CART services.[10] In its analysis of the regulation, the department uses the CART system as an example of an effective auxiliary aid or service in a courtroom for a person who is deaf or hard of hearing and uses speech to communicate.[11] The Justice Department regulation also makes it clear that the individual with a disability cannot be charged for the auxiliary aid provided by a state or local court:

> A public entity may not place a surcharge on a particular individual with a disability . . . to cover the costs of measures, such as the provision of auxiliary aids or program accessibility, that are required to provide that individual . . . with the nondiscriminatory treatment required by the Act or this part.[12]

Any states laws permitting state judges to assess the cost of interpreter services as "court costs" are in violation of the ADA. In its analysis to the ADA regulation, the Justice Department has explicitly addressed the issue of court costs:

> The Department [of Justice] has already recognized that imposition of the cost of courtroom interpreter services is impermissible under Section 504 . . . Accordingly, recouping the costs of interpreter services by assessing them as part of court costs would also be prohibited.[13]

Complaints against State and Local Courts

Despite the ADA and Section 504, some judges refuse to provide deaf and hard of hearing people with the equal access promised by law. In these instances, lawsuits against the courts and the judges have been necessary to ensure compliance. In Indiana, for instance, Cindy Clark filed a small claims action in a state court. She asked the judge to appoint a qualified interpreter at no cost. The judge refused, stating that "the court will hear evidence by way of written documents rather than verbal communication or signing." Clark sued the state of Indiana and the county court judge in a federal court, claiming discrimination under the ADA and Section 504. The case was settled when the Indiana Supreme Court agreed to amend its own trial rules in order to comply with the ADA. The county court agreed to provide an interpreter for Clark's small claims court proceeding and further agreed that the fee would not be assessed against Clark regardless of the outcome of the case.[14]

In Ohio, a deaf man was a defendant in a criminal proceeding in a county court. A county judge ordered him to pay more than $200 for the interpreter who was present during his hearings. The man filed a complaint in an Ohio federal court, claiming violations of the ADA and Section 504. In response to the lawsuit, the county judge entered an order relieving the man of the obligation to pay for interpreter fees. The county court also adopted a new policy that provided that "All parties and witnesses who appear before the court, who are deaf, shall be afforded a properly certified and trained interpreter at County expense . . . No interpreter's fee shall be taxed as court costs against any deaf parties or witness."[15]

The repercussions of a court's or a judge's failure to provide auxiliary aids and equal access are, in many cases, the denial of justice. As a result of violations of the ADA and Section 504 in the courtroom, deaf parents have unfairly and needlessly lost their children. In one child custody case, a court refused to provide real-time captioning or a suitable alternative during trial for a father who was unable to hear the proceedings.[16] In a case that truly gives meaning to the phrase "justice delayed is justice denied," the father did not see his daughter for five years. He brought a Title II ADA complaint against the county and the county court in a federal district court. The jury awarded him $400,000.

Even deaf lawyers have to fight for communication access so that they can litigate. Kentucky had an explicit policy of refusing to provide communication access (e.g., via interpreters) to deaf attorneys when they appeared for their court proceedings. Under Kentucky's discriminatory policy, Teri Mosier, a deaf attorney, was effectively limited in her ability to practice law.[17] The NAD and a private law firm filed an ADA and Section 504 lawsuit against Kentucky on Mosier's behalf. The defendants settled the federal complaint and agreed to update their policy to provide interpreters when necessary for deaf attorneys to be able to communicate effectively in court.

Deaf and hard of hearing jurors are also entitled to communication access in state courts. In *People v. Guzman,* the New York Supreme Court concluded that the presence of a deaf juror did not rob the criminal defendant's right to a fair trial.[18] However, some state courts have refused to accept deaf jurors despite federal laws. An Ohio court ruled that because a deaf juror was not able to discern the demeanor, speech patterns, and voice inflections of a key piece of evidence presented on an audiotape, she was not qualified to serve as a juror on this precise case.[19]

Federal Courts

It is ironic that deaf and hard of hearing participants in federal court have fewer rights to access than litigants in state courts. The ADA and Section 504 do not apply to the federal court system. However, there is some recourse for these participants in federal court proceedings. For instance, the Court Interpreter Act requires that, in any criminal or civil action initiated by the federal government, the court must appoint a qualified interpreter for a deaf party or witness.[20] Under this law, the service is paid for by the government, whether or not the person needing the service is indigent. When an interpreter is to be provided, the director of the Administrative Office of the United States Courts determines the qualifications required of court-appointed interpreters. Each district court must maintain a list of certified interpreters in the office of the clerk of the court. In preparing such lists, the director of court administration must consult organizations of and for deaf people, including the National Association of the Deaf and the Registry of Interpreters for the Deaf.[21] If an interpreter is unable to communicate effectively with the defendant, party, or witness, the court's presiding officer must dismiss that interpreter and obtain the services of another.

The shortcoming of this law is that it requires the appointment of interpreters only in criminal and civil cases initiated by the federal government. If, on the other hand, a private party files a suit, this law does not require the federal court to provide an interpreter. However, since 1996 the Administrative Office of the United States Courts addressed this shortcoming by extending interpreter services to *all* federal court proceedings. Section 255 of the *Guide to Judiciary Policy* provides as follows:

§ 255.10 General Policy
(a) As adopted in September 1995, it is the policy of the Judicial Conference that all federal courts provide reasonable accommodations to persons with communications disabilities (JCUS-SEP 95, p. 75). This policy provides for services in addition to those required by the Court Interpreters Act (28 U.S.C. § 1827).
(b) Under 28 U.S.C. § 1827(l), a judge *may* [emphasis in the original] provide a sign language interpreter for a party, witness or other participant in a judicial proceeding, whether or not the proceeding is instituted by the United States.
(c) Under Judicial Conference policy, a court *must* [emphasis in the original] provide sign language interpreters or other auxiliary aides and services to participants in federal court proceedings who are deaf, hearing-impaired or have communication disabilities and *may* [emphasis in the original] provide these services to spectators when deemed appropriate.
(d) For information on policies for employees with disabilities, see: Guide, Vol 12, Ch 2 (Fair Employment Practices).

§ 255.20 Sign Language Interpreters and Other Auxiliary Aids and Services
(a) Requirement
    Each federal court is required to provide, at judiciary expense, sign language interpreters or other appropriate auxiliary aids and services to participants in federal court proceedings who are deaf, hearing-impaired, or have other communications disabilities. The court will give primary consideration to a participant's choice of auxiliary aid or service.
(b) Real-time reporting
    (1) When deemed appropriate by a court, computer-assisted real-time reporting is one of the services that may be provided under these guidelines, but solely in furtherance of the limited purposes for which the guidelines have been adopted. Thus,

real-time reporting should be provided only for as long as necessary and for those specific purposes required by a participant; for example, only for the duration of a deaf witness's testimony.

(2) Real-time reporting is to be used solely to assist in communication and is not to be used in lieu of conventional means of producing the official record.

(3) Real-time services provided under these guidelines will be limited to a video display of spoken words, and may not include enhancements such as key-word searching or the provision of unedited daily transcripts.

(4) Courts may not use this policy as an authorization to purchase and install real-time court reporting equipment in the courtroom. Such purchase is governed by Judicial Conference policy on court reporting.

(c) Definitions

(1) "Participants" in court proceedings include parties, attorneys, and witnesses. The services called for under these guidelines are not required to be provided to spectators, although courts may elect to do so in situations when deemed appropriate, for example, a court may provide an interpreter to the deaf spouse of a defendant so that the spouse may follow the course of the trial.

(2) "Court proceedings" include trials, hearings, ceremonies and other public programs or activities conducted by a court.

(3) "Primary consideration" means that the court is to honor a participant's choice of auxiliary aid or service, unless it can show that another equally effective means of communication is available, or that use of the means chosen would result in a fundamental alteration in the nature of the court proceeding or an undue financial or administrative burden.

(4) "Auxiliary aids and services" include: qualified interpreters; assistive listening devices or systems; or other effective methods of making aurally delivered materials available to individuals with hearing impairments.

§ 255.30 Provision for and Payment of Juror Services

(a) When an individual is found to be legally qualified to serve as a juror, but has a communications disability, payment for services necessary to address the communications disability should be made from the jury fee appropriation.

(b) Services provided under these guidelines include a sign language interpreter or other appropriate auxiliary aids.

(c) The determination of whether a prospective juror with a communications disability is legally qualified to serve as a juror is one for the judgment of the trial court under the Jury Selection and Service Act, 28 U.S.C. §§ 1861, et seq., and that determination is not governed or affected by these guidelines.

§ 255.40 Procedures

(a) Each court is required to identify a specific office or individual(s) to serve as access coordinator from whom participants in court proceedings may request auxiliary aids or services.

  (1) The access coordinator must be familiar with the judiciary's policy of providing reasonable accommodations to persons with communications disabilities to ensure that the policy is properly implemented.

  (2) The access coordinator must have a ready working knowledge of the types of auxiliary aids and services available to serve the needs of disabled persons and of the local sources from which auxiliary aids and services may be procured.

  (3) Personnel in each court are to be instructed as to the judiciary's policy and the identity and location of the access coordinators in their particular court.

  (4) Each court will appropriately publicize the identity and location of its access coordinator through, for instance:
    + courthouse signs,
    + bulletin board announcements,
    + pamphlets, and
    + announcements in the local press.

(b) Courts may, but are not required to, establish specific procedures through which requests for auxiliary aid services are to be submitted, such as requiring that they be submitted to the access coordinator in writing or that they be submitted in advance of the court proceeding involved. Courts may also establish procedures through which persons dissatisfied with the court's proposed provision of auxiliary aids and services may seek review or reconsideration.

   (1) Any such procedures must be appropriately publicized.

   (2) These guidelines are not intended to extend or modify existing law.

§ 255.50 Reporting

In all situations in which services are provided under these guidelines, regardless of whether any costs are incurred, courts are to file reports with the AO on forms provided for this purpose. See: Guide, Vol 5, § 370.

§ 255.60 Funding

Except as noted above in § 255.30, payment for sign language interpreters or other auxiliary aids should be from the general authorization. See: Guide, Vol 5, § 410.[22]

As this policy guide indicates, the communication access services that must be provided for participants and jurors are not required for spectators. However, the federal courts could elect to do so in situations where they deem it appropriate. In addition, although a CART system may be provided, the policy requires that these services be provided only for the duration of a deaf or hard of hearing person's participation in the proceedings. Deaf and hard of hearing jurors are also entitled to communication access under this policy.

In addition to this policy guidance, at least one federal court has ruled that being deaf did not automatically disqualify a person from jury service.[23] According to the court, having an interpreter present did not mean a deaf juror did not meet the requirement of understanding and speaking English. Furthermore, the presence of an interpreter did not deprive the criminal defendant of his or her right to a fair trial. The court also found that a deaf juror's alleged inability to evaluate the demeanor of witnesses during their testimonies did not impair the juror's overall ability to perceive and evaluate evidence.

ATTORNEYS' OBLIGATIONS TO DEAF CLIENTS

Another key element to equal access in the legal system is the difficulty many deaf and hard of hearing people have in retaining lawyers who are able to respond to their clients' specialized needs while providing legal representation. In a profession where fact counts, it is crucial that lawyers and their clients be able to communicate freely and completely and to minimize misunderstandings. Yet, too many lawyers try to evade their legal obligations to provide effective communication with deaf and hard of hearing clients.

Every state has adopted rules of professional conduct that obligate lawyers to represent their clients competently and zealously. It is difficult to imagine how a lawyer who fails to communicate effectively with a client could satisfy this duty. In addition to this ethical responsibility, attorneys have a statutory duty to provide effective communication to deaf clients under Title III of the ADA, which grants people with disabilities the right to equal access to public accommodations.[24]

Title III of the ADA specifically includes lawyers' offices in the definition of public accommodations and requires them to provide deaf and hard of hearing clients with sign language interpreters and other auxiliary aids or services that are necessary for effective communication.[25] In the legal setting, lipreading and writing notes back and forth are seldom effective methods of communication with sign language users. The risk of miscommunication is too great in this context. An attorney who relies on these methods with clients who use ASL cannot be assured of communicating effectively or accurately with the client.[26]

The analysis to this regulation makes it clear that both Congress and the Justice Department expect "that public accommodation(s) will consult with the individual with a disability before providing a particular auxiliary aid or service."[27] The analysis further states that "It is not difficult to imagine a wide range of communications involving areas such as health, legal matters, and finances that would be sufficiently lengthy or complex to require an interpreter for effective communication."[28]

A public accommodation may avoid having to provide an auxiliary aid or service only if it can demonstrate that providing the aid or service would fundamentally alter the nature of the service or constitute an undue burden or expense. However, even if an attorney's office is able to demonstrate that a fundamental alteration would be required or an undue burden imposed in the provision of a particular auxiliary aid, the lawyer must be prepared to provide an alternative auxiliary aid.[29]

Whether or not the provision of a particular auxiliary aid would constitute an "undue burden" is not always a simple matter. The undue burden standard is applied on a case-by-case basis. Undue burden is not proven just by showing that the cost of the auxiliary aid is greater than the income the lawyer or other private business would receive from a deaf client. Instead, undue burden must be proven by a number of factors, including the financial resources of the law firm as a whole.[30] Therefore, it is possible for a lawyer to be responsible for providing auxiliary aids even for pro bono clients if the cost of the aid would not be an undue burden.

The Justice Department does not permit an attorney or other place of public accommodation to charge a person with a disability for the cost of the auxiliary aid.[31] Therefore, billing the deaf client for interpreter services as a "client cost" is not permissible. Title III of the ADA and the Justice Department's ADA regulations and analysis mandate that attorneys be responsible for ensuring effective communication with their deaf clients, including the costs thereof, and that costs may not be passed on to the client.

EQUAL ACCESS IN LAW ENFORCEMENT

Deaf and hard of hearing people are subject to gross violations of their personal and constitutional liberties if subjected to law enforcement without the assurance or provision of effective communication. If arrested for a crime, such individuals can face serious barriers when it comes to expressing innocence. A deaf or hard of hearing victim who is asked to tell the story of a rape or an assault without an interpreter is twice victimized. Unlike other arrestees, these persons might not be permitted to contact an attorney or family member simply because there is no effective way to do so due to the absence of accessible equipment. Although the ADA and Section 504 offer protections to ensure that these persons will have equal access to communication in such situations, those measures are meaningless if law enforcement agencies are unaware of the requirement to provide this access.

Effective Communication under the ADA

Title II of the ADA prohibits discrimination against people with disabilities in state and local government services, programs, and activities.[32] Law enforcement agencies are covered under Title II because they are programs of state or local governments. The ADA affects all of the ways that police officers and deputies interact with the public, including but not limited to receiving citizen complaints; questioning witnesses; arresting, booking, and holding suspects; and providing emergency services.[33]

Pursuant to Title II, police officers must ensure effective communication with individuals who are deaf or hard of hearing. The form of communication to be provided—whether it be a qualified sign language interpreter, written communications, or something else—depends on the situation and the parties involved. If a deaf person asks a police officer for directions to a destination, a notepad and pencil might be sufficient. However, if a deaf person who has primary fluency in sign language is being interrogated, the law enforcement officer involved may have to provide an interpreter to ensure effective communication. It also depends on the specific communication needs of the deaf or hard of hearing individual, given that the person may not know sign language and may prefer lipreading.

According to Title II regulations, law enforcement officers should consider the nature, length, complexity, and context of the communication and the deaf or hard of hearing person's usual mode of communication when determining whether an interpreter or some other form of auxiliary aid or service is necessary for effective communication.[34] In addition, law enforcement officers must give primary consideration to the requests of deaf and hard of hearing individuals with respect to what auxiliary aids or services they require for effective communication.[35] The Department of Justice cautions that "Police officers should be careful about miscommunication in the absence of a qualified interpreter. A nod of the head may be an attempt to appear cooperative in the midst of a misunderstanding, rather than consent or a confession of wrongdoing."[36]

Title II regulations defines the term "qualified interpreter" to mean "an interpreter who, via a video remote interpreting (VRI) service or an on-site appearance, is able to interpret effectively, accurately, and impartially, both receptively and expressively, using any necessary specialized vocabulary. Qualified interpreters include, for example, sign language interpreters, oral transliterators, and cued-language transliterators."[37] The regulations also state that it is impermissible to ask deaf or hard of hearing persons to provide their own interpreter or to ask any person accompanying them to interpret except in rare circumstances.[38] The Department of Justice goes further in its guidance material, advising against the "use [of] family members or children as interpreters . . . [as t]hey may lack the vocabulary or the impartiality needed to interpret effectively."[39]

Example Cases

Oklahoma state law requires that interpreters be provided to deaf defendants upon arrest.[40] In one instance, however, a deaf man arrested for a misdemeanor was kept in jail for two days without being given an interpreter. The Oklahoma Supreme Court found that the state law applies to city police departments and that because the deaf man could not understand his rights or communicate with those who could help him, he was forced to stay in jail longer than a hearing person in the same situation. The city was found to be in violation of state law.[41]

In another case, Joseph Serio, a deaf man, alleged that the city of Milwaukee and its police officers violated Section 504 by failing to provide an interpreter throughout the course of his arrest and subsequent processing.[42] The officers were investigating Serio's alleged violation of an antiharassment restraining order secured by his former girlfriend. When the officers went to Serio's home, they unsuccessfully attempted to communicate with him through his hearing son. They then attempted to communicate with Serio by using written notes, which also proved unsuccessful. Serio asked for an interpreter, but his request was denied. The police officers arrested him for violating the restraining order and took him to jail. He made at least one written request for an interpreter, but an interpreter was never provided.

Serio was released on bail the next day. He sued the city of Milwaukee and the police officers, claiming that they violated Section 504 by failing to provide an interpreter. A jury awarded Serio $65,000 for compensatory damages and $90,000 for punitive damages. A Wisconsin appeals court affirmed, finding that "credible evidence was presented to the jury that at several points during his arrest and processing Serio requested an . . . interpreter [and t]he City never provided one." The court rejected the city's request for a new trial and did not accept the city's argument that having interpreters present during the trial made the jury unfairly sympathetic to Serio and that the excessive punitive damage award was not "in the interest of justice."[43]

INTERPRETER COMPETENCE

Securing qualified interpreters in law enforcement and court environments is critical. In its analysis of regulations for both Section 504 and the ADA, the Justice Department determined that recipients of federal funds as well as state and local governments (which include the court systems and the police) must use qualified interpreters to ensure that deaf and hard of hearing defendants are advised of their rights and receive a fair trial. Given the complex terminology used in courtrooms and other legal settings, the standard for a qualified interpreter is more stringent and thus requires more formal training in the intricate legal terms and concepts to ensure effective and accurate communication with deaf and hard of hearing individuals.

Despite the clear mandate for qualified interpreters who are able to interpret effectively, accurately, and impartially, police departments have attempted to use staff members who claim to know sign language to act as an "interpreter." A person who can only fingerspell or who has taken only one or two classes in sign language is not qualified. It is impossible for a person with such limited knowledge of sign language to communicate the complex information typically conveyed in legal settings.

In Virginia, where state law requires the appointment of qualified interpreters in court matters, an unskilled and uncertified interpreter was provided to a deaf rape victim testifying at a preliminary hearing.[44] The judge proceeded with the hearing even though the interpreter informed the court that he was not skilled in sign language. When the prosecutor asked the victim what had happened, she gave the sign for "forced intercourse." The interpreter translated this sign erroneously as "made love," an altogether different sign and concept. The legal effect of the interpreter's mistake was devastating. Later, when the victim answered "blouse" in response to the prosecutor's question about what she had been wearing, the interpreter told the court, "short blouse," creating the impression that the victim had dressed provocatively. At the jury trial, a truly qualified interpreter was provided.

Effective enforcement of the right to a qualified interpreter is extremely important. It will require a continuing effort to raise the awareness of judicial and administrative judges and court clerks about relevant laws and the communication patterns of deaf people.

MIRANDA RIGHTS

In the landmark decision *Miranda v. Arizona*, the U.S. Supreme Court recognized that questioning by police in the station house or jail is inherently coercive and undermines the Fifth Amendment privilege against self-incrimination.[45] As a result of this decision, police are now required to "effectively inform" accused people of their constitutional rights before any questioning can take place. If an accused person wants to waive his or her rights, the waiver must be voluntary, knowing, and intelligent. Without the use of a qualified interpreter, most deaf people would not be able to fully understand their rights, and any waiver of these would not be voluntary, knowing, and intelligent.

The standard written advice-of-rights form given to suspects before questioning requires a sixth-to eighth-grade reading comprehension level. The listening comprehension level of people who can hear usually exceeds their reading comprehension level.[46] However, the reading level required by the *Miranda* warnings and advice-of-rights forms remains far above the reading comprehension of many deaf people, for whom English is a second language. Police officers need to ensure that deaf people receive an explanation of their rights through the use of a qualified sign language interpreter.

The conceptual and linguistic difficulties posed by the *Miranda* requirement cannot be overcome by a direct word-for-word translation into sign language. As is true for translations between two languages, concepts presented in English can be difficult to present in ASL, and vice versa. Moreover, fingerspelling important legal terms will not generally increase understanding, especially if the accused deaf person has a low reading level.[47] To be understood, the complex English terms and their meanings must be carefully and clearly explained in clear ASL concepts. A qualified interpreter is fundamental at this point. Appropriate translations by qualified interpreters suited for both the individual involved and the legal situation allow deaf defendants to understand these rights.

One case illustrates the problem of communicating the *Miranda* advice of rights to a deaf defendant. David Barker, a deaf man with a reading comprehension level at grade 2.8, was charged with murder.[48] The charges were dropped, but when Barker was in custody for unrelated charges a year later, police questioned him extensively about the original murder through written notes. The police questioned him without either a sign language interpreter or advice of counsel. After several hours of questioning, Barker signed the *Miranda* waiver of rights and then a confession. When Barker was interrogated a month later with an interpreter, he showed confusion when answering questions. Asked whether he had understood the *Miranda* advice of rights, he replied in sign language, "a little bit." He also referred to promises allegedly made by the police guaranteeing hospitalization.

The court suppressed the first confession as being involuntary and suppressed a second confession on the grounds that the original promise of hospitalization continued to influence him, making the second confession involuntary. The court wrote as follows:

> There was additionally offered testimony by experts in the field of sign language for the deaf that the expression "Constitutional rights," being an abstract idea, is extremely difficult to convey to the deaf, especially, as in this case, when the educational level of the individual is so curtailed. There was testimony that the warning, "Do you understand that you have the right to have an attorney present at all times during the questioning?" may well have been signed, and understood as "Do you understand it is all *right* to have an attorney present?" which obviously is far from the actual portent of the warning.[49]

ACCESS TO PRISON PROGRAMS AND ACTIVITIES

Once in prison to serve their terms, deaf people are frequently denied basic due process rights and access to rehabilitation programs simply because prison staff cannot communicate with them. Both Title II of the ADA and Section 504 apply to state prisons, given that they receive federal funding and are agencies of state government.

Nevertheless, a number of important discrimination complaints have been lodged by deaf inmates. For example, a deaf and blind prisoner in a state prison in Arizona could not communicate effectively with prison guards and other prison personnel. He could not talk to prison counselors or medical staff when he was ill. He was charged with breaking a prison rule that he was never properly informed of, and he could not understand the testimony against him at the disciplinary hearing or explain his version of what had happened. When he sued the state prison system, the case was dismissed by an Arizona federal court. The U.S. Court of Appeals for the Ninth Circuit held that the prisoner could bring his complaint to court under Section 504 and the Fourteenth Amendment of the Constitution. The court upheld the Justice Department's Section 504 regulations, which require prison systems to provide auxiliary aids for deaf individuals to give them equal access to prison programs and activities.[50]

In Maryland, a deaf inmate in the state prison system was denied an interpreter at a disciplinary hearing and was therefore unable to present a defense.[51] The disciplinary board took away "good time" days that would have led to earlier release, and it transferred him from his minimum security location to a maximum security facility for psychological evaluation. The state psychologist there could not communicate with him and therefore could not competently evaluate him. The prisoner filed a lawsuit in a Maryland federal court requesting a court order requiring the state to provide an interpreter to any deaf inmate who faces administrative charges. The suit argued that, without a qualified interpreter, a deaf inmate who uses sign language cannot testify or question witnesses and is thereby denied his or her constitutional right to a fair hearing.

The federal court approved a consent decree that provided interpreters for deaf prisoners in many situations of prison life:

+ at adjustment team hearings
+ when officials give notice that a disciplinary report is being written
+ whenever a deaf inmate is provided counseling or psychiatric, psychological, or medical care
+ in any on-the-job or vocational training or any educational program

This consent decree is an excellent model of how to provide deaf prisoners both their basic due-process rights and access to needed counseling, medical services, and rehabilitation programs.[52]

In response to the discrimination complaints brought by prisoners with disabilities, state and local governments began challenging these lawsuits on the ground that neither the ADA nor Section 504 applied to prisons. In 1998 a unanimous U.S. Supreme Court held that the ADA did in fact apply to prisons and that the prisons had to make their services, programs, and activities accessible to inmates with disabilities.[53] Immediately after that decision, a Texas federal court applied the same legal principle to a deaf person who had been arrested. The arrestee alleged that city police officers failed to provide an interpreter at the time of his arrest, that he appeared before two different judges for probable cause and bond hearings without interpreter services, and that he remained in a county lockup for two weeks without interpreter services. The defendants contended that the ADA and Section 504 did not apply to pretrial arrest and detention, but the Texas federal court disagreed and held that the ADA applies to all programs, activities, and services of state and local governments.[54]

An increasing number of cases have been filed against state prisons for failing to provide effective communication in all aspects of prison as well as equal access to programs and services such as employment opportunities. A deaf man filed suit and later settled for $150,000 with the Oregon Department of Corrections for failing to provide interpreters and limiting his employment opportunities to menial jobs.[55] Cases have also been brought against the federal prisons for similar violations.[56]

Telecommunications Access

Title II of the ADA and Section 504 require equal access to telecommunications in all state and local government agencies where the public has telephone access. The definition of auxiliary aids and services includes various forms of telecommunications as necessary to provide access to telephone services, such as TTYs, captioned telephones, and videophones.[57] With the advent of videophones and captioned telephones, however, TTYs are increasingly obsolete, and many deaf and hard of hearing individuals no longer use them. As a result, when deaf and hard of hearing individuals need to make telephone calls from jails or prisons, a TTY may not be of any benefit, and videophones or other telecommunications devices may be required.

In fact, a group of deaf inmates filed a lawsuit against the Virginia Department of Corrections for failure to provide videophones so that they could make calls to family, attorneys, and others on an equal basis as their hearing peers.[58] When the case was settled in 2010, it marked the first time a state prison began providing videophones to deaf inmates, and further litigation is occurring to ensure the same happens throughout the country.

Similarly, deaf individuals must have direct access to 911 or similar emergency telephone services, including emergency response centers, which must be equipped to receive calls from TTYs and computer modem users without relying on third parties or state relay services. In addition, public safety answering points (PSAPs) must accept relay calls as well, pursuant to the ADA.[59]

In addition to TTYs and relay calls, several jurisdictions are experimenting with text as an alternative method of contacting PSAPs in case of emergency. Such communities include Frederick, Maryland, and Vermont. As this book is going to press, the Federal Communications Commission has engaged in notices of rule making seeking to mandate text-to-911 capability by December 31, 2014.[60]

Notes

1. *Terry v. State*, 21 Ala. App. 100, 105 So. 386, 387 (Ct. App. 1925).
2. 28 C.F.R. §35.160(b); 75 *Fed. Reg.* 56163.
3. 28 C.F.R. §35.130(f). See analysis by the U.S. Department of Justice at 56 *Fed. Reg.* 35,705 (July 26, 1991). Imposition of the cost of courtroom interpreter services as court costs is impermissible under Section 504.
4. 28 U.S.C. §1827.
5. 42 U.S.C. §12131. See also 29 U.S.C. §794.
6. See "Nondiscrimination on the Basis of Disability in State and Local Government Services," ADA Title II, Part 35, (September 15, 2010); "Communication Access with Police and Law

Enforcement," 28 C.F.R. Part 35, 56 *Fed. Reg.* 35,694 (July 26, 1991), updated 56 *Fed. Reg.* 35,716. See also "Nondiscrimination; Equal Employment Opportunity; Policies and Procedures," 28 C.F.R. Part 42, 45 *Fed. Reg.* 37,820 (June 3, 1990).

7. 45 *Fed. Reg.* at 37,630.
8. 45 *Fed. Reg.* at 37,631.
9. 28 C.F.R. §35.160.
10. 28 C.F.R. §35.104.
11. 56 *Fed. Reg.* at 35,712.
12. 28 C.F.R. §35.130(f).
13. 56 *Fed. Reg.* at 38,705–38,706.
14. *Clark v. Bridges*, No. IP 93-877-C (D. Ind. Sept. 23, 1994).
15. *Shafer v. Judkins*, No. C-193-887 (S.D. Ohio, Aug. 16, 1994).
16. Ibid.
17. *Mosier v. Kentucky*, 675 F. Supp. 2d 693 (E.D. Ky 2009).
18. *People v. Guzman*, 478 N.Y.S. 2d 455 (N.Y. Sup. Ct. 1984), aff'd, 76 N.Y. 2d 1, 555 N.E. 2d 259 (1990).
19. *State v. Speer*, 124 Ohio St. 3d 564 (Ohio Sup. Ct. 2010).
20. 28 U.S.C. §1827.
21. National Association of the Deaf, 8630 Fenton Street, Suite 820, Silver Spring, MD 20910, (301) 587-1788, nadinfo@nad.org, www.nad.org; Registry of Interpreters for the Deaf, 333 Commerce Street, Alexandria, VA 22314, (703) 838-0030, www. rid.org.
22. Judicial Conference Policy and Procedures, General Management and Administration, vol. 5, ch. 2, §§255.10–255.60 (Services to the Hearing Impaired and Others with Communication Disabilities), http://www.uscourts.gov/FederalCourts/ UnderstandingtheFederalCourts/DistrictCourts/CourtInterpreters/ court-interpreter-guidance.aspx.
23. *United States v. Dempsey*, 830 F. 2d 1084 (10th Circuit, 1987).
24. 42 U.S.C. §§12181–12183.
25. 42 U.S.C. §12181(7)(F).
26. According to 28 C.F.R. §36.303(c)(1), "A public accommodation shall furnish appropriate auxiliary aids and services where necessary to ensure effective communication with individuals with disabilities."
27. See 56 *Fed. Reg.* at 35,567, quoting H.R. 485, 101st Cong., 2d Sess., pt. 2, at 107 (1990).
28. 56 *Fed. Reg.* at 35,567.
29. 28 C.F.R. §36.303(g).
30. 28 C.F.R. §36.104.
31. 28 C.F.R. §36.301(c).

32. 28 C.F.R. §§35.101–35.102.
33. 28 C.F.R. §35.130.
34. 28 C.F.R. §35.160(b)(2). See also U.S. Department of Justice, Civil Rights Division, "Effective Communication," January 31, 2014, http://www.ada.gov/effective-comm.htm.
35. 28 C.F.R. §35.160(b)(2).
36. U.S. Department of Justice, Civil Rights Division, "Communicating with People Who Are Deaf or Hard of Hearing: ADA Guide for Law Enforcement Officers," January 2006, http://www.ada.gov/lawenfcomm.htm. See also U.S. Department of Justice, Civil Rights Division, "Guide for Law Enforcement Officers: When In Contact With People Who Are Deaf or Hard of Hearing," http://www.ada.gov/wendell_city/wendell_attd.htm.
37. 28 C.F.R. §35.104.
38. 28 C.F.R. §35.160(c).
39. U.S. Department of Justice, Civil Rights Division, "Communicating with People Who Are Deaf or Hard of Hearing: ADA Guide for Law Enforcement Officers."
40. 63 Oklahoma St. T. §2410.
41. *Kiddy v. City of Oklahoma City,* 576 P. 2d 298 (Okla. Sup. Ct. 1978).
42. *Serio v. City of Milwaukee,* 186 Wis. 2d 575, 522 N.W. 2d 36 (Wisc. Ct. App. 1994).
43. Ibid.
44. *Commonwealth v. Edmonds* (Va. Cir. Ct., Staunton, 1975).
45. *Miranda v. Arizona,* 384 U.S. 436 (1966).
46. McCay Vernon, Lawrence J. Raifman, and Sheldon F. Greenberg, "The Miranda Warnings and the Deaf Suspect," *Behavioral Sciences and the Law* 14 (1996): 121–35; McCay Vernon, "Violation of Constitutional Rights: The Language-Impaired Person and the Miranda Warnings," *Journal of Rehabilitation of the Deaf* 11 (4): 1–8.
47. McCay Vernon and Joan Colely, "Violation of Constitutional Rights: The Language-Impaired Person and the Miranda Warnings" April 1978, https://www.courts.wa.gov/programs_orgs/pos_interpret/content/signLanguageMaterials/VernonandCole.pdf.
48. *State of Maryland v. Barker,* Crim. nos. 17,995 and 19,518 (Md. Cir. Ct., Dec. 8, 1977).
49. Ibid.
50. *Bonner v. Lewis,* 857 F. 2d 559 (9th Cir. 1988).
51. *Pyles v. Kamka,* 491 F. Supp. 204 (D. Md. 1980).
52. Ibid. See also *Clarkson v. Coughlin,* 898 F. Supp. 1019 (S.D.N.Y. 1995); *Duffy v. Riveland,* 98 F. 3d 447 (9th Cir. 1996).

53. *Pennsylvania Department of Corrections v. Yeskey,* 524 U.S. 206, 118 U.S. 1952 (1998).
54. *Gordon v. City of Houston, Harris County, and State of Texas,* No. 98-0394 (S.D. Tex. June 18, 1998).
55. *Baldridge v. Oregon Department of Corrections,* Case No. 1204-04976 (Multnomah County Dist. Ct. 2012).
56. See, for example, *Heyer v. United States Bureau of Prisons,* Case No. 5:11-CV-318 (E.D. N.C., 2011).
57. 28 C.F.R. §35.104.
58. *Minnis v. Virginia Department of Corrections,* No. 1:10-CV-96, U.S. District Court (E.D. Va. 2010), settlement.
59. 28 C.F.R. §35.161.
60. See Federal Communications Commission, "Facilitating the Deployment of Text-to-911 and Other NG 911 Apps," May 12, 2014, http://www.fcc.gov/document/facilitating-deployment-text-911-and-other-ng-911-apps; Federal Communications Commission "Text-to-911 Policy Statement and Second FNPRM," January 31, 2014, http://www.fcc.gov/document/text-911-policy-statement-and-second-fnprm.

Chapter 10

Video Media

Television has become our major source of entertainment, news, and information. The Nielsen Company reports that the average American watches nearly five hours of television each day.[1] Americans are also increasingly viewing televised media on the Internet and mobile devices. Without captioning, however, televised and video media provide little benefit or enjoyment for individuals who are deaf or hard of hearing. Captions provide essential access to national and worldwide current events, local and community affairs, and entertainment, bringing this population into the cultural and political mainstream of our society. Federal captioning legislation has made it possible for these viewers to have access to nearly all forms of television programming and a significant amount of online programming.

THE BENEFITS OF CAPTIONING

Captioned programming has made it possible for millions of people who are deaf or hard of hearing to see what is being broadcast on televised media. Televised captioning has taken two forms: *open captioning,* which involves broadcasting captions on a regular television signal to all receivers and which cannot be turned off by the viewer, and *closed captioning,* which involves transmitting the captions on a special television signal that requires the use of a decoder-adapter on the receiver. Today almost all captions are closed.

The potential audience that can benefit from closed captioning is quite significant. At the time the Telecommunications Act of 1996 was passed, the National Captioning Institute (NCI) estimated that nearly 100 million Americans would directly benefit from closed-captioned TV.[2] This estimate included 28 million deaf and hard of hearing persons, 30 million Americans for whom English is a second language,[3] 12 million young children learning to read, 27 million illiterate adults,[4] and 3.7 million remedial readers.

Studies have consistently demonstrated the benefits of captioning for children and adults who are learning English or learning to read. A report commissioned by the Pew Charitable Trust in Philadelphia found that closed captioning has "a startling effect" on non-English-speaking children's ability to learn English words.[5] Most of the students in the study were from Southeast Asia. Similarly, results of a study at the University of Maryland showed that captioning improved word recognition for students with learning disabilities.[6] In addition, a Los Angeles English teacher turned off the sound on closed-captioned programs to force her high school students to read the captions in order to understand the television shows. She reported marked improvement in the students' literacy skills.[7]

The number of senior citizens with hearing disabilities who are taking advantage of closed captions is also growing. It is well established that the population of the United States as a whole is aging. According to the Department of Health and Human Services, the share of Americans over sixty-five years of age increased by 18 percent between 2000 and 2011, an increase of 6.3 million people, and the number of Americans forty-five to sixty-four years of age, who will reach sixty-five in the next two decades, increased by 33 percent.[8] At the same time, researchers at Gallaudet University estimate that more than half of all the deaf and hard of hearing people in our country are over sixty-five.[9] A significant number of these individuals will require closed captioning to benefit from television programing.

THE HISTORY OF TELEVISED CAPTIONING

In 1972 the Public Broadcasting Service (PBS), a nonprofit, non-commercial television network, first introduced captioning with the nationally broadcast cooking show *The French Chef.* The captioning was done by WGBH, the PBS station in Boston, Massachusetts. This program and a few others available only on public television had open captions. By late 1973 WGBH was also providing open captions for the *ABC Evening News,* a half-hour program that daily took five staff people five hours to caption.

In 1972 PBS began developing a closed-captioning system.[10] In 1975 PBS filed a petition with the FCC to reserve a segment of the television broadcast signal known as "Line 21" for transmitting closed captions. Line 21 is the last line in the vertical blanking interval (VBI) before the actual television picture begins. Television closed captions are included in this video signal as invisible data. The captions are then decoded and generated into visual characters that are displayed on the television screen through a television set with a built-in decoder chip or a separate decoding device.

Since 1976 the FCC has reserved Line 21 for closed-captioned transmissions. In 1979 Congress created the nonprofit National Captioning Institute to offer closed-captioning services to the broadcast television industry using Line 21.[11] Closed-captioned television services began the following year, when the NCI entered into a cooperative agreement with ABC, NBC, PBS, and Sears, Roebuck and Co.[12] Under this agreement, NBC, ABC, and PBS each captioned sixteen hours of programming per week, and Sears manufactured and sold decoders. In 1984 CBS also began transmitting closed captions using both Line 21 and its own teletext technologies.[13] Over the next decade, the number of television programs with captions grew dramatically, and by 1989 the entire prime-time schedule on CBS, NBC, and ABC was captioned.[14] In all, by 1990 approximately 290 hours of programming were closed-captioned each week.[15]

FEDERAL LEGISLATION

Despite the significant growth in captioned programming in the 1980s, the vast majority of cable programming, local news programming, late-night programming, and daytime programming remained without captioning as late as 1990. In 1991 approximately 72 percent of all Americans listed television as their primary news source.[16] However, only 150 out of 1,450 broadcast affiliates closed-captioned their local news programs that year.[17]

Many attributed the networks' resistance to increasing the number of captioning hours to the fact that only a limited number of Americans owned devices that could decode captions on their televisions. In fact, in order to decode captions in the 1980s, individuals were required to purchase expensive and cumbersome external decoder equipment that connected to their televisions. The cost and difficulties of installing these decoders kept sales down, and as of June 1990, only three hundred thousand decoders had been sold to the American public.[18] With so small a viewing public, many networks did not have the commercial incentive to fund new captioned programs. For example, in proceedings before the Commission on Education of the Deaf (COED) in the 1980s, ABC claimed that increased decoder usage would be necessary for captioning to become self-sustaining:

> [If] decoders were more widely used and viewership to grow, the marketplace can be relied upon to increase captioning because more viewers would be reached at a decreased per capita cost. Increased decoder ownership—not just more captioning—is required for a strong, self-sustaining captioning service.[19]

In response, the COED recommended that Congress pass a law requiring all new televisions to have built-in decoder circuitry capable of receiving and displaying closed captions.[20]

CAPTIONING DECODERS

In an effort to expand the caption-viewing audience and thereby create the necessary economic incentives for networks to caption more of their programs, Congress heeded the COED recommendation. In 1990 it enacted the Television Decoder Circuitry Act (TDCA).[21] The new law required all television sets with screens thirteen inches or larger, manufactured in or imported into the United States after July 1, 1993, to be capable of displaying closed-captioned television transmissions without the aid of external equipment.[22] This meant that televisions of this size would have to be equipped with internal decoder circuitry, which came to be known as a "decoder chip." In part, the law was patterned after the All Channel Receiver Act of 1962, which had mandated the inclusion of UHF tuners in all television sets.[23] Prior to that law, UHF transmissions had also been available to consumers only through a special adapter attached to their televisions.

Passage of the TDCA did in fact result in the growth of the captioning audience. By 1995 twenty-five million television sets equipped with decoder circuitry had been sold in the United States, providing closed captioning to as many as sixty million American homes. After passage of the TDCA, the number of captioned programs also increased somewhat. In the early 1990s captioning was added to certain children's programs, late-night talk shows, national sports programs, and premium cable stations.

Pursuant to the TDCA, the FCC has adopted display standards for built-in closed-captioning decoder circuitry.[24] These standards are intended to enable the television viewer to enjoy the benefits of the latest innovative technologies for high-quality closed captioning. For example, the FCC requires the use of technology that allows captions to appear anywhere on the screen. This feature allows for better identification of who is speaking during a television program. Additionally, several features that had proven effective in the separate decoder, such as a black background, are now required in new televisions containing the decoder circuitry.[25]

Because of the rapid changes in television technology, the drafters of the TDCA sought to make certain that any new television technologies, such as high-definition and other forms of digital TV, would be capable of transmitting closed captions. A section was included in the TDCA requiring the FCC to take appropriate action to ensure that as new technologies are developed, closed captioning will continue to be available to television viewers without the need to use a separate decoder.[26]

On July 21, 2000, the FCC heeded this legislative directive and amended its rules to require closed-captioning display capability in digital television receivers.[27] As a result, digital television receivers with picture screens larger than thirteen inches, as well as those with widescreen displays measuring at least 7.8 inches vertically, were required to include built-in, closed-captioning decoder circuitry as of July 1, 2002.[28] The FCC rules also include provisions allowing users to choose and alter the color, size, font, background opacity, and character edges of their captioning on digital captioning decoders.[29]

Section 203(a) of the Twenty-First Century Communications and Video Accessibility Act of 2010 (CVAA) expanded coverage to smaller television screens by requiring that an apparatus designed to receive or play back video programming and that uses a picture screen of any size be equipped with built-in caption decoder circuitry or the capability of displaying captioned video programming. However, this requirement does not apply if the picture screen is smaller than thirteen inches and if complying with the requirements is not achievable.[30] For more information, see the later section on IP Closed Captioning.

CLOSED CAPTIONING ON TELEVISION

Congressional Action

In the early 1990s Congress decided to revisit federal requirements for the provision of cable services to the American public. Deaf and hard of hearing consumers seized this opportunity to secure a provision in the pending bill to expand television captioning requirements. They successfully pointed to the cable industry's consistent failure to caption more of its programs. In response, Congress enacted Section 305 of the Telecommunications Act in 1996, establishing extensive requirements for the provision of closed captions on television programming.[31]

The 1996 Telecommunications Act applied the new captioning mandates to all programming providers and owners that transmit video programming to customers' homes, including broadcasters, cable operators, satellite operators, and other programming distributors. It directed the FCC to set up a transition schedule for captioning two categories of television programming: (1) *new programming* (programming first published or exhibited after the effective date of the FCC's captioning rules) and (2) *prerule programming* (programming first published or exhibited prior to the effective date of such FCC rules). Congress set different access standards for these two categories, requiring television programmers both to make all new programming "fully accessible" through the provision of closed captions and to "maximize" the accessibility of prerule programming. This latter category includes, for example, old reruns, as well as new made-for-TV movies that were shown before the FCC's rules became effective. As noted later, the FCC's captioning rules became effective on January 1, 1998, setting the dividing line for the new and prerule categories.

Section 305 authorized the FCC to exempt certain types of programming from the captioning requirements. Specifically, Congress gave the FCC permission to exempt programs under the following three conditions:

1. The FCC may exempt, by rule, closed captioning on programs, classes of programs, or services if the provision of captions would be economically burdensome to the video programming provider or owner of that programming.
2. The FCC may exempt closed captioning where the provision of captions would be inconsistent with contracts in effect on February 8, 1996.
3. The FCC may grant individual exemptions from the closed-captioning requirements in response to petitions for such exemptions, where the provision of captions would result in an undue burden for a video programming provider or owner.

FCC Captioning Order

On August 22, 1997, the FCC established an elaborate schedule of deadlines by which compliance with the captioning mandates was to be achieved, together with permissible exemptions from the captioning rules.[32] Dissatisfied with many of the possible exemptions, the National Association of the Deaf and several other consumer groups challenged the rules, asking the FCC to strengthen the requirements for captioning access. Among other things, these groups asked the FCC not to limit captioning to only 95 percent of new programming and not to exempt Spanish language programming, overnight programming, and short advertisements. Yet at the same time, several television stations requested that the FCC impose even more exemptions than were contained in the 1997 order. For example, networks sought exemptions for home shopping programming, all instructional programming on public television stations, and interactive game shows.

On September 17, 1998, the FCC rejected virtually all requests by networks for new exemptions and granted several of the consumer requests for enhanced captioning access.[33] The final FCC rules concern new, prerule, and Spanish-language programming.

New Programming

As of January 1, 2006, the FCC requires that 100 percent of all new, nonexempt television programming be captioned.[34] The FCC decided that, in order to meet this obligation, beginning January 1, 1998, each channel was required to caption (during each calendar quarter) the following: 450 hours of programming within the first two years (by December 31, 2001), 900 hours within four years, and 1,350 hours within six years. The remaining programming that was not exempt had to be captioned within eight years.[35]

If a station already captioned more programming than it was required by the transition schedule, it was *not* permitted to reduce the amount of captioning in accordance with the above schedules. Rather, programming providers had to continue providing captioning "at a level substantially the same" as the average level they provided captioning during the first six months of 1997.[36]

Prerule Programming

As of January 1, 2008, the FCC requires programmers to caption 75 percent of all prerule programming,[37] at least 30 percent of such programming had to be captioned by January 1, 2003.[38]

The FCC has yet to reevaluate its decision to require captioning for only 75 percent of this type of programming.

Spanish-Language Programming

As of January 1, 2010, the FCC requires programmers to caption 100 percent of their new, nonexempt Spanish-language programs and 75 percent of their nonexempt, prerule programs after January 1, 2012.[39] The FCC adopted benchmarks for this type of programming as follows: 450 hours of *new, nonexempt* programming per channel had be captioned during each calendar quarter by the end of 2003; 900 hours had to be captioned by the end of 2006; and 1,350 hours had to be captioned by the end of 2009. Thirty percent of *prerule nonexempt* programming had to be captioned beginning January 1, 2005.

Exemptions

To avoid imposing an economic burden on program providers, the FCC has exempted the following types of programming from all of the captioning requirements:

- all advertisements under five minutes in duration
- late-night programming shown between the hours of 2 a.m. and 6 a.m. local time
- programming in a language other than English or Spanish
- primarily textual programming, such as program channel schedules and community bulletin boards
- promotional programming and brief programming used as a bridge between full-length programs
- public service announcements (PSAs) under ten minutes in duration; however, all federally funded PSAs, regardless of length, must be captioned as mandated under the ADA
- locally produced and distributed nonnews programming with limited repeat value, such as parades and high school sports
- video programming produced for the instructional television fixed service, which is distributed to individual educational institutions, and locally produced instructional programming that is narrowly distributed to individual educational institutions
- nonvocal musical programming such as a symphony or ballet
- new networks during the first four years of their operation[40]

Small programming providers that have annual gross revenues of up to $3 million are exempted altogether from the closed-captioning rules.[41] Moreover, all programming providers are permitted to limit their expenditures on captioning to 2 percent of their annual gross revenues.[42]

In addition to the foregoing exemptions, programming providers may petition the FCC for individual exemptions from the captioning requirements if they can show that compliance with these requirements would result in an undue burden (be "economically burdensome").[43] After receiving fewer than seventy-five undue burden petitions between 1997 and mid-2005, the FCC received about six hundred undue burden petitions between October 2005 and August 2006.[44] The FCC granted individual exemptions to Anglers for Christ Ministries, Inc., New Beginning Ministries, and then 301 others under the *Anglers Order,* most of which were never placed on public notice prior to being granted.[45] In November 2006 the FCC placed 494 petitions on public notice.[46] The NAD and other organizations strongly opposed nearly all of the petitions placed on public notice. In October 2011 the FCC reversed 298 of the exemptions granted under the *Anglers Order,* clarified its standard of review, and replaced "undue burden" with "economically burdensome."[47]

To make an economically burdensome determination, the FCC must consider the following four factors: (1) the nature and cost of the closed captions for the programming; (2) the impact on the operation of the provider or program owner; (3) the financial resources of the provider or program owner; and (4) the type of operations of the provider or program owner.[48] Petitioners are also required to meet specific evidentiary standards. The NAD and other organizations continue to oppose petitions that fall short of the economically burdensome standard or lack sufficient evidence that compliance with the closed-captioning requirements would be economically burdensome.

In January 2011 several deaf and hard of hearing consumer groups filed a petition asking that the FCC eliminate the broad class captioning exemptions mentioned earlier.[49] These exemptions are inconsistent with Congress's vision of full accessibility and continue to deny deaf and hard of hearing Americans access to televised content. The groups noted that the costs and challenges of captioning have greatly decreased since 1997 and maintained that these broad exemptions are thus no longer appropriate. The FCC has yet to publicly consider this petition.

Finally, reruns of a captioned program must be shown with the captions intact only if the program has not been edited before it is reshown. Editing, typically done for new commercial breaks, disrupts the timing of captions. The consequence is that the captions for an edited program must be reformatted for the captions to make sense. The FCC has decided not to require reformatting of captions for the time being but has indicated a willingness to review this decision in the future.

Quality Standards

Although the Telecommunications Act is silent on the issue of ensuring high standards of captioning quality, many consumer groups urged the FCC to promulgate quality standards to ensure *full access* to television programming. Among other things, these groups sought standards to ensure comprehensive captioning of background sound effects, real-time captioning for live news broadcasts, accuracy in spelling and typing, proper synchronization of captions with audio content, and no obstruction of other textual messages (such as emergency warnings and names of speakers that appear on the screen).

The FCC has also decided, for the time being, not to issue standards for the nontechnical aspects of quality. However, the rules do require programming distributors to deliver closed captions intact and to monitor their equipment in order to ensure the technical quality of the closed captions transmitted.[50] Previously, no such requirements existed, and often captions were often unintentionally stripped during the transmission of programming, to the dismay and frustration of caption viewers.

In July 2004 the NAD and several other deaf and hard of hearing organizations petitioned the FCC to initiate a rule-making procedure to establish quality standards for closed captioning as well as necessary enforcement mechanisms.[51] Many deaf and hard of hearing people continue to experience poor-quality captions with errors such as incorrect spelling, missing words, garbled captions, timing delays, and technical problems. These usually result in a lack of access to video programming and misunderstandings.

In addition, the FCC has established special rules for the captioning of live news broadcasts. There are two ways of providing textual information for live news programs: *real-time captioning* and the *electronic newsroom captioning technique* (ENCT). Real-time captioning uses live individuals to simultaneously caption the entire audio portion of a program, while ENCT uses special equipment to convert prescripted news materials transmitted via a teleprompter into closed captions. Because ENCT is tied to what comes over the teleprompter, typically this method does not provide captioning for live interviews, banter among anchor persons, field reports, sports and weather updates, and other late-breaking stories that are not prescripted.

Consumer groups representing the interests of people who are deaf or hard of hearing have long complained that ENCT is not an adequate method of providing television access. In its original 1997 captioning order, the FCC issued rules that would have permitted the use of ENCT for all television programmers. When consumers challenged this part of the FCC's 1997 order, the FCC revised its requirements for access to live new shows. The FCC now will not allow the four major national television broadcast networks (CBS, Fox, NBC, and ABC) and their affiliates in the top twenty-five television markets (i.e., typically the largest cities) to count programs captioned with ENCT toward compliance with the FCC's captioning transition schedule.[52] National nonbroadcast networks (e.g., HBO, CNN, and other cable or satellite networks) that serve at least 50 percent of the total number of households subscribing to television programming services will also not be permitted to count ENCT toward their captioning requirements.[53] Due to this exception, many deaf and hard of hearing people who live outside the top twenty-five markets receive inferior and oftentimes no captioning on live programs such as those monitoring natural disasters or terrorist events. In January 1997 a universal captioning petition was filed by consumer groups, asking the FCC to disallow the use of ENCT to satisfy captioning requirements.[54] The universal captioning as well as captioning-quality petitions remained pending as this book went to print.

IP Closed Captioning

Congressional Action

In the late 2000s the NAD and other disability organizations recognized that people with disabilities were often unable to benefit from many of the advances in communications and video programming delivered using Internet Protocol (IP). These new technologies were increasingly becoming central to our everyday lives, both in the workplace and at home, such as streaming video content over the Internet through Netflix, Hulu, and news stations' websites. Congress recognized these barriers and that the industry was not providing much-needed access for people with disabilities, such as adding closed captions to online programming that had already been shown on television with captions.

On June 26, 2009, U.S. Representative Edward Markey (D-MA) introduced the Twenty-First Century Communications and Video Accessibility Act of 2009 (H.R. 3101) to ensure that individuals with disabilities have access to emerging Internet protocol–based communication and video programming technologies in this century.[55] A Senate version was later introduced in May 2010 by Senator Mark Pryor (D-AR) and Senator John Kerry (D-MA).[56] The CVAA passed Congress and was signed into law by President Barack Obama on October 8, 2010. It was supported by more than three hundred national, state, and community-based organizations.[57]

In the CVAA, Congress amended section 713(c) of the Communications Act to require captioning for video programming shown on the Internet after being shown on television with captions.[58] This new law instructed the FCC to create a schedule of deadlines for different types of online programming. Moreover, recognizing that requiring captions online means nothing if the relevant technology is not also required to support captions,

Section 203 of the CVAA requires that all physical devices designed to receive and play back video programming, including smartphones, tablets, personal computers, and television set-top boxes, must support captions.[59]

Deaf and hard of hearing consumers have long complained about the difficulty of turning on closed captions on television and devices and particularly about one common cable box that requires users to turn the device off before one can enter a menu screen to access the captioning controls. Addressing this concern, the CVAA requires the closed-captioning mechanism on such devices to be accessible through a mechanism that is reasonably comparable to a button, key, or icon designated to activate the closed captioning.[60] The FCC has yet to release its rules on accessing captioning controls, but the NAD is hopeful that the FCC rules will make it much easier to turn captions on and off and to change their color, size, and so forth.

FCC IP Captioning Order

On January 13, 2012, the FCC established an elaborate schedule of deadlines for IP closed captioning by which compliance with the mandates is to be achieved, and the FCC refrained from creating any new categorical exemptions aside from what is already exempted on television.[61] The FCC rules require video programming owners (VPOs) to provide video programming distributors (VPDs) and video programming providers with captions for their IP-delivered video programs.[62] In turn, VPDs and VPOs must enable the rendering (or pass-through) of all of the captions to the end users.[63] Moreover, the quality of the captions shown online must be of at least the same quality as the captions for the same programming when shown on television.[64] The rules also include provisions allowing users to choose and alter the color, size, font, background opacity, and character edges of their captioning on digital captioning decoders.

Unfortunately, the FCC decided to limit coverage of the IP captioning rules to full-length programming shown on television and currently exempt coverage of video clips. The NAD and other consumer groups were very disappointed with this exemption as there is no language in the CVAA that authorizes the FCC to limit its rules to full-length programming. A great deal of online video programming is in the form of video clips, such as those on news websites that cover important information about natural disasters or terrorist attacks. The NAD and other deaf and hard of hearing organizations promptly filed a petition for reconsideration of this decision.[65] As this book went to press, the FCC was seriously considering the petition to require captioning of video clips but had not yet done so.[66]

Apparatus Deadline

The FCC requires that all physical devices that are manufactured after January 1, 2014, and are designed to receive and play back video programming to support captions.[67] Such devices include but are not limited to smartphones, tablets, personal computers, and television set-top boxes. The deadline for these devices applies only to the date of manufacture and not to the date of importation, shipment, or sale.[68]

Schedule of IP Captioning Deadlines

The rules require the following schedule for each category of new video programming to begin full captioning compliance:

+ Prerecorded programming that is not edited for Internet distribution must be captioned when shown online if shown on TV with captions on or after September 30, 2012.
+ Live and near live programming, which is programming that was recorded within twenty-four hours of being broadcast on television, must be captioned when shown online if shown on TV with captions on or after March 30, 2013.
+ Prerecorded programming that is edited for Internet distribution must be captioned when shown online if shown on TV with captions on or after September 30, 2013.

This means that by September 30, 2013, 100 percent of new video programming shown on television with captions must be captioned when shown online. By contrast, archival video programming that is already available online but shown or reaired on television must be shown online with captions according to the following deadlines:

+ The programming must be captioned within forty-five days of the date it is shown on television with captions on or after March 30, 2014.
+ The programming must be captioned within thirty days of the date it is shown on television with captions on or after March 30, 2015.
+ Such programming must be captioned within fifteen days of the date it is shown on television with captions on or after March 30, 2016.

Similarly to television programming providers, under the CVAA, online video programming providers and video programming owners may petition the FCC for exemptions based on economic burden.[69]

Access to Online Video Programming under the ADA

The scope of the CVAA IP captioning rules is limited and applies only to programming first shown on television with captions and then later online. However, an enormous amount of online video programming has never been shown on television. Such CVAA-exempt programming includes thousands of newly released movies and programs, including Web-only shows, which are available online via live streaming through video subscription services such as Netflix or on demand where individual rentals can be purchased and streamed to individual devices. Even though these programs may be exempt from the CVAA, they are nonetheless covered under the Americans with Disabilities Act.

On June 16, 2012, the NAD sued Netflix, Inc., in the U.S. District Court for the District of Massachusetts, alleging that the failure of Netflix to caption all of its *Watch Instantly* programs violates the mandate of the ADA that all "places of entertainment" provide "full and equal enjoyment" for people with disabilities.[70] The NAD successfully argued that the ADA applies to Website-only businesses like Netflix, and the District Court of

Massachusetts was the first court in the country to hold that the ADA applies to Web-only businesses.[71] Judge Ponsor explained that:

> [i]t would be irrational to conclude that persons who enter an office to purchase services are protected by the ADA, but persons who purchase the same services over the telephone or by mail are not. Congress could not have intended such an absurd result.[72] . . .
>
> In a society in which business is increasingly conducted online, excluding businesses that sell services through the Internet from the ADA would run afoul of the purposes of the ADA and would severely frustrate Congress's intent that individuals with disabilities fully enjoy the goods, services, privileges and advantages, available indiscriminately to other members of the general public.[73]

Following this ruling, the NAD and Netflix reached a settlement agreement, and Netflix agreed to make 100 percent of its online streaming videos accessible by 2014.

Other online video programming distributors have made similar efforts to caption more of their online content. For instance, in June 2013 Apple committed to ensuring that iTunes TV and movie offerings will contain closed captioning or subtitles, with every movie and TV episode in the iTunes catalog captioned or subtitled, by June 2015.[74] The NAD is committed to working with online video programming distributors to ensure that all of their content is accessible to deaf and hard of hearing people.

EMERGENCY CAPTIONING

In 1977 the FCC adopted a rule requiring television broadcasters to present emergency bulletins both visually and aurally when using the Emergency Broadcast System.[75] Prior to this time, during emergencies, television stations would interrupt the sound portion of the television signal to make oral announcements, but the picture would continue without any indication that something was wrong. Sometimes the words "Emergency Bulletin" would appear on the screen, and an off-camera announcer would read the details of the urgent situation. The deaf viewer, unable to understand what was said, could not make realistic plans for safety. For example, when fires ravaged wide sections of California in 1970, officials used loudspeakers and radio and television broadcasts to warn residents to evacuate threatened areas. Several deaf people burned to death because they could not hear the loudspeakers or the radio bulletins and because the television announcements gave no visual information about the danger. Their deaths might have been prevented if the warnings had also been provided visually.

These and similar tragedies prompted appeals to the FCC. Thousands of letters from people all over the country convinced the FCC to adopt a visual warning rule. The later revised rule states the following:

> Any emergency information transmitted by a TV or
> Class A TV station in accordance with this section shall be
> transmitted both aurally and visually or only visually.
> TV and Class A TV stations may use any method of visual
> presentation which results in a legible message conveying
> the essential emergency information. Methods which may
> be used include, but are not necessarily limited to, slides,
> electronic captioning, manual methods (e.g., hand printing)
> or mechanical printing processes. However, when an
> emergency operation is being conducted under a national,
> State or Local Area Emergency Alert System (EAS) plan,
> emergency information shall be transmitted both aurally
> and visually unless only the EAS codes are transmitted as
> specified in § 11.51(b) of this chapter.[76]

In 1997 the FCC expanded its requirements for access to emergency information to cable television networks, establishing what is called the "Emergency Alert System."[77] The requirement to create this system comes from the Cable Television Consumer Protection and Competition Act of 1992. The act directed the FCC to ensure that viewers of video programming on cable systems are provided with the same emergency information as is provided by the Emergency Broadcast System (EBS). The FCC's rules required all cable operators serving five thousand or more customers to provide the full EAS message in both audio and visual formats on *all* channels. Systems with ten thousand or more subscribers began meeting this obligation on December 31, 1998, while systems with five thousand to ten thousand subscribers had until October 1, 2002, to comply.[78] The FCC created looser obligations for systems with fewer than five thousand subscribers.

Although the EBS and EAS requirements for visual access to televised emergency information were intended to ensure access by deaf and hard of hearing individuals, these systems were required only for national emergencies and are merely voluntary for local emergencies. As a result, televised information about emergencies was often left uncaptioned. For example, even though the EBS visual warning rule had been in effect for several years, in 1989, during the San Francisco and Los Angeles earthquakes and Hurricane Hugo, local stations failed to provide captions to accompany their reports. Similarly, information about bombings, tornadoes, blizzards, and other emergencies throughout the nation commonly have not been captioned.

To remedy this situation, in 1998 the FCC initiated a proceeding to ensure that all televised emergency information is captioned.[79] Much to the relief of deaf and hard of hearing people everywhere, on April 14, 2000, the FCC adopted rules requiring that all broadcasters, cable operators, and other multichannel video programming distributors make local emergency information that is provided in the audio portion of the programming accessible to deaf and hard of hearing people.[80] They may do so through the use of captioning or visual presentations such as open captioning, crawls, or scrolls on the screen.[81] Despite a series of notices from the FCC, numerous local television stations continued to fail to provide access to emergency information. In 2005, under pressure from the NAD, deaf and hard of hearing organizations, and deaf and hard of hearing people around the country, the FCC decided to investigate several complaints and fined several stations in San Diego, California, and Washington, DC, and one in Florida for failing to provide access to emergency information.[82] Further, to ensure that deaf and hard of hearing people can read the visual emergency announcement, in 2006 the FCC explained that video programming distributors must make sure that nothing blocks the closed captioning during emergency announcements and also that the captions do not block any visual emergency information.[83] This 1998 proceeding, which was an extension of the FCC's closed-captioning proceeding, addresses the need to provide real-time captioning for *all* live emergency news information regardless of whether the EBS or the EAS is used.

Filing an FCC Complaint

Consumers may file disability access complaints with the FCC related to: (1) accessibility of emergency information on television, (2) closed captioning on television, and (3) closed captioning of television programs streamed or downloaded from the Internet. The 2000C complaint form can be filled out online at the FCC website.[84]

DVDS and Videotapes

There is no clear law requiring production companies that sell or rent DVDs or videotapes to add captions. Fortunately, the vast majority of DVDs and videotapes sold and rented in the United States are voluntarily captioned or subtitled. Given the advent of streaming video via the Internet and the decrease in the use of DVDs and videotapes, the majority of efforts in captioning legislation and litigation have focused on streaming videos.

Notes

1. Nielsen Company, *Free to Move between Screens: The Cross Platform Report* (March 2013), 9, http://www.nielsen.com/content/dam/corporate/us/en/reports-downloads/2013%20 Reports/Nielsen-March-2013-Cross-Platform-Report.pdf.
2. National Captioning Institute, "Nearly 100 Million Americans Can Benefit from Watching Captioned TV," *NCI FYI Fact Sheet*, 1996.
3. "[F]orty percent of the 60,000 closed captioning decoders sold in 1989 were to people for whom English is a second language" (Sy DuBow, "The Television Decoder Circuitry Act – TV For All,"

Temple Law Review 64 [1991]: 614). See also Dennis Kelly, "TV Closed-Captions Fight Illiteracy," *USA Today,* July 11, 1990, 6D.

4. Studies have shown that closed captioning is an effective tool in teaching literacy skills. See Rita Bean and Robert Wilson, "Using Closed Captioned Television to Teach Reading to Adults," *Reading Research and Instruction* 28(4) (1989): 27–37. See also Forrest P. Chisman, *Jump Start: The Federal Role in Adult Literacy* (Southport, CT: Southport Institute for Policy Analysis, 1989), http://www.caalusa.org/jumpstart.pdf.

5. Dennis Kelly, "TV Closed-Captions Fight Illiteracy."

6. Patricia Koskinen, Robert Wilson, Linda Gambrell, and Carl Jensema, "Closed Captioned Television: A New Technology for Enhancing Reading Skills of Learning Disabled Students," *Spectrum: Journal of School Research and Information* 4(2) (1986): 9–13.

7. Dennis Kelly, "TV Closed-Captions Fight Illiteracy."

8. Department of Health & Human Services, Administration on Aging, "A Profile of Older Americans: 2012,", http://www.aoa.gov/Aging_Statistics/Profile/2012/docs/2012profile.pdf.

9. Ross E. Mitchell, "Can You Tell Me How Many Deaf People There Are in the United States?" (Gallaudet Research Institute, February 2005), http://research.gallaudet.edu/Demographics/deaf-US.php.

10. In the early 1980s the Greater Los Angeles Council on Deafness, Inc., brought a class action suit against Community Television of Southern California to mandate open captioning. See *Greater Los Angeles Council on Deafness, Inc., v. Community Television of Southern California,* 719 F. 2d 1017, 1019 (9th Cir. 1983). The council argued that because Community Television received federal funds, it should provide open captioning under Section 504 of the Rehabilitation Act of 1973. Both the U.S. District Court and the U.S. Court of Appeals for the Ninth Circuit ruled that Section 504 of the Rehabilitation Act does not mandate that federally funded television programs be produced and broadcast with open rather than closed captions. The courts both noted that the U.S. Department of Education helped originate closed captioning and required all programs it funded to be produced with closed captions. Further, as a condition of its grants, the department required that public stations transmit closed captions on all programs that had been produced with closed captions. See also *Community Television v. Gottfried,* 459 U.S. 498 (1983), which states that Section 504 does not require the FCC to impose a greater obligation on public licensees than on commercial licensees to provide special programming for individuals with hearing disabilities.

11. Commission on Education of the Deaf, *Toward Equality: Education of the Deaf,* (Washington, D.C.: U.S. Government Printing

Office, 1988), 13. The COED was a temporary federal commission created in the 1980s to study and make recommendations on improving educational opportunities for deaf Americans.

12. Ibid.; See also Sy DuBow, "The Television Decoder Circuitry Act – TV for All," for a general discussion of the history of closed captioning.

13. Commission on Education of the Deaf, *Toward Equality: Education of the Deaf.*

14. S. Rep. No. 393, 101st Cong., 2d Sess. 2 (1990).

15. H. Rep. No. 767, 101st Cong., 2d Sess. 5 (1990).

16. The FCC's *In the Matter of Implementation of Video Description of Video Programming, Notice of Proposed Rulemaking,* MM Docket No. 99-339 at 1 (November, 1999), cites the Roper Starch [Organization], *America's Watching: Public Attitudes toward Television* (New York: Network Television Association, National Association of Broadcasters, 1997), 1-2.

17. S. Rep. No. 393, 101st Congress, 2d Sess. 2 (1990), citing Caption Center Survey, WGBH, Boston, MA (1990).

18. *TV Decoder Circuitry Act of 1989: Hearing Before the Subcommittee on Communications,* 101st Cong., 2d Sess. at 67 (1990), (in statement of John Ball, president of the National Captioning Institute).

19. Commission on Education of the Deaf, *Toward Equality: Education of the Deaf,* (Washington, D.C.: U.S. Government Printing Office), 119.

20. Ibid., 120.

21. *Television Decoder Circuitry Act,* Pub. L. 101-431, 104 Stat. 960 (1990); 47 U.S.C. §303(u); 47 U.S.C. §330(b).

22. In 1988, 96 percent of new television sets had thirteen-inch screens or larger. *TV Digest* (September 11, 1989): 12.

23. 47 U.S.C. §303(s).

24. *In the Matter of Amendment of Part 15 of the Commission's Rules to Implement the Provisions of the Television Decoder Circuitry Act of 1990,* Report and Order, Gen. Docket No. 91-1 (adopted April 12, 1991; released April 15, 1991). The standards cover the use of color characters, italics, upper- and lowercase characters, smooth scrolling, caption size, and compatibility with cable scrambling technology.

25. The FCC pointed out that "it is essential that television receivers display captions that are readable. By providing a black background, the legibility of the caption is assured" (FCC, *FCC Record* 6(9) [1991]: 2430).

26. 47 U.S.C. §330(b).

27. *In the Matter of Closed Captioning Requirements for Digital Television Receivers,* Report and Order, FCC 00-259, ET Docket

No. 99-254, MM Docket No. 95-176, (released July 31, 2000). See also FCC, "FCC Adopts Technical Standards for Display of Closed Captioning on Digital Television Receivers," July 21, 2000, http://transition.fcc.gov/Bureaus/Mass_Media/News_Releases/2000/nrmm0031.html.

28. *In the Matter of Closed Captioning Requirements for Digital Television Receivers* at Summary of Requirements.

29. Ibid.

30. *Twenty-First Century Communications and Video Accessibility Act,* Pub. L. 111-260, 124 Stat. 2751 at 203(a) (2010). See also *In the Matter of Closed Captioning of Internet Protocol-Delivered,* MB Docket No. 11-154 at §IV (2012).

31. *Telecommunications Act,* Pub. L. 104-104, 110 Stat. 56 (1996). Section 305 of the Act added a new section (Section 613, Video Programming Accessibility) to the *Communications Act of 1934* (47 U.S.C. §613 [1996]).

32. *In the Matter of Closed Captioning and Video Description of Video Programming, Implementation of Section 305 of the Telecommunications Act of 1996, Video Programming Accessibility,* Report and Order, FCC 97-279, MM Docket No. 95-176 (1997).

33. *In the Matter of Closed Captioning and Video Description of Video Programming, Implementation of Section 305 of the Telecommunications Act of 1996, Video Programming Accessibility,* Order on Reconsideration, FCC 98-236, MM Docket No. 95-176 (1998).

34. 47 C.F.R. §79.1(b)(1)(iv).

35. The FCC divides the year into three-month blocks; each channel must meet these captioning requirements every quarter.

36. 47 C.F.R. §79.1(b)(5).

37. Any programming produced or shown before January 1, 1998, falls into this "prerule" category.

38. 47 C.F.R. §79.1(b)(2).

39. 47 C.F.R. §79.1(b)(3), (b)(4).

40. 47 C.F.R. §§79.1(a)(1), (d) et seq.

41. 47 C.F.R. §79.1(d)(12).

42. 47 C.F.R. §79.1(d)(11).

43. *In the Matter of Anglers for Christ Ministries, Inc.,* Memorandum Opinion and Order, Order, and Notice of Proposed Rulemaking, FCC 11-159, CGB-CC-0005, CGB-CC-0007, CG Docket No. 06-181, CG Docket No. 11-175 §IV at 16–17 (2011).

44. Ibid. at §II ¶ 5.

45. Ibid.

46. Ibid. at §II ¶ 15.

47. Ibid. at §I ¶ 1. The *Twenty-First Century Communications and Video Accessibility Act of 2010* uses the phrase "economically burdensome" instead of the old "undue burden"; however, the FCC interpreted the terms as synonymous (at §III ¶ 36).
48. *In the Matter of Interpretation of Economically Burdensome Standard*, CG Docket No. 11-175 (2012).
49. *In the Matter of Telecommunications for the Deaf and Hard of Hearing, Inc., et al., Petition to Amend the Commission's Rules to Eliminate Class Exemptions*, Petition for Rulemaking (2011).
50. 47 C.F.R. §79.1(c).
51. *In the Matter of Closed Captioning of Video Programming, Description of Video Programming, Closed Captioning Quality Standards,* Petition for Rulemaking, Docket RM-11065 (2004).s.
52. 47 C.F.R. §79.1(e)(3).
53. Ibid. As an example, the FCC explains that if the combined national subscribership of all multichannel programming providers (cable, satellite, and wireless cable) is eighty million households, then nonbroadcast networks that serve at least forty million households would be covered by this rule.
54. *In the Matter of Telecommunications for the Deaf and Hard of Hearing, Inc., et. al.*
55. U.S. House Committee on Energy and Commerce, *The Twenty-First Century Communications and Video Accessibility Act of 2010, Report [to Accompany H.R. 3101]*, H. Rpt. 111-563 (2010).
56. *Equal Access to 21st Century Communications Act*, S. 3304 (2010); COAT Press Releases, "Senate Bill Introduced: "Equal Access to 21st Century Communications Act" (S. 3304)," May 5, 2010, http://www.coataccess.org/node/7159.
57. NAD, "NAD Celebrates Passage of the 21st Century Act on Capitol Hill," December 1, 2010, http://nad.org/news/2010/12/nad-celebrates-passage-21st-century-act-capitol-hill. The Coalition of Organizations for Accessible Technology (COAT) led the effort to pass the CVAA. COAT is made up of more than three hundred organizations and was led by five steering-member organizations: the NAD, the American Association of People with Disabilities, the American Council of the Blind, the American Foundation for the Blind, and Communication Service for the Deaf. See also www.coataccess.org.
58. *Twenty-First Century Communications and Video Accessibility Act of 2010*, Pub. L. 111-260, 124 Stat. 2751, at 202(b) (2010).
59. Ibid., at 203(a) (2010).
60. Ibid., at 204(a) (2010).
61. *In the Matter of Closed Captioning of Internet Protocol-Delivered Video Programming: Implementation of the Twenty-First Century*

Communications and Video Accessibility Act of 2010, Report and Order, MB Docket no. 11-154, FCC 12-9 §I and §III at ¶ 67 (2012).

62. Ibid. §I and §III at ¶ 15.

63. Ibid. at §I and §IV at ¶ 26.

64. Ibid. at §I and §III at ¶ 36.

65. *In the Matter of Closed Captioning of Internet Protocol-Delivered Video Programming: Implementation of the Twenty-First Century Communications and Video Accessibility Act of 2010*, Petition for Reconsideration of the Commission's Report and Order, MB Docket no. 11-154 (2012).

66. *In the Matter of Closed Captioning of Internet Protocol-Delivered Video Programming: Implementation of the Twenty-First Century Communications and Video Accessibility Act of 2010*, Order on Reconsideration and Further Notice of Proposed Rulemaking, FCC 13-84, MB Docket no. 11-154 §III at ¶ 30 (2013); Lily Bond, "FCC Considers Extending Closed Captioning Requirements to Video Clips," May 12, 2014, http://www.3playmedia.com/2014/05/12/fcc-considers-extending-closed-captioning-requirements-video-clips/.

67. *In the Matter of Closed Captioning of Internet Protocol-Delivered Video Programming*, Order on Reconsideration and Further Notice of Proposed Rulemaking, FCC 13-84 §IV at ¶ 23.

68. Ibid.

69. *In the Matter of Closed Captioning of Internet Protocol-Delivered Video Programming*, FCC 12-9 §IV at ¶ 29.

70. Complaint for Declaratory and Injunctive Relief, *NAD v. Netflix, Inc.* (D. Mass.) at 2 (June 16, 2011).

71. *NAD v. Netflix, Inc.*, C.A. No. 11-CV-30168-MAP, Docket No. 43 (D. Mass.) (2012).

72. *Carparts Distrib. Ctr. v. Auto. Wholesaler's Assoc.*, 37 F.3d 12, 19 (1st Cir. 1994).

73. Ibid. at 7.

74. NAD, "Apple Committed to Captioning of iTunes Movies and TV Shows," June 17, 2013, http://nad.org/news/2013/6/apple-committed-captioning-itunes-movies-and-tv-shows.

75. 47 C.F.R. §73.1250(h).

76. Ibid.

77. *In the Matter of Amendment of Part 73, Subpart G, of the Commission's Rules regarding the Emergency Broadcast System*, Second Report and Order, FCC 97-338, FO Docket No. 91-301, FO Docket No. 91171 (1997).

78. *Cable Television Consumer Protection and Competition Act*, Pub. L. No. 102-385 §16(b), 106 Stat. 1460, 1490 (1992).

79. *In the Matter of Closed Captioning and Video Description of Video Programming, Implementation of Section 305 of the*

Telecommunications Act of 1996, Video Programming Accessibility, Notice of Proposed Rulemaking, FCC 97-4, MM Docket No. 95-176 (1997).

80. *In the Matter of Closed Captioning and Video Description of Video Programming*, Second Report and Order, FCC 00-136, MM Docket No. 95-176 (2000). See also FCC, "Reminder to Video Programming Distributors of Obligation to Make Emergency Information Accessible to Persons with Hearing Disabilities," DA 01-1930 (August 13, 2001).

81. FCC, "Reminder to Video Programming Distributors of Obligation to Make Emergency Information Accessible to Persons with Hearing Disabilities."

82. See *In the Matter of Midwest Television, Inc., Licensee of KFMB-TV, San Diego, CA*, Notice of Apparent Liability for Forfeiture, File No. EB-04-TC-061, DA 05-455 (2005); *In the Matter of Channel 51 of San Diego, Inc., Licensee of KUSI-TV, San Diego, CA*, Notice of Apparent Liability for Forfeiture, File No. EB-04-TC-067, DA 05-456 (2005); *In the Matter of McGraw-Hill Broadcasting Company, Inc., Licensee of KGTV, San Diego, CA*, Notice of Apparent Liability for Forfeiture, File No. EB-04-TC-068, DA 05-457 (2005); *In the Matter of NBC Telemundo License Co., Licensee of WRC-TV, Washington, DC*, Notice of Apparent Liability for Forfeiture, File No. EB-04-TC-101, DA 05-1512 (2005); *In the Matter of ACC Licensee, Inc., Licensee of WJLA-TV, Washington, DC*, Notice of Apparent Liability for Forfeiture, File No. EB-04-TC-100, DA 05-1511 (2005); *In the Matter of Waterman Broadcasting Corp. of Florida, Inc., Licensee of WBBH-TV, Fort Myers-Naples, FL, Montclair Communications, Inc., Licensee of WZVN-TV, Fort Myers-Naples, FL*, Notice of Apparent Liability for Forfeiture, File No. EB-04-TC-145 and EB-04-TC-150, DA 05-2258 (2005).

83. *Obligation of Video Programming Distributors to Make Emergency Information Accessible to Persons with Hearing Disabilities Using Closed Captioning*, Public Notice, DA 06-2627 (2006).

84. To file a complaint visit the FCC's Consumer Help Center, www. fcc.gov/complaints, select "Access by People with Disabilities to Communications Services and Equipment," and then file Form 2000C (http://www.fcc.gov/accessibility-complaints-form-2000c) in your preferred format.

Chapter 11

Telecommunication Services

Historically, deaf and hard of hearing people have been unable to access the majority of our nation's telecommunications products and services. Even today, a considerable number of these products and services depend on auditory and verbal input and output. Rapid and efficient telecommunications services, readily available to almost all hearing Americans, have been largely denied to those who are deaf or hard of hearing. For most of the twentieth century the telephone network created unnecessary barriers of expense and difficulty for deaf and hard of hearing people, limiting their ability to communicate with family, friends, businesses, government, and social service providers. However, numerous developments over the past two decades have begun to erode these obstacles.

The Telecommunications Act of 1996 requires manufacturers of telecommunications products and providers of telecommunications services to ensure that their products and services are accessible to individuals with disabilities, if doing so would be readily achievable.[1] Additionally, deaf and hard of hearing people who in the past used TTY relay services now have access to several newer forms of telecommunications relay service (TRS) such as video relay service (VRS), captioned telephone service (CTS), and Internet protocol (IP) relay service. They can also enjoy TRS at home, at their workplace, at school, in public spaces with Wi-Fi connections, and even on mobile devices.

REGULATION OF TELECOMMUNICATIONS

Telephone companies are public utilities whose rates and practices are regulated by federal and state agencies. The one that regulates interstate telephone practices is the Federal Communications Commission (FCC). Each state also has its own agency that regulates the operations of telephone companies within the state. Those agencies are usually called public utility commissions (PUCs). The FCC and the state PUCs work to ensure that telephone companies operate in the public interest by providing adequate and nondiscriminatory service to the public for a fair price.

Telecommunications Relay Services

Telecommunications relay services enable people who use TTYs, videophones, or other nonvoice terminal devices to have conversations with people who use conventional voice telephones. The calls are relayed back and forth by a third party who, with TTY or IP relay users, reads what the TTY user types and types what the voice telephone user says. With VRS calls, the third party is a sign language interpreter who is connected to the deaf or hard of hearing person using video conferencing technology. The interpreter relays a call by speaking to the hearing person and signing to the deaf or hard of hearing person. In the early 1980s, private relay systems began to develop around the country, linking TTYs to the public telecommunications network. Most of these private programs were funded with donations and staffed with volunteers. Unfortunately, funding shortages caused most of these state and private programs to impose call restrictions on relay users. Few programs relayed interstate calls, and many placed limitations on the length, number, and time of day that calls could be made. Even with these restrictions, the demand for relay services was overwhelming. The tremendous need for relay services eventually resulted in the passage of two federal laws requiring relay services.

Telecommunications Accessibility Enhancement Act

The first of these laws is the Telecommunications Accessibility Enhancement Act (TAEA) of 1988.[2] The TAEA requires the federal government to provide relay services for calls to, from, and within the federal government. The federal relay system has been in existence since 1986. It was originally established by the Architectural and Transportation Barriers Compliance Board (Access Board) and operated by the U.S. Treasury Department. Before the passage of the TAEA, however, the federal relay system had been poorly publicized and understaffed. The TAEA transferred authority for its operations to the General Services Administration and added staff to accommodate many more users. In addition to enlarging the federal relay program, the TAEA ordered the publication of federal TTY numbers in a government-wide directory and directed both houses of Congress to develop a policy on placing TTYs in members' offices.

Title IV of the Americans with Disabilities Act

The second piece of legislation requiring relay services is Title IV of the Americans with Disabilities Act (ADA). Title IV has required all telephone companies to provide intrastate and interstate relay services throughout the United States since July 26, 1993.[3] To implement Title IV, the FCC issued rules that require relay services to be functionally equivalent to conventional voice telephone services. Functional equivalence is defined as follows:

+ Relay services must be provided twenty-four hours a day, seven days a week for all local and long-distance calls.
+ TTY relay systems must accept calls in both the Baudot and ASCII computer formats.
+ TTY relay calls must be relayed verbatim unless one of the relay parties requests that the messages be summarized or that an ASL call be interpreted.
+ Individuals using any form of relay services may not be charged any more for their calls than voice telephone users

are charged for calls with the same points of origination and destination.

+ No restrictions may be placed on the type, length, or number of calls made by any relay user. This means that relay systems must be capable of handling third-party numbers, calling cards, collect calls, and all other calls normally handled by telephone companies. The burden of proving that relaying a particular kind of call is not techno-logically possible rests on the telephone companies. This requirement also allows relay callers to request relay operators, commonly referred to as communication assis-tants (CAs), to make several calls for them each time they call into a relay center.[4]

+ The CAs must also maintain the complete confidentiality of relayed conversations. They are prohibited from keeping records of relayed conversations beyond the length of the telephone call. However, under Section 705 (a) of the Communications Act of 1934, the CAs may be required to disclose interstate or foreign conversations when directed to do so by a court-issued subpoena or upon the demand of some other lawful authority.

+ TTY relay and IP relay CAs are required to have competent skills in grammar, typing, spelling, and relay etiquette. In addition, these particular CAs must be sufficiently acquainted with American Sign Language and with the cultures of the various communities that their relay systems are intended to serve.

Relay Service Providers

Under the ADA, telephone companies are responsible for provid-ing relay services wherever they provide conventional telephone services. In addition, individual states may take on this responsi-bility by having their state relay programs certified by the FCC. Both telephone companies and states are permitted to provide relay services individually through a competitively selected vendor or together with other telephone companies or states.

A state that wishes to receive certification to operate its own relay system must submit documentation to the FCC proving that its program will (1) meet or exceed all of the operational, technical, and functional minimum standards contained in the FCC's regulations; (2) provide adequate procedures and remedies to enforce the state program; and (3) not conflict with federal law where its program exceeds the minimum standards contained in the FCC regulations.

When a state requests certification, the FCC must give the public notice and an opportunity to comment on that request. Once it is granted, certification remains in effect for a five-year period. A state may apply to the FCC for recertification one year before its certification expires. Alternatively, the FCC may revoke or suspend a state's certification if that state's practices do not follow the FCC's minimum guidelines. Internet-based TRS providers must obtain certification from the FCC.

Currently, all fifty states, the District of Columbia, and U.S. territories have individual, state-certified relay programs. With the exception of California and Virginia, each of these states has selected single relay providers to handle local relay calls. Some of these states have their own relay centers physically located within their borders; others share regional centers centrally located among three or four states. Virginia has two providers providing different kinds of relay service. California is presently the only state that allows its residents to choose among several relay providers for local calls. In addition to these intrastate relay call options, consumers in all states have their choice of several relay providers to handle long-distance (toll) calls. Several companies provide Internet-based TRS in video relay service, IP relay, and IP captioned telephone service.

7-1-1 Uniform Dialing

When the relay mandates took effect, each state relay program had its own relay access telephone number. A deaf or hard of hearing person who traveled to another state had to know the number used in that state in order to connect to the relay service. It was very difficult to find each state's relay access telephone number in the days before the Internet became widespread.

In October of 1993 the National Center for Law and Deafness (NCLD), formerly of Gallaudet University, filed a petition for rule-making with the FCC, requesting that the commission allocate the digits 7-1-1 for nationwide relay access. The NCLD argued that access to relay services was confusing and difficult for individuals who traveled across state borders. The petition sought a single nationwide access number to make relay access "convenient, fast, and uncomplicated" and to reduce the number of digits that needed to be dialed. Sometime after the NCLD filed this petition, Hawaii and Canada independently began using 711 for relay access.[5] In February 1997 the FCC ultimately granted the NCLD's petition and directed 711 to be reserved for relay access on a nationwide basis.[6] Although this FCC action reserved the code, it did not mandate that every state use it for access to their relay programs. In July 1998 Bell Atlantic announced that it would start using 711 for TTY relay access in its states within two years.[7] Three years later, in August 2000, the advocacy work of the NAD and other organizations paid off when the FCC required all telecommunication carriers to implement 711 dialing for TTY relay services in every state by October 1, 2001.[8]

Enforcement

Consumers who are not satisfied with a state relay service should first file their complaints with the state agency responsible for implementing the relay program. The state then has 180 days in which to resolve the complaint. If the consumer is still not satisfied, a complaint can be filed with the FCC. If the issue is with an Internet-based relay service, such as VRS or IP relay, the consumer should file a complaint with the FCC or the relay provider. The FCC accepts complaints through an online complaint system. A telephone company that violates the ADA's relay provisions may be ordered to begin compliance immediately and may have to pay damages for the violation. The FCC Disability Rights Office website has a list of TRS points of contact for complaints as well as complaint log summaries.

Relay Services

With the passing of the ADA, states started providing relay services to deaf and hard of hearing people throughout the country. These non-Internet-based relay services are funded by the states, with the exception of interstate relay calls. These relay services include text-to-voice TTY-based TRS, where deaf and hard of hearing people use TTYs to connect to relay operators; speech-to-speech relay services, where people with speech disabilities connect to CAs who are specially trained in understanding people with speech disorders; and captioned telephone services where deaf and hard of hearing callers can listen and speak for themselves on calls but are assisted by a CA who provides real-time captions of what the other party says. These forms of relay services can be accessed only through the public switched telephone network (traditional telephone services) and not through the Internet.

Internet-Based Services

In May 1998 the FCC began a proceeding to expand its minimum standards for relay services. In that proceeding, the commission issued a notice of proposed rulemaking that suggested ways to broaden the definition of "telecommunications relay services."[9] Historically, the FCC interpreted Title IV of the ADA to require only TTY-to-speech and speech-to-TTY services. Under this definition, companies that provided relay services were able to receive reimbursement from the FCC only for providing relay services to calls between TTY and voice telephone users. However, technological advancements made other types of relay services possible. In fact, the ADA requires that the FCC encourage the use of existing technology and the development of new technology.[10] Accordingly, in the first few years of the new century, the FCC decided to include the provision of video relay service, Internet protocol relay, and Internet protocol captioned telephone service (IP CTS) as reimbursable forms of Internet-based TRS. At the time of this writing, the FCC was considering adding Internet protocol speech-to-speech (IP STS) as a covered and mandated relay service.

Video Relay Service

Video Relay Service is an Internet-based telecommunications relay service that allows deaf and hard of hearing people who use American Sign Language (ASL) to communicate with voice telephone users through video conferencing technology.[11] These individuals are able to use ASL to communicate with the CA through video conferencing, and the CA speaks what is signed to the other party and then relays in ASL what the other party says in response. The video relay service has been extremely beneficial to deaf and hard of hearing people who use ASL to communicate as it allows them to make relay calls in their native language. Because signing is much faster and more natural than typing, VRS also cuts down the length of their relay calls.

Like all other relay services, VRS must be provided twenty-four hours a day and seven days a week.[12] As of this writing, VRS providers must answer 80 percent of all incoming calls within 180 seconds, measured on a daily basis.[13] In 2014 the FCC has sought to significantly reduce the speed-of-answer requirement for VRS to 85 percent of calls within thirty seconds.[14] Moreover, VRS CAs employed by providers must be qualified interpreters who are able to interpret effectively, accurately, and impartially, both receptively and expressively, using any necessary specialized vocabulary.

Internet Protocol Relay Service

The IP relay service is an Internet-based telecommunications relay service that allows deaf and hard of hearing individuals to communicate with voice telephone users in text using an Internet-connected device. The deaf or hard of hearing person communicates with the CA through text, and the CA relays the call between the deaf or hard of hearing caller and the other party. Many users connect to the IP relay through a computer, tablet, or smartphone and even over the wireless telephone network. The IP relay service must be provided 24/7, and 85 percent of IP relay calls must be answered within ten seconds.[15]

Internet Protocol Captioned Telephone Service

The IP captioned telephone service, one of the newer forms of relay service, allows deaf and hard of hearing callers to make phone calls with the assistance of captions. These deaf and hard of hearing callers are able to make calls to another party and listen and talk to that other party just like on a conventional telephone, but the CA will supplement the call by providing the deaf or hard of hearing caller with captions of what the other party says.[16] The IP CTS, which uses the Internet instead of the public switched telephone system, must be provided 24/7, and currently 85 percent of calls must be answered within ten seconds.[17]

Additional Access to Relay Services

TRS providers may provide voice carryover (VCO) as well as hearing carryover (HCO) options as part of their telecommunications relay service. VCO allows the deaf or hard of hearing caller to speak directly to the other party but receive responses through the CA in text or even ASL. By contrast, HCO allows the caller to listen to the other party but respond in ASL or text through the operator. These options recognize that each deaf or hard of hearing person has unique communication needs that require different services to effectively relay that person's calls. The FCC also permits TRS providers to provide TRS in other languages, such as Spanish, as there are numerous Spanish speakers in the United States. At this time, Spanish is the only language other than English in which text and VRS relay services are provided.

Equipment Distribution Programs

While many relay providers provide relay service equipment and/or software free of charge directly to consumers, some states have equipment distribution programs to ensure their deaf and hard of hearing residents have equal access to telecommunications. These programs distribute specialized equipment, such as TTYs and telephone amplifiers, to these individuals free of charge or at a discount. Some states set income qualifications for individuals wishing to receive such equipment. Other states merely require certification that the individual is deaf or hard of hearing.[18]

The Twenty-First Century Communications and Video Accessibility Act of 2010 (CVAA) created the National Deaf-Blind Equipment Distribution Program (NDBEDP), which provides specialized equipment to low-income individuals who are deaf-blind so that they can effectively access the Internet and advanced communications. The FCC certifies one entity per state for the local distribution of equipment for this population. A list of the provider in each state can be found on the FCC website. Deaf-blind individuals who want to obtain specialized equipment through the NDBEDP should contact their state distributor.

HEARING AID COMPATIBILITY

Hearing-aid-compatible telephones utilize a switch to block out background sounds and high-pitched squeals that can occur with incompatible telephones. The switch enables the hearing aid wearer to pick up sound waves generated by the electromagnetic field of the telephone receiver. Telephones with the required amount of electromagnetic field are considered to be compatible with hearing aids.

Until the early 1980s, most telephones were hearing aid compatible. Before that time, most Americans rented their phones from AT&T; these rented phones had strong electromagnetic fields. In the 1980s, new equipment companies began manufacturing and selling telephones directly to consumers. Many of these telephones did not have a strong enough electromagnetic field to be compatible with hearing aids.

Telecommunications for the Disabled Act

In 1982 Congress took steps to rectify this situation. It passed the Telecommunications for the Disabled Act, which stated that compatibility between telephones and hearing aids was necessary to accommodate the needs of individuals with hearing loss.[19] The act directed the FCC to establish uniform technical standards for hearing aid compatibility. It created a mandate for all "essential telephones" to be compatible with hearing aids. Congress defined "essential" phones as coin-operated phones, phones for emergencies, and phones frequently needed by deaf and hard of hearing individuals. Finally, it directed that telephone equipment be labeled so that consumers would be aware of the compatibility between telephones and hearing aids.

Hearing Aid Compatibility Act

In the years following passage of the Telecommunications for the Disabled Act, consumers insisted that the definition of essential telephones was far too narrow to meet the needs of hearing aid users. Spearheaded by the Organization for Use of the Telephone (OUT), consumers succeeded in obtaining passage of the Hearing Aid Compatibility Act in 1988 (HAC Act).[20] The HAC Act required that all telephones manufactured after August 16, 1989, be compatible for use with hearing aids. On May 18, 1989, the FCC promulgated regulations directing compliance with the new law.[21]

After the HAC Act was passed, hearing aid wearers were still concerned that the FCC had not taken adequate steps to reduce the number of incompatible telephones that had been installed in workplaces and other institutions prior to the 1989 manufacturing deadline. As a result of consumer persistence on this matter, the FCC issued a rule in 1990 to again expand the availability of HAC telephones. The new rule changed the definition of essential telephones to require that telephones located in common areas of the workplace and all credit-card-operated telephones be compatible with hearing aids by May 1, 1991.[22] In 1992 the FCC again broadened its rules to require HAC telephones in *all* areas of the workplace and in *all* hotel, motel, and hospital rooms.[23] These rules, set to go into effect on May 1, 1993, were indefinitely suspended by the FCC at the last minute as a result of hundreds of last-minute complaints from businesses around the country. The businesses stated that compliance with the 1992 rules would be too difficult.[24]

In 1995 the FCC gathered together various representatives from consumer organizations, industry, and the government to revise the HAC rules. After extensive deliberations, the Hearing Aid Compatible Negotiated Rulemaking Committee recommended various ways for the FCC to strengthen its HAC mandates. On July 3, 1996, the FCC released rules that adopted these recommendations.[25]

The FCC's hearing aid compatibility rules now contain the following mandates:

+ All workplace telephones (other than those in common areas, which are subject to the requirements noted earlier) were required to be HAC by January 1, 2000, with the exception of telephones purchased between January 1, 1985, and December 31, 1989. Moreover, telephones in workplaces with fewer than fifteen employees were given until January 1, 2005 to be HAC.
+ All telephones in hotels and motels were required to be HAC by January 1, 2000. However, hotels and motels that were required to replace telephones purchased between January 1, 1985, and December 31, 1989, were given until 2001 and 2004 to comply, depending on the number of guest rooms they had.
+ All telephones utilized to signal emergency situations in confined settings, such as hospitals and residential healthcare facilities, were required to be HAC as of November 1, 1998.

All telephones, including cordless telephones, that are manufactured in or imported into the United States after January 1, 2000, must have volume control.[26] These telephones allow the telephone user to control the loudness of the other person's voice.[27] When Congress passed the HAC Act in 1988, it temporarily exempted wireless telephones from these requirements and gave the FCC criteria to follow and allowed the agency to use its discretion for when to end this exemption. After years of petitioning for coverage of wireless phones, the FCC determined in August 2003 that a general exemption of wireless phones had an adverse effect on deaf and hard of hearing individuals and that limiting the exemption was in the public interest.[28]

The FCC's wireless hearing aid compatibility rules now contain the following mandates for hearing aids operating in both acoustic and inductive coupling. The acoustic coupling mode uses a hearing aid to amplify sounds, including those from a telephone, while inductive coupling uses a hearing aid only to receive signals from magnetic fields generated by telecoil-compatible telephones (using the "T" setting on many hearing aids).[29]

- Each handset manufacturer must meet at least an M3 rating for one-third of the handset models that it offers to the service providers.[30]
- Each wireless service provider must meet at least an M3 rating for 50 percent or eight of the handset models it offers to consumers, whichever is less.[31]
- Each handset manufacturer must offer at least two T3-rated handset models . . . In addition, manufacturers have to ensure that one-third of their handset models . . . meet at least a T3 rating.[32]
- Each wireless service provider must meet at least a T3 rating for one-third or ten of the handset models it offers to consumers, whichever is less.[33]
- The FCC allows a *de minimis* exception to the preceding requirements for wireless service providers and manufacturers that offer two or fewer digital handsets in the United States as well as requiring those that offer three digital wireless handsets in the United States to just make one HAC handset available.[34]
- Accessible handsets must be explicitly labeled and include detailed information in the package. Since 2009 manufacturers and service providers must include information about their HAC phones on their websites.[35]
- Retail stores owned or operated by wireless service providers must allow in-store testing of accessible phones.[36]

Hearing aid compatibility complaints may be filed with the FCC, and consumers may use the FCC's online complaint form.

TELECOMMUNICATIONS ACT OF 1996

In the 1990s our nation entered a new era of telecommunications advances. Talk of the information superhighway and the release of new telecommunications devices, including wireless services, pagers, and interactive telephone systems, alerted deaf and hard of hearing consumers, as well as consumers with disabilities, of the need for a law that would ensure access to all of these new technologies.

After several years of negotiating with federal legislators, these consumers got their wish. On January 8, 1996, Congress enacted Section 255 of the Telecommunications Act of 1996. For the first time in U.S. history, a federal law requires telecommunications manufacturers and service providers to make their equipment and services accessible to individuals with disabilities where it is readily achievable to do so.[37] The new law also requires manufacturers and service providers to make their products and services compatible with peripheral devices and specialized customer premises equipment, such as TTYs, where it is readily achievable to do so. The FCC defines "readily achievable" as "easily accomplishable and able to be carried out without much difficulty or expense."[38] In determining whether an access feature is readily achievable, the FCC will balance the costs and nature of the access feature with the resources available to a company on a case-by-case basis. Often it is readily achievable to provide access if access is incorporated during the research and development stages of creating a product or service. Since then, Section 255 has made a profound difference in the ability of new technologies and services to reach Americans with disabilities.

Congress directed the Access Board, in conjunction with the FCC, to issue guidelines for achieving compliance by telecommunications equipment manufacturers. To obtain assistance in creating these guidelines, in June 1996 the Access Board developed the Telecommunications Access Advisory Committee (TAAC), a federal advisory team that comprised consumer and industry representatives. The TAAC presented its recommendations to the Access Board in January 1997. The Access Board used these recommendations to develop its Section 255 guidelines, which were released on February 3, 1998. Approximately one and a half years later, the FCC issued its own rules, designed to enforce compliance with Section 255 by both equipment manufacturers and service providers. For the most part, these rules mirror the Access Board's guidelines.

The FCC's rules require telecommunications manufacturers and service providers to identify and address the accessibility needs of individuals who are deaf and hard of hearing throughout the product design, development, and fabrication of their products and to do so as early and consistently as possible. The rules recognize the need to incorporate access early in design processes in order to avoid expensive and burdensome retrofits later on. In developing processes to identify accessibility barriers, manufacturers and service providers may engage in a number of actions. For example, if a company conducts market research, product testing, or pilot demonstrations for a particular product, it should include individuals with disabilities in these activities to help identify their needs. By consulting this population, manufacturers will get a better idea of the need to provide visual cues or vibrations for products (e.g., pagers) that may otherwise provide only aural cues.

The FCC's rules also require new telecommunications equipment and services to be compatible with peripheral devices and specialized equipment that are commonly used by individuals with disabilities. Examples are TTYs, videophones, visual signaling devices, and amplifiers. Under this mandate, products that offer voice communication (such as wireless phones) must provide a standard connection point for TTYs. In addition, these products must have a feature that enables users to alternate between using speech and TTY signals. The compatibility requirement also requires that telecommunications devices have a connection point so that they can be hooked up to audio-processing devices (such as amplifiers) that are used for telecommunications functions.

In addition to requiring *access* to telecommunications products and services, the FCC's rules require that deaf and hard of hearing people be able to *use* these products and services. The new rules define "usability" as access to product information (such as user manuals, bills, and technical support) that is functionally equivalent to information available to individuals without disabilities. For example, when a product is accompanied by an instructional video, the video should be provided with captions. Companies that comply with Section 255 may not impose any additional charges for providing such access.

The FCC's Section 255 rules are broad in scope. The rules cover virtually every type of telecommunications equipment, including telephones, videophones, pagers, wireless devices, fax machines, answering machines, telecommunications software, and business systems. Similarly, they cover all types of telecommunications services, including call waiting, speed dialing, call forwarding, computer-provided directory assistance, call monitoring, caller identification, call tracing, and repeat dialing.

Enforcement of the Section 255 rules is primarily through informal and formal consumer complaints filed with the FCC. These complaints may be filed with the FCC, and consumers may use the FCC's online complaint form.

Twenty-First Century Communications and Video Accessibility Act of 2010

Congress recognized that the evolving communications technologies of the twenty-first century were leaving behind people who are deaf and hard of hearing as well as people with disabilities. Although the Telecommunications Act of 1996 and other laws mandated access to more traditional telephone communication technologies, many Americans with disabilities have been unable to fully utilize advanced communications services (ACS) such as email and other Internet-based communications. Thus Congress passed the Twenty-First Century Communications and Accessibility Act of 2010 to ensure that people with disabilities are able to access emerging communications technologies. The NAD played a key role in the passing of the CVAA.

Examples of ACS include the following: (1) interconnected voice-over-Internet-protocol (VoIP) service, (2) noninterconnected VoIP service, (3) electronic messaging service, and (4) interoperable video conferencing service.[39] As required by Section 255, manufacturers are responsible for making sure that their ACS services and equipment are accessible to people with disabilities unless not achievable.[40] When determining achievability, the FCC considers the financial and technical challenges of making the product accessible. Further, entities are given flexibility in how they make their products accessible—they can either provide built-in accessibility features or use third-party applications or peripheral devices that are available to consumers at a nominal cost.[41] Although the FCC has granted some waivers and not all of the ACS rules have been adopted, such as for interoperable video conferencing service, full compliance was required by October 8, 2013.[42]

NOTES

1. Pub. L. No. 104-104, 110 Stat. 56 (1996), codified at 47 U.S.C. §255.
2. Pub. L. No. 100-542, 102 Stat. 2721 (1988), codified at 40 U.S.C. §762.
3. *Americans with Disabilities Act*, Title IV, Pub. L. No. 101-336, 104 Stat. 327, codified at 47 U.S.C. §225 (1990).
4. *In the Matter of Telecommunications Services for Individuals with Hearing and Speech Disabilities and the Americans with Disabilities Act of 1990*, Report and Order and Request for Comments, CC Docket No. 90-571, FCC 91-213 (1991).
5. For technical reasons, Hawaii requires dialing a "1" before the three-digit code.
6. *In the Matter of the Use of N11 Codes and Other Abbreviated Dialing Arrangements*, First Report and Order and Further Notice of Proposed Rulemaking, CC Docket No. 92-105, FCC 97-51 (1997).
7. Verizon Communications, "Bell Atlantic to Make Calling Easier for Customers Who Are Deaf, Hard of Hearing," July 8, 1998, http://www.verizon.com/about/news/press-releases/bell-atlantic-make-calling-easier-customers-who-are-deaf-hard-hearing/. Verizon Communications (formerly Bell Atlantic) provides wireless telephone service to residents in all 50 U.S. states and Puerto Rico.
8. *In the Matter of the Use of N11 Codes and Other Abbreviated Dialing Arrangements*, Second Report and Order, CC Docket No. 92-105 at ¶ 3 and 32 (2000).
9. *In the Matter of Telecommunications Relay Services and Speech-to-Speech Services for Individuals with Hearing and Speech Disabilities*, Notice of Proposed Rulemaking, CC Docket No. 98-67, FCC 98-90 (1998).
10. Title IV of the ADA codified at 47 U.S.C. §225.

11. 47 C.F.R. §64.601(a)(27).
12. 47 C.F.R. §64.604(a).
13. Ibid.
14. 47 C.F.R. §64.604(b)(2).
15. Ibid.
16. 47 C.F.R. §64.601(a)(16).
17. 47 C.F.R. §64.604(b)(2).
18. Additional information about the various state equipment distribution programs may be obtained by contacting the State of Maryland Department of Budget and Management, 45 Calvert Street, Annapolis, MD 21401.
19. 47 U.S.C. §610(d); *Hearing Aid Compatibility Act*, Pub. L. No. 100-394 (1988).
20. *Hearing Aid Compatibility Act*, Pub. L. No. 100-394 (1988).
21. *In the Matter of Access to Telecommunications Equipment and Services by the Hearing Impaired and Other Disabled Persons*, First Report and Order, CC Docket No. 87-124, FCC 89-137 (1989), 54 *Fed. Reg.* 21,429 (May 18, 1989), codified at 47 C.F.R. Part 68.
22. 47 C.F.R. § 68.112(b)(4).
23. 47 C.F.R. § 68.112 (b)(5); 47 C.F.R. § 68.112 (b)(6).
24. *In the Matter of Access to Telecommunications Equipment and Services by the Hearing Impaired and Other Disabled Persons*, First Report and Order.
25. *In the Matter of Access to Telecommunications Equipment and Services by the Hearing Impaired and Other Disabled Persons*, Memorandum Opinion and Order and Further Notice of Proposed Rulemaking, CC Docket No. 87-124, FCC 90-133 (1990), 55 *Fed. Reg.* 28,762, codified at 47 C.F.R. Part 68.
26. *In the Matter of Access to Telecommunications Equipment and Services by the Hearing Impaired and Other Disabled Persons*, Report and Order, CC Docket No. 87-124, FCC 92-217 (1992), 57 *Fed. Reg.* 27,182 (June 18, 1992), codified at 47 C.F.R. Part 68.
27. *In the Matter of Access to Telecommunications Equipment and Services by the Hearing Impaired and Other Disabled Persons*, Order, CC Docket No. 87-124, FCC 93-191 (1993).
28. FCC, "Hearing Aid Compatibility for Wireless Telephones," www.fcc.gov/guides/hearing-aid-compatibility-wireless-telephones.
29. FCC, "Consumer Guide: Hearing Aid Compatibility for Wireless Telephones," January 9, 2012, http://transition.fcc.gov/cgb/consumerfacts/hac_wireless.pdf.
30. Ibid.
31. Ibid.

32. Ibid.
33. Ibid.
34. Ibid.
35. Ibid.
36. 47 C.F.R. §20.19(c)(4).
37. Pub. L. No. 104-104, 110 Stat. 56 (1996), codified at 47 U.S.C. §255.
38. 63 *Fed. Reg.* 5607 (February 3, 1998), codified at 36 C.F.R. Part 1193.
39. *Twenty-First Century Communications and Video Accessibility Act*, Pub. L. 111-260 §716 (2010).
40. Ibid.
41. *In the Matter of Implementation of Sections 716 and 717 of the Communications Act of 1934, as Enacted by the Twenty-First Century Communications and Video Accessibility Act of 2010,* Report and Order and Further Notice of Proposed Rulemaking, CG Dockets No. 10-213 and 10-145 and WT Docket No. 96-198, FCC 11-151 at ¶ 13 (released Oct. 7, 2011).
42. Ibid. at ¶ 23.

Index

ABC, 219, 220, 228
Access Board. *See* Architectural and Transportation Barriers Compliance Board
accommodation. *See also* auxiliary aids and services
cost vs. benefit of, 2
defense of undue burden. *See* undue burden defense
defense of undue hardship, 31, 159–60
employment reasonable accommodation, 30, 154–57
housing reasonable modifications and accommodations, 179–80
methods of communication, 1
Rehabilitation Act, Section 504, 59–60
Acoustical Society of America (ASA), 87
ADA. *See* Americans with Disabilities Act of 1990
ADA Accessibility Guidelines (ADAAG), 47, 97
ADA Amendments Act of 2008 (ADAAA), xii, 26, 28, 29, 32–33, 152, 171

administrative enforcement employment discrimination, 166
burden of proof on employer, 154
Rehabilitation Act, Section 501 (federal employee), 151, 167–70
Rehabilitation Act, Section 503 (federal contractor), 151, 170–71
Rehabilitation Act, Section 504, 63, 172
state and local government (ADA Title II), 39
Administrative Office of the United States Courts, 197–98
advanced communications services (ACS), 258–59
Advocacy Center for the Elderly and Disabled, 106
affirmative action, 163–65, 167, 170, 171
agencies. *See* federal government; Rehabilitation Act of 1973; state and local governments (ADA Title II)

Alabama Board
  of Pharmacy, 156
alerting devices, 24, 155, 156
 accessible smoke alarms,
  156, 182
 on campus and in college
  classrooms, 114
 telephone flashers, 131
 visual alarm systems
  doorbell system, 183
  in new buildings, 48
Alexander v. Choate (1985), 108
All Channel Receiver Act of
  1962, 221
American National Standards
  Institute (ANSI), 87
American Sign Language (ASL),
  2, 6, 11, 15, 79, 84–85, 91,
  92, 246
 of *Miranda* rights, 208
 video relay service enabling use
  of, 250
American Society for Deaf
  Children, 88
Americans with Disabilities Act
  of 1990 (ADA), 25–52. *See
  also* ADA Amendments Act
  of 2008 (ADAAA)
 definition of "individual with
  disability," 26–29
 definition of "substantially
  limits," 27, 33
 education, specialized
  instruction, 75
 EEOC amendments to reflect
  ADA Amendments Act. *See*
  ADA Amendments Act of
  2008 (ADAAA)
 employment (Title I), 26, 29–32
  disability, definition of
   person with. *See* definition
   of "individual with a
   disability"
  employers covered, 29, 150

 employment discrimination
  prohibited, 30, 150
 enforcement provisions, 31–32,
  150, 167
 undue hardship defense, 31,
  159–60
 online video programming,
  access to, 232–33
 overview, 25–26
 public accommodation
  (Title III), 26, 39–50
 auxiliary aids, 21, 41–42, 49,
  109, 213n26
 conferences and
  performances, 46
 decoders and captioning,
  42–46
 DOJ regulations implementing,
  49–50
 enforcement, 48
 examinations and courses, 47
 existing vs. new facilities,
  47–48
 lawyers' offices, 202
 private healthcare providers
  and hospitals, 122
 private schools and educational
  programs for children and
  adults, 95, 107
 service animals, use of, 47
 undue burden defense, 42, 111,
  115, 203
 state and local courts, access to,
  192–95
 state and local governments
  (Title II), 26, 33–39
 accessibility of, 34–35
 auxiliary aids and services,
  36–39
 definition of "discrimination,"
  35–36
 filing complaints, 39
 public colleges and
  universities, 107

public school system, 95
state universities, 106
telecommunications
    (Title IV), 50–51,
    245–46, 249
amplification equipment.
    See hearing aids and
    amplification equipment
Anglers Order, 226
ANSI/ASA S12.60-2002, 87
Architectural and Transportation
    Barriers Compliance Board
    (Access Board), 47, 54, 55,
    87, 245, 256
    Telecommunications Access
    Advisory Committee
    (TAAC), 256
Architectural Barriers Act of
    1968, 25, 54
Argenyi v. Creighton University
    (2013), 109–11, 112
Arizona prison system, deaf
    persons in, 209–10
ASA (Acoustical Society of
    America), 87
ASL. *See* American Sign
    Language
assistive listening systems,
    20–21, 37, 41, 48, 61, 87,
    91, 155
assistive technology and
    services, schools providing,
    86–88
attorneys. *See* legal system and
    lawsuits
autism spectrum disorder, 86,
    98n30
automated-attendant
    systems, 50
auxiliary aids and services. *See
    also specific types of aids
    and services*
in courts, 192–95, 200–201
failure to provide, 1–2

hospitals and healthcare
    providers, 128–29
    ADA, 122–23
    Rehabilitation Act Section 504,
    120–21
public accommodation (ADA
    Title III), 41–42, 49, 109
public housing, 181
Rehabilitation Act
    regulations, 61
schools providing assistive
    technology and services,
    86–88, 91, 96
state and local governments
    (ADA Title II), 36–39, 109
universities and colleges
    providing assistive
    technology and services,
    107, 108–11
vocational rehabilitation
    agency's obligation to pay
    for, 112–13

Barker, David, 208–9
Bates v. UPS (2007), 162
Bell Atlantic 711 service, 248
bills of rights
    Deaf and Hard of Hearing
    Children's Bills of Rights
    (DCBR), 73, 89–95. *See also*
    Education
    Rehabilitation Act, 53
blindness. *See* Deaf-blind
    individuals
*Board of Education of Hendrick
    Hudson Central School
    District v. Rowley* (1982),
    76–77, 96
Bronk v. Ineichen (1995), 183
Brown v. Board of Education
    (1954), 71
*Bryant v. Better Business Bureau
    of Greater Maryland*
    (1996), 157

Cable Television Consumer
    Protection and Competition
    Act of 1992, 234
California relay service, 247
Camenisch v. University of Texas
    (1980), 111
captioning, 18–22, 155
  assistive listening systems,
    20–21, 37, 41
  background, 217
  benefits of, 217–18
  closed, 20, 37, 41, 61, 217
  development of, 219
  IP, 229–33
  quality standards, 227–29,
    248*n*25
  television, 51, 219, 222–29
  consumer complaints, 236
  decoders, 37, 41, 42–46, 61,
    216, 220–22
  development of, 219, 248*n*24
  DVDs and videotapes, 108, 236
  electronic newsroom
    captioning technique
    (ENCT), 228–29
  emergency, 233–36
  FCC captioning order for IP,
    230–32
  FCC captioning order for
    television, 223–30
  exemptions, 225–27
  live news broadcasts, 228
  new programming, 224
  prerule programming, 224–25
  Spanish-language
    programming, 225
  federal legislation, 220
  FM broadcast technology, 22
  history of televised
    captioning, 219
  induction loop technology, 21
  infrared light technology, 22
  movies, 43–44
  open, 20, 37, 41, 61, 217

public accommodation (ADA
    Title III), 42–46
public service
    announcements, 51
  real-time, 17, 19–20, 61
  streaming video, 234, 236
  telephones, 211, 243
CART system. *See*
    communication access
    realtime transcription
    (CART) services
CAs (communication assistants),
    246, 250–51
CASE (Conceptually Accurate
    Signed English), 2
CBS, 219, 228
Certified Deaf Interpreters
    (CDIs), 9, 17–18. *See also*
    interpreters
Charmatz, Marc, xi
churches, ADA Title III
    exemption, 41
Civil Rights Act of 1964
    Title VI, 63
    Title VII, 32, 166
Civil Rights Act of 1991,
    32, 166
Civil Service Reform Act of
    1978, 164
Clark, Cindy, 195–96
class action lawsuits
  for mental health services,
    140–45
  for open captioning, 237*n*10
closed captioning.
    See captioning
CNN, 228
Coalition of Organizations
    for Accessible Technology
    (COAT), 240–57
cochlear implants, 21–22,
    28–29, 137, 152
COED. *See* Commission on
    Education of the Deaf

cognitive impairments or mental illness. *See* health care and social services

colleges. *See* oostsecondary and continuing education

Commission on Education of the Deaf (COED), 85, 220, 238*n*11

communicating with people who are deaf or hard of hearing, 1–38

barriers to communication, 3–6. *See also specific legislative acts*

captioning, 18–22. *See also* captioning

common communication styles, 2–3. *See also specific methods of communication*

solutions for communication, 6–18. *See also* interpreters

telecommunications, 22–24. *See also* telecommunications

communication access real-time transcription (CART) services, 19, 87, 96, 109, 111, 113, 155, 201

in courts, 193, 195, 198–99

communication assistants (CAs), 246, 250–51

Communications Act of 1934, 246

Community Television v. Gottfried (1983), 237*n*10

compensatory damages. *See* remedies

complaint procedure

ADA

Title I (employment), 167

Title II (state and local governments), 39

Title III (public accommodation), 48

housing, 185–86

Rehabilitation Act

Section 501 (federal employee), 167–70

Section 504 (federal financial assistance), 57, 64, 65–67

telecommunications (FCC complaints), 236, 248, 255, 258

computer use, 19–20, 230, 231. *See also* Internet

Conceptually Accurate Signed English (CASE), 2

conferences and performances, accessibility to

ADA, 46

Rehabilitation Act, Section 504, 62–63

Connecticut Association of the Deaf, 132

construction. *See* existing facilities; new facilities

continuing education courses and professional examinations, 114–15

Court Interpreter Act of 1979, 192, 198

court reporters, 193

courts. *See* legal system and lawsuits

C-Print captioning, 19

Creighton University, 109–11, 112

criminal procedure, 203–4

cued speech, 3, 85, 91

CVAA. *See* Twenty-First Century Communications and Video Accessibility Act of 2010

damages. *See* remedies

DCBR (Deaf and Hard of Hearing Children's Bills of Rights). *See* education

Deaf and hard of hearing people

education discrimination. *See* education; postsecondary and continuing education

employment discrimination. *See* employment

health care discrimination. *See* health care and social services

housing discrimination. *See* housing

methods of communication, 1. *See also specific methods*

number in United States, 1

social services discrimination. *See* health care and social services

telecommunications services. *See* telecommunications

Deaf-blind individuals

equipment distribution to, 252

IDEA category, 75–76

interpreters for, 16–17

mental health services for, 139

decoders. *See* captioning

defendants, interpreters for, 18, 196, 205

defenses. *See also* undue burden defense

employment discrimination, 157–60. *See also* undue hardship defense of employers

definition of "individual with a disability"

ADA, 26–29, 151–52

"regarded as having an impairment," 152

ADA Amendments Act, 32–33

Rehabilitation Act, Section 503, 152

Rehabilitation Act, Section 504, 28

"qualified person with a disability," 58, 152

Department of Education, US

creation of, 69n6

Rehabilitation Act, Section 504 and, 63, 64, 65, 96, 107

Department of Health, Education, and Welfare, US (HEW), 55, 63, 69n6

Department of Health and Human Services (HHS), US

complaints against mental health facilities, 141–42

creation of, 69n6

on population of Americans over 65 years old, 218

Rehabilitation Act, Section 504 and, 61, 62, 63, 64, 65

Department of Housing and Urban Development, US (HUD), 178, 180, 185

Department of Justice (DOJ)

ADA Title II regulations. *See* state and local governments

court access for individuals with hearing impairments, regulations on, 193–95

housing accommodations and modifications, 180

movie captioning, proposed rule on, 43

public accommodations, 2010 amendments to DOJ regulations, 49–50

Rehabilitation Act enforcement powers, 63

Section 504 regulations, 55, 61

website accessibility regulations, 44

Department of Transportation, US (DOT), 162–63

deposit for loan of special equipment, 42

DeVinney v. Maine Medical Center (1977), 144–45

digital television and
    captioning, 222
disability, definition of person
    with. *See* definition
    of "individual with a
    disability"
discrimination prohibition
employment. *See* employment
    housing, 178–79, 182–85
    public accommodation (ADA
        Title III), 39–40, 48
    Rehabilitation Act, 25, 58–63
    state and local governments
        (ADA Title II), 35–36
Down syndrome, 86
due process rights, 210. *See also*
    education
DVD captioning, 236

early intervention services,
    73–75, 91
EBS (Emergency Broadcast
    System), 233, 234
education, 71–99. *See also*
    Individuals with Disabilities
    Education Act of 1990
    (IDEA); postsecondary and
    continuing education
    ADA, applicability to, 75,
        95–97
    Deaf and Hard of Hearing
        Children's Bills of Rights
        (DCBR), 73, 89–95
    appropriate assessments, 91
    availability of same language
        mode peers, 90
    common elements, 90–91
    early intervention services, 91
    emphasis on communication, 90
    equal opportunity to benefit
        from all services and
        programs, 90
    implementation and
        outreach, 92
    interaction with deaf and
        hard of hearing adult role
        models, 90
    placement, curriculum, and
        program development, 92
    qualified professionals, 90
    selection of language
        medium, 91
    unique elements, 91–92
    free, appropriate public
        education, 76–77
    individualized educational
        program (IEP), 75, 78–89
    annual review, 80
    appropriate language medium,
        84–85
    appropriate placement, 85–86
    assistive technology and related
        services, 86–88
    attendees required at IEP
        meeting, 82
    contents of, 81–82
    decisions and appeals on,
        94–95
    development of, 83–84
    due process hearing on,
        92–94
    interpreters' qualifications, 84
    procedural rights, 78, 83
    qualified professionals, 88–89
    individualized family service
        plan (IFSP), 73–75
    infants and toddlers,
        73–75, 91
    least restrictive environment,
        77, 86, 98–99*n*30
    mainstreaming, 77
    oral method vs. sign language
        in, 84
    procedural rights, 78, 83
    procedural safeguards (due
        process), 92–93
    Rehabilitation Act, Section 504,
        75, 95–97

residential schools, 77
special education, 77, 80
teacher certification, 89
students ages 3–21, 75–89
Education Department, US.
    See Department of
    Education, US
Education for All Handicapped
    Children Act of 1975, 25.
    See now Individuals with
    Disabilities Education Act of
    1990 (IDEA)
EEOC. *See* Equal Employment
    Opportunity Commission
effective communication
    accommodation for. *See*
    accommodation; auxiliary
    aids and services
    attorneys to provide, 202
    colleges and universities, 102,
    109, 130n28
    courts and public entities, 194
    government agencies, 36–37
    healthcare system, 119, 123–24,
    125, 128–29, 136
    interpreters and, 8, 9, 16
    legal system, 168, 194, 202,
    204–6
    public accommodations, 41, 49
    public housing, 181
    schools, 96, 97
elderly with hearing
    disabilities, 218
electronic messaging service, 258
electronic newsroom captioning
    technique (ENCT), 228–29
email, 22, 149, 155, 258
emergency alerts. *See* alerting
    devices
Emergency Alert System on
    television stations, 234
Emergency Broadcast System
    (EBS), 233, 234
emergency captioning, 233–36

emergency hospital care, 129
emergency telephone
    services, 212
employment, 149–75
    ADA Title I, 26, 29–32, 150
    discrimination prohibited,
    30, 150
    employers covered, 29, 150
    enforcement provisions,
    31–32, 150, 167
    exemptions, 29
    undue hardship defense, 31,
    159–60
    affirmative action, 163–65
    background, 149–51
    benefits for employees with
    disabilities, 156
    defenses, 157–60
    direct threat to safety, 157–58
    undue hardship, 31, 159–60
    disability, definition of
    person with. *See* definition
    of "individual with a
    disability"
    enforcement procedures,
    167–72
    ADA, 31–32, 150, 167
    Rehabilitation Act, Section
    503, 150–51, 170–71
    Rehabilitation Act, Section
    504, 150–51, 167–70, 172
    state laws, 172–73
    essential functions of job,
    153–54
    federal contractors
    (Rehabilitation Act, Section
    503), 54, 56, 150–51, 163
    federal jobs, 164–65
    Rehabilitation Act, Section
    501, 151, 164–65
    insurance coverage of
    employees with
    disabilities, 156
    medical examinations, 160–63

pre-offer inquiries about
disability, 160, 161
qualification standards, tests,
and other criteria, 160–63
reasonable accommodations,
154–57
Rehabilitation Act provisions,
150–51. *See also*
Rehabilitation Act of 1973
remedies, 166–67
state laws, 172–73
right to sue letter, 167
ENCT (Electronic newsroom
captioning technique),
228–29
enforcement provisions. *See also*
administrative enforcement;
complaint procedure;
remedies
ADA
Title I (employment), 31–32,
150, 167
Title III (public
accommodation), 48
housing, 180
Rehabilitation Act
Section 501 (federal employee),
150–51
Section 503 (federal
contractor), 150–51, 170–71
Section 504 (federal financial
assistance), 63–67, 150–51,
167–70, 172
telecommunications, 248, 255
English language. *See* spoken
English
environmental factors affecting
communication, 6
Equal Employment Opportunity
Commission (EEOC), 29
amendments to reflect ADA
Amendments Act. *See* ADA
Amendments Act of 2008
(ADAAA)

discrimination filing with, 150,
166, 167
Interpretive Guidance
on preemployment inquiries
and medical examinations,
161–62
on reasonable
accommodations, 155
right to sue letter, 167
equal opportunity provisions.
See also affirmative action;
discrimination prohibition
ADA, 25, 101
DCBR specifying for deaf
and hard of hearing
children, 90
Rehabilitation Act, Section 504,
59, 101
examinations
continuing education
courses and professional
examinations, 114–15
medical examinations for
employment, 160–63
public accommodation
(Title III), 47
existing facilities
public accommodation
(Title III), 47–48
removal of structural
communication barriers
in, 107
school modifications, 97

facial expression, 84
Fair Housing Act (FHA), 177–79
Fair Housing Amendments Act
of 1988 (FHAA), 177–78,
179, 181
Federal Communications
Commission (FCC), xii,
219, 221–23
accessing captioning controls,
need for rules on, 230

advanced communications
    services (ACS), 258–59
captioning order, 221, 223–27,
    239n35, 240n53
digital televisions, 222
new technologies required to
    accommodate captioning,
    221–22
certification for local
    distribution of specialized
    equipment, 252
Disability Rights Office
    website, 248
emergency captioning, visual
    warning rule, 233–36
filing complaint, 236, 248,
    255, 258
FM broadcast frequencies
    designated by, 22
hearing aid compatibility
    standards (HAC rules),
    253–54
IP captioning order, 230–32
quality standards, 227–29,
    238nn24–25
readily achievable
    determination, 256, 258–59
relay services rules, 251
telecommunications
    complaints, 248, 255, 258
    equipment manufacturers
        guidelines, 231, 256–58
    HAC telephones, 253–54
    regulation, 244
    wireless hearing aid
        compatibility rules, 254–55
text-to-911 capability
    rulemaking, 212
federal contractors. See
    Rehabilitation Act of 1973,
    Section 503
federal employees. See federal
    government; Rehabilitation
    Act of 1973, Section 501

federal financial recipients. See
    Rehabilitation Act of 1973,
    Section 504
federal government
    ADA Title II exemption, 35
    Office of Personnel
        Management's guidelines
        on reasonable
        accommodation, 157
    Rehabilitation Act. See also
        Rehabilitation Act of 1973
    Section 501, applicability
        of, 151
    Section 504, applicability of,
        57–58, 151
    Section 508, applicability of,
        67–68
federally funded programs. See
    Rehabilitation Act of 1973,
    Section 504
Federal Motor Carrier Safety
    Administration, 163
FHA (Fair Housing Act), 177–79
FHAA (Fair Housing
    Amendments Act of 1988),
    177–78, 179, 181
fifth Amendment rights, 207–8
fingerspelling, 14, 84, 85
fire alarms. See alerting devices
FM broadcast technology, 22
foreign languages, translation
    into ASL, 18
Fourteenth Amendment, 210
Fox, 228
Freedom of Information Act
    (FOIA) requests, 57

Gallaudet University on persons
    over 65 years old who are
    deaf or hard of hearing, 218
General Services Administration,
    68, 245
Georgia Office of
    Deaf Services, 144

Gillespie v. Dimensions Health Corp. (2005), 135
Grantham v. Moffett (1998), 105–7
Greater Los Angeles Council on Deafness, Inc., class action filed by, 237*n*10
grievance procedure (Rehabilitation Act, Section 504), 64
Guide to Judiciary Policy (federal courts), 198

handicap, defined for fair housing purposes, 178
HBO, 228
Health, Education, and Welfare Department, US. *See* Department of Health, Education, and Welfare, US (HEW)
Health and Human Services Department, US. *See* Department of Health and Human Services (HHS), US
health care and social services, 119–48
ADA, 119, 122–25
agency responsibilities, 125
background, 119–20
hospitals, 125–34
  auxiliary aids and services, 128
  communication barriers, 126
  compliance issues, 129–32
  direct care staff, 135–37
  emergency care preparation, 129
  National Association of the Deaf guidelines, 132–34
  planning for deaf and hard of hearing patients, 127–29
  qualified interpreters, use of, 136. *See also* effective communication

Rehabilitation Act, Section 504, applicability of, 57
stressful situations, 126–27
video remote interpreting systems, 134–35
mental health, 137–45
appropriate treatment, 146*n*33
interpreter for deaf person with mental illness, 16, 17–18
legal action for, 140–45
specialized programs for deaf people, 139–40, 146*n*33
Rehabilitation Act, Section 504, 119, 120–21
Hearing Aid Compatibility Act in 1988 (HAC Act), 253
Hearing Aid Compatible Negotiated Rulemaking Committee, 254
hearing aids and amplification equipment, 21–22, 28–29, 137
ADA coverage of deaf individuals who use, 152
in courts, 193
hearing-aid-compatible telephones, 61, 155, 252–55
safety issues in employment and, 158
in schools, 85, 87
wireless hearing aid compatibility rules, 254–55
hearing carryover (HCO), 251
hospitals. *See* health care and social services
hotels, public accommodation requirements for, 48
housing, 177–89
accessible smoke alarms, 182
discrimination experienced by deaf and hard of hearing people, 182–85
discrimination prohibited, 178–79

Fair Housing Act (FHA),
    177–79
Fair Housing Amendments Act
    of 1988 (FHAA), 177–78,
    179, 181
filing complaints, 185–86
handicap, definition of, 178
penalties, 180
public housing requirements,
    180–81
reasonable modifications and
    accommodations, 179–80
state and local housing laws,
    181–86
testers to find housing
    discrimination, 183–85
Housing and Urban
    Development Department,
    US. See Department
    of Housing and Urban
    Development, US (HUD)
Howard v. Alabama Board of
    Pharmacy (2009), 156
HUD (US Department of
    Housing and Urban
    Development), 178, 185

IDEA. See Individuals with
    Disabilities Education Act of
    1990
immigrants, 18
Indiana courts, 195–96
individualized educational
    program (IEP). See education
individualized family service plan
    (IFSP), 73–75
individual plan for employment
    (IPE, formerly individual
    written rehabilitation
    plan), 112
Individuals with Disabilities
    Education Act of 1990
    (IDEA), 25, 58, 71–73

free, appropriate public
    education, 76–77
general entitlements, 76–89
"hearing impairment"
    categories, 75–76
individualized educational
    program (IEP), 78–89
infants and toddlers with
    disabilities, 73
least restrictive environment,
    77, 86, 98–99n30
procedural rights, 78, 83
procedural safeguards (due
    process), 92–93
student records, parental rights
    to inspect, 94
students ages 3–21, 75–89
individual with a disability. See
    Americans with Disabilities
    Act of 1990 (ADA);
    definition of "disability";
    Rehabilitation Act of 1973
individual with cognitive
    impairment or mental illness.
    See health care and social
    services
induction loop technology, 21
infants and toddlers with
    disabilities, services for,
    73–75, 91
infrared light technology, 22
instant messaging, 155
International Association of
    Parents of the Deaf (now
    American Society for Deaf
    Children), 88
Internet
closed captioning, 229–33
Internet protocol captioned
    telephone service (IP CTS),
    249, 251
Internet protocol (IP) relay,
    23–24, 243, 249

Internet protocol speech-to-
speech (IP STS), 250
relay services, 50, 249–51
website accessibility, 44–45
interpreters. *See also* auxiliary
aids and services
certified deaf interpreters, 9
DCBR specifying, 90
federal court lists of, 197
IEP specifying, 89
Civil Service examination
requirements, 164
court system, 193–96
competence of interpreter,
206–7
costs not to include interpreter
costs, 54*n*20, 198, 212*n*3
for defendants, 18, 196, 205
federal court list of certified
interpreters, 197
for suspects, 18, 206
for witnesses, 18
for deaf-blind individuals,
16–17
employment discrimination
when deaf person denied
interpreter at interview or
job training, 30
IEP including, 87, 89
for immigrants, 18
for individuals with cognitive
impairments or mental
illness, 16, 17–18
oral interpreters, 9–10
public accommodation not
allowed to charge for cost
of, 203
sign language interpreters, 7–9
best practices in using, 12–13
guidelines when using, 14–15
locating, 11–12
qualified interpreter, according
to DOJ, 36, 61–62, 205

unqualified, dangers of using,
15–16
use of, 7–11
video remote interpreting. *See*
video remote interpreting
IPE (individual plan for
employment), 112
iTunes TV and movie
offerings, 234

*Jones v. Illinois Department
of Rehabilitation Services*
(1982), 112
judicial enforcement. *See* legal
system and lawsuits
jurors, deaf and hard of hearing,
197, 200, 201–2
Jury Selection and Service Act of
1968, 200
Justice Department. *See*
Department of Justice (DOJ)

Kentucky courts, 196
Kerry, John, 229
Kirkingburg v. Albertsons
(1999), 27, 28
*K.M. v. Tustin Unified School
District* (2013), 96

Legal Advocacy Project
for Hearing Impaired
People, 143
legal system and lawsuits,
191–215
access to courts, 192–202
federal courts, 197–202
state and local courts, 192–97
attorneys
deaf attorneys, 196
obligations to deaf clients,
202–3
background, 191–92
court costs

not to include interpreter costs,
54*n*20, 198, 212*n*3
state and local courts, 194
defendants, interpreters for, 18,
196, 205
effective communication under
ADA, 194, 204–5
example cases, 205–6
employment suits
ADA Title I, 167
burden of proof on
employer, 154
Rehabilitation Act, Section 501
(federal employee), 167–70
Rehabilitation Act, Section 503
(federal contractor), 170–71
housing discrimination, 185–86
IEP suits by parents, 95
interpreter competence, 206–7
jurors, deaf, 197, 200, 201–2
law enforcement, equal access
in, 203–6
mental health services, lawsuits
for, 140–45
Miranda rights, 207–9
prison programs and activities,
access to, 209–12
Rehabilitation Act
Section 503 (federal
contractor), 166–67, 175*n*55
Section 504 (federal financial
assistance), 67, 151
Line 21, 219
lipreading, 3, 193, 202. *See also*
speechreading
literacy skills and closed
captioning, 218, 237*n*4
local government. *See* state and
local governments
local laws. *See* state and local
laws

Maine Medical Center, 144–45
mainstreaming, 77

Markey, Edward, 229
Maryland prison system, deaf
persons in, 210
medical examinations for
employment, 160–63
mental health. *See* health care
and social services
mental retardation, 138
Milwaukee arrest
of deaf man, 206
Miranda rights, 207–9
Morton v. UPS (2001), 162
Mosier, Teri, 196
movie captioning, 20, 43–44
Murphy v. United Parcel Service
(1999), 27, 28

National Association of the Deaf
(NAD)
on alerting devices, 182
CVAA passage, role in, 258
deaf attorney, lawsuit on behalf
of, 196
DOT advocacy for deaf
drivers, 163
FCC captioning order
challenged by, 224, 226, 227
IP captioning, 231
Grantham v. Moffett
role, 106
history of, xi
hospital guidelines, 132–35
Law Center, 131
Legal Defense Fund, 143
on movie captioning, 43–44
Netflix suit by, 232–33
Position Statement on
Mental Health Interpreting
Services with People Who
Are Deaf, 139
Position Statement on Mental
Health Services, 139
qualified interpreters, provided
for court lists, 197

sign language interpreter
certification, 8
*Standards of Care for the
Delivery of Mental Health
Services to Deaf and Hard of
Hearing People,* 138–39
Supplement on Culturally
Affirmative and Linguistically
Accessible Services, 139
testers to find housing
discrimination, 183–85
video remote interpreters,
guidelines for, 11
on website accessibility, 45
National Board of Medical
Examiners, 115
National Captioning Institute
(NCI), 216, 219
National Center for Law and
Deafness (NCLD), xi–xii,
248. *See now* Law and
Advocacy Center
National Deaf-Blind Equipment
Distribution Program
(NDBEDP), 252
National Fair Housing
Alliance, 184
National Interpreter Certification
(NIC), 8, 9
natural disasters, emergency
captioning of warnings,
233–36
NBC, 219, 228
NCI (National Captioning
Institute), 216, 219
NCLD (National Center for Law
and Deafness), xi–xii, 248.
See now Law and Advocacy
Center
Netflix, 232–33
new facilities
public accommodation
(Title III), 47–48
school construction, 97

New York Hospital Codes,
Rules, and Regulations, 125
No Child Left Behind Act of
2002, 72, 89
notetakers, 6, 37, 41, 61, 63,
106, 109, 131
note writing, limitations of, 5–6,
202, 206

Office for Civil Rights, 65, 97,
141–42
Office of Federal Contract
Compliance Programs
(OFCCP), 170–71
Office of Personnel
Management's guidelines
on reasonable
accommodation, 157
Ohio courts, 196
Ohio Department of Mental
Health, 142
Oklahoma law on interpreters
for deaf criminal
defendants, 205
online video programming,
233–34
open captioning.
See captioning
oral interpreters, 9–10
oral method vs. sign language in
educational settings, 84
Oral Transliteration Certificate
(OTC), 10
Oregon prison system, deaf
persons in, 211
Organization for Use of the
Telephone (OUT), 253

parents' rights
Deaf and Hard of Hearing
Children's Bills of Rights
(DCBR), 89–95
individualized educational
program (IEP), 78–89

individualized family service
plan (IFSP), 73–75
parent teacher association (PTA)
programs, 97
pattern-or-practice
discrimination, 48
pay discrimination. *See*
employment
penalties. *See* enforcement
provisions
personal computers, 230, 231
Pew Charitable Trust, 216
pidgin signed English, 85
*Pinnacle Holdings, Inc., EEOC
v.,* 157
police officers, communication
with, 203–6
postsecondary education, 101–17
ADA, applicability of, 101,
106–7
auxiliary aids and services,
107–11
institution's obligation to pay
for, 111–12
vocational rehabilitation
agency's obligation to pay
for, 112–13
campus life, 113–14
continuing education
courses and professional
examinations, 114–15
recruitment, admissions, and
matriculation, 102–3
example cases, 103–7
Rehabilitation Act, Section 504,
applicability of, 57, 64, 101,
104, 107
prison programs and activities,
access to, 209–12
private clubs, ada Title III
exemption, 41
Pryor, Mark, 229
PSAPs (Public safety answering
points), 212

PTA (Parent teacher association)
programs, 97
public accommodation (ADA
Title III), 26, 39–50
auxiliary aids, 21, 41–42, 49,
109, 213n26
conferences and
performances, 46
decoders and captioning, 42–46
DOJ regulations implementing
(2010 amendments), 49–50
enforcement, 48
examinations and courses, 47
existing vs. new facilities, 47–48
lawyers' offices, 202
private facilities and nonprofit
organizations, 27, 39–40
private healthcare providers and
hospitals, 122
private schools and educational
programs for children and
adults, 95, 107
service animals, use of, 47
undue burden defense, 42, 111,
115, 203
public agencies. *See* federal
government; state and local
governments (ADA Title II)
Public Broadcasting Service
(PBS), 219
public housing requirements,
180–81
Public Law 94-142. *See* Individuals
with Disabilities Education
Act of 1990 (IDEA)
public safety answering points
(PSAPs), 212
public school education. *See*
education
public transportation (ADA Title
II), 26, 34
public utility commissions
(PUCs), 244
punitive damages. *See* remedies

real-time captioning, 17, 19–20, 228. *See also* communication access realtime transcription (CART) services

reasonable accommodation. *See* accommodation

Registry of Interpreters for the Deaf (RID), 8, 9, 11, 197

Rehabilitation Act of 1973, 53–69
background, 53
discrimination prohibited in federal employment, federally conducted programs and activities, and federal contractors, 25, 58–63
employment specific issues. *See* employment
Section 501 (federal employment), 54, 150–51, 163, 164–65
rehabilitation counselors, guidance for hiring, 165–66
Section 502, 54
Section 503 (federal contractors), 54, 56, 150–51, 163
enforcement provisions, 170–71
private right to sue rulings, 175n55
remedies, 166–67
Section 504 (federal financial recipients), 53, 54, 55–67, 150
accommodation or assistance, 59–60
administrative enforcement, 63, 172
applicability to federally funded programs and activities, 56–58

assurance of compliance form agreeing to obey, 172
communication barriers, 60–62
complaint procedure, 64, 65–67
definition of "qualified person with a disability," 58
education, specialized instruction, 75
enforcement provisions, 63–67, 150–51, 167–70, 172
equal opportunity provisions, 59
healthcare providers, 119
internal grievance procedure, 64
judicial enforcement, 67
nondiscrimination vs. affirmative action, 163
prisoners' right to auxiliary aids, 210
program accessibility, 62–63
self-evaluation, 64
special or different treatment that stigmatizes person with disabilities, 60
state and local courts, access to, 192–95
telecommunications access, 211
Section 508 (electronic and information technology accessible to deaf federal employees and those who need government information), 53, 55, 67–68
synopsis, 54–55
vocational rehabilitation agency's obligation to pay for auxiliary aids and services, 112–13
rehabilitation counselors, guidance for federal hiring, 165–66

relay services, 23–24, 50–51,
120, 131, 156, 212, 243–47,
249–51
religious organizations, ADA
Title III exemption, 41
remedies. *See also* enforcement
provisions
employment violations, 32,
166–67
state laws, 172–73
public accommodation
violations, 48
residential schools, 77
Revenue Reconciliation Act of
1990, 124
right to sue letter, 167
*Rizzo v. Children's World
Learning Center* (1999), 158
Rowley case. *See Board of
Education of Hendrick
Hudson Central School
District v. Rowley* (1982)

Sabino, Vincent, 46
safety, as reason not to employ
persons with disability,
157–58
Schedule A appointment, 164
*Schornstein v. N.J. Division of
Vocational Rehabilitation
Services* (1982), 112
Sections 504 and 508. *See
Rehabilitation Act of 1973*
self-evaluation of
Rehabilitation Act,
Section 504 compliance, 64
self-incrimination privilege,
207–8
Serio, Joseph, 206
service animals, use of, 47, 155,
182–83
7-1-1 uniform dialing, 247–48
Signing Exact English (SEE),
2, 79

sign language, defined, 84
sign language interpreters, 7–16.
See also interpreters
smartphones, 230, 231
smoke alarms, 24, 182. *See also*
alerting devices
social media, xii. *See also*
internet
social services. *See* health care
and social services
*Southeastern Community
College v. Davis* (1979),
104–5, 106
Spanish language
captions for programs, 225
relay services, 251
speechreading, 3
limitations of, 3–5
in schools, 85
spoken English, 2–3, 5, 9
in bilingual education of deaf
students, 84–85
interpreter using, 14
stadiums and sporting events,
20, 45–46, 48
*Standards of Care for the
Delivery of Mental Health
Services to Deaf and Hard
of Hearing People* (NAD),
138–39
state and local courts. *See* legal
system and lawsuits
state and local governments
(ADA Title II), 26, 33–39
accessibility of, 34–35
auxiliary aids and services, DOJ
requirements for, 36–39, 109
definition of "discrimination,"
35–36
filing complaints, 39
healthcare providers and
hospitals, 122
law enforcement agencies, 204
public school systems, 95

qualified interpreter, according to DOJ, 36, 61–62, 205
state universities and colleges, 106–7
telecommunications access, 211
undue burden defense, 38–39, 111
state and local laws
civil rights laws, 125
education standards, 72–73
employment remedies, 172–73
housing, 181–86
social service agencies, 125
state relay programs, 246–47
Strathie v. Department of Transportation (1983), 158
streaming video, 234, 236
suspects, interpreters for, 18, 206
Sutton v. United Airlines (1999), 27, 28

TAAC (Telecommunications Access Advisory Committee), 256
tablet computers, 230, 231
tactile signed communications, 16–17
TAEA (Telecommunications Accessibility Enhancement Act of 1988), 245
TDCA (Television Decoder Circuitry Act of 1990), 221
TDDs. *See* telecommunications devices for deaf people
telecoil circuit ("T" switch), 21
telecommunications, 37, 243–61. *See also* videophones
ADA Title IV, 50–51, 245–46, 249
alerting devices. *See* alerting devices
amplified telephones. *See* hearing aids and amplification equipment

complaints and enforcement, 248, 255
equipment distribution programs, 251–52
hearing aid compatibility, 61, 252–56
prison programs and activities, access to, 211–12
regulation of, 244–52
Rehabilitation Act regulations, 61
relay services (TRS), 23–24, 50–51, 120, 131, 156, 212, 243–47, 249
Telecommunications Access Advisory Committee (TAAC), 256
Telecommunications Accessibility Enhancement Act of 1988 (TAEA), 245
Telecommunications Act of 1996, 216, 222, 243, 255–58
Section 255, 256–58
Section 305, 222–23
Telecommunications devices for deaf people (TDDs), 6, 22, 41
Telecommunications for the Disabled Act of 1982, 252–53
Telephone services. *See* Hearing aids and amplification equipment; Telecommunications
teletypewriters (ttys), 22, 24, 48, 61, 97, 114, 155, 181, 211–12, 244–45, 256, 257
television captioning. *See* captioning
Television Decoder Circuitry Act of 1990 (TDCA), 221
Terry v. State (1925), 191
testmasters, 115

Texas criminal system, deaf
   persons in, 211
text messaging, 22
Title I (ADA). *See* employment
Title II (ADA). *See* state and
   local governments
Title III (ADA). *See* public
   accommodation
Title IV (ADA). *See*
   telecommunications
Title VII (Civil Rights Act of
   1964), 32, 166
Title VIII. *See* Fair Housing Act
   (FHA)
Total Communication program,
   99*n*30
Transportation Department, US
   (DOT), 162–63
TRS. *See* telecommunications,
   relay services
truck drivers, 162–63
TTYs. *See* teletypewriters
Tugg v. Towey (1994), 143
Twenty-First Century
   Communications and Video
   Accessibility Act of 2010
   (CVAA), xii, 108, 222,
   229–30, 232, 240*n*57, 252,
   258–59

UHF transmissions, 221
undue burden defense
   ADA Title II, 38–39, 111
   ADA Title III (public
      accommodation), 42, 111,
      115, 203
   Rehabilitation Act
   Section 504, 111, 112
   Section 508, 68
   television captioning, 226,
      240*n*47
undue hardship defense of
   employers, 31, 159–60
uniform dialing, 247–48

Uniform Federal Accessibility
   Standards, 97
universities. *See* postsecondary
   and continuing education
University of Alabama, 111
University of Maryland, 216
University of Texas, 111
UPS cases, 162
US Department of ___. *See*
   department *by specific name*

Vernon, McCay, 138
victims of crime, 204
video media, 217–42. *See also*
   captioning
videophones (VPs), 23, 61, 97,
   114, 121, 130, 140, 155,
   211–12, 257
video relay service (VRS), 23–24,
   243, 250
video remote interpreting
   (VRI), 10–11, 36, 50, 61,
   134–35, 205
videotape captioning, 236
videotext displays, 37, 41, 61
Virginia
   prison inmates, access to
      videophones, 212
   relay service, 247
vocational rehabilitation
   agencies
   deaf unit funding, 140
   obligation to pay for auxiliary
      aids and services, 112–13
voice carryover (VCO), 251
Voice-over-Internet-protocol
   (VoIP) service, 258

website accessibility, 44–45
welfare offices. *See* health care
   and social services
WGBH (PBS station in
   Boston), 219
Wilzack, Doe v. (1986), 143

wireless hearing aid
compatibility rules, 254–55
wireless technologies, 21
witnesses, interpreters for, 18
Workforce Investment Act of
1998, 68

written communication, 61. *See
also* notetakers; note writing
Miranda rights, 208
Wyatt v. Stickney (1972), *aff'd
sub nom. Wyatt v. Aderholt*
(1974), 141